Flannery O'Connor and Stylistic Asceticism

Flannery O'Connor and Stylistic Asceticism

Rachel Toombs

☞PICKWICK *Publications* · Eugene, Oregon

FLANNERY O'CONNOR AND STYLISTIC ASCETICISM

Copyright © 2022 Rachel Toombs. All rights reserved. Except for brief quotations in critical publications or reviews, no part of this book may be reproduced in any manner without prior written permission from the publisher. Write: Permissions, Wipf and Stock Publishers, 199 W. 8th Ave., Suite 3, Eugene, OR 97401.

Pickwick Publications
An Imprint of Wipf and Stock Publishers
199 W. 8th Ave., Suite 3
Eugene, OR 97401

www.wipfandstock.com

PAPERBACK ISBN: 978-1-6667-3221-4
HARDCOVER ISBN: 978-1-6667-2563-6
EBOOK ISBN: 978-1-6667-2564-3

Cataloguing-in-Publication data:

Names: Toombs, Rachel, author.

Title: Flannery O'Connor and stylistic asceticism / by Rachel Toombs.

Description: Eugene, OR : Pickwick Publications, 2022 | Includes bibliographical references and index.

Identifiers: ISBN 978-1-6667-3221-4 (paperback) | ISBN 978-1-6667-2563-6 (hardcover) | ISBN 978-1-6667-2564-3 (ebook)

Subjects: LCSH: O'Connor, Flannery—Criticism and interpretation.

Classification: PS3565.C57 Z90 2022 (print) | PS3565.C57 Z90 (ebook)

10/04/22

© 1951 Flannery O'Connor. Reprinted by permission of the Mary Flannery O'Connor Charitable Trust via Harold Matson-Ben Camardi, Inc. All rights reserved. Unpublished material quoted in Chapter 4.

© 2021 John Wiley and Sons. Portions of Chapters 2, 5, and 6 appear in Rachel Toombs, "'Almost Imperceptible Intrusions of Grace': On Flannery O'Connor's Fiction and Readerly Entanglement," *Heythrop Journal* 62, no. 5 (2021) 900–915. Used with permission.

To Ralph C. Wood

Contents

Acknowledgments | ix
Abbreviations | xi

Introduction | 1

Chapter 1: A Style Too Demanding?: Caroline Gordon, the New Criticism, and Flannery O'Connor's *Wise Blood* | 20

Chapter 2: Flannery O'Connor's Grotesque as Moments of Excess | 41

Chapter 3: On Stories Sparely Wrought | 68

Chapter 4: Genesis 32 and *Wise Blood*: The Wounded Victor and the Blinded Convert | 90

Chapter 5: Reading Spare Stories | 119

Chapter 6: Blessed Wounds of Reading: "The River," "The Enduring Chill," "Parker's Back" | 139

Conclusion: Stylistic Asceticism | 161

Bibliography | 167
Index | 173

Acknowledgments

FLANNERY O'CONNOR ONCE WROTE that a "story that is any good can't be reduced, it can only be expanded. A story is good when you continue to see more and more in it, and when it continues to escape you. In fiction two and two is always more than four" (MM, 102). As this is a book that aims to speak of a particular kind of reading event, it seems fitting to thank the two figures that have most impacted my ability to attend to good stories: my mother, Eileen Toombs, and my *doktorvater*, Ralph C. Wood. My mother prioritized regular visits to the public library growing up so that my sister and I might find friends in books. Ralph modelled to me both in the classroom and in his scholarship how to return again and again to a story in order to see more and more in it.

A number of further thanks are in order. I am grateful to Natalie Carnes for helping me draw together the seemingly odd pairing of Flannery O'Connor and biblical Hebrew narrative through the writings of Jean-Louis Chrétien and the relationship of wounding and blessing. I am grateful to Gavin Hopps, who suggested to me the term "stylistic asceticism" after reflecting on a guest lecture I gave to the Institute for Theology, Imagination, and the Arts (ITIA) at the University of St. Andrews in February 2018. I also want to thank Bill Bellinger, Luke Ferretter, and Jonathan Tran for the productive feedback to my dissertation upon which this book is based. More broadly, I thank Baylor University's Department of Religion, and in particular Jim Nogalski, for not only allowing but enthusiastically supporting my interdisciplinary work. I would like to thank The Donald A. Driskell Endowed Fund for the Glenn O. and Martell B. Hilburn Endowed Graduate Research Scholarship, whose funding provided the means for archival work at Flannery O'Connor archives at George College & State

ACKNOWLEDGMENTS

University's Flannery O'Connor Special Collection and Emory University's MARBL's Flannery O'Connor and Sally Fitzgerald collections. The time I spent in those archives was both invaluable and a delight.

For years now, Mandy Brobst-Renaud, Rebecca Poe Hays, and Lacy Crocker Papadakis have been constant and faithful companions in writing and in life. You three know just how much you mean to me, I am pleased to put even a hint of that gratitude in print. I also want to thank my many brilliant colleagues and friends for their feedback on this project over the years, in particular Thomas Breedlove, Nicholas Krause, and Matthew Rothaus Moser. A special note of gratitude to Anna Beaudry who did the indexing for this book. Additionally, I am grateful to Egg Breedlove for her friendship.

Finally, I want to thank my husband, Lance Green, for the many, many ways he is in my corner. I love you, LG.

Abbreviations

CW *Collected Works*. New York: Literary Classics of the United States, 1988.

HB *The Habit of Being*. Edited by Sally Fitzgerald. New York: Farrar, Straus & Giroux, 1979.

MM *Mystery and Manners: Occasional Prose*. Edited by Sally Fitzgerald and Robert Fitzgerald. New York: Farrar, Straus & Giroux, 1969.

Introduction

The Difficulty of Flannery O'Connor's Fiction

O'CONNOR'S MOST WELL-KNOWN SHORT story, "A Good Man Is Hard to Find," narrates a family road trip to Florida turned blood-bath when their car careens off the road and into a ditch only to find an escaped convict and his two cronies. As the family is methodically sent off into the woods to be shot, the convict Misfit and genteel grandmother are foregrounded at the side of the road discussing, of all things, Jesus Christ. The story abruptly comes to climactic end when the grandmother reaches tenderly toward the Misfit only to receive three swift shots to the chest with the Misfit's disconcerting proclamation: "She would of been a good woman . . . if it had been somebody there to shoot her every minute of her life" (CW, 153). While unsettling, "A Good Man Is Hard to Find" is also humorous, leaving readers unnerved at the end of a horrific story that made them laugh out loud as much as, if not more than, it made them lament.[1] This play between humor and violence appears throughout O'Connor's writing and leaves readers unsure whether to laugh or cry—or both. O'Connor's style of storytelling does not make readers' task easy, as it characteristically fails to explain, justify, or remedy the acts of violence that often and suddenly erupt in the stories' climactic moments.

O'Connor's fiction frequently puzzles readers for two central reasons: its strange style of narrating climactic moments without recourse to cause or motive and its peculiar use of violence as a means of redemption. While

---

1. A recording of O'Connor reading "A Good Man Is Hard to Find" is available online and the audible chuckles of the crowd heighten the play of the comic and tragic in the story: https://youtu.be/sQT7y4L5aKU.

some critics celebrate O'Connor's spare climactic narrations and use of violence as key aspects of her distinctive quality as a fiction writer, others identify these same qualities as deficiencies and distractions from otherwise powerful stories.[2] Rowan Williams picks up on these two disparate responses to the discomfiting effect of O'Connor's storytelling: "O'Connor deliberately confuses our sympathies in ways that not every critic seems to recognise. . . . We are not given a stable judgement in the way the story is told."[3] As Williams highlights, these destabilizing narratives prevent readers from reducing O'Connor's stories to formulaic meaning even as they invite readers to go deeper. Readers must inhabit the world of the text rather than reach easy conclusions that leave them disengaged from the stories. Just as the characters are confronted with the ironic truth "that the gift of life is the gift of daily 'terror', the terror of being aware of reality in the light of God," readers too must be so confronted through O'Connor's violent and difficult narrative style if they hope to grapple with her stories.[4]

In this book, I demonstrate that O'Connor's recourse to grotesque action and spare narration in climactic moments offers a profound fictional embodiment of the theological truth that God's blessing is often also a wounding. I show that this surprising integration of skeletal style and disturbing violence is not unique to O'Connor. On the contrary, it may help illumine her deep saturation in the narrative world of Scripture. As I demonstrate, biblical Hebrew narrative often employs similar means of narrating events, requiring readers to discern for themselves how characters are similarly wounded in their blessing and blessed in their wounding. These inferential demands on readers opens them up to an analogous sort of wounding and blessing.

I refer to O'Connor's spare style of narration as "stylistic asceticism."[5] I use this term with ample awareness of the theological baggage that comes with it. I heed Robert Fitzgerald's warning, a close friend of Flannery O'Connor's, that she herself would be "sardonic of the word *ascesis*."[6] But, like Fitzgerald, I also cannot get away from the fittingness of ascesis to

---

2. Among those who identify O'Connor's style as detrimental are Joann Halleran McMullen and Sarah Gordon, discussed later in this chapter.

3. Williams, *Grace and Necessity*, 123.

4. Williams, *Grace and Necessity*, 121.

5. I am grateful to Gavin Hopps in first suggesting this term as a means of capturing my proposal of the theological impact of O'Connor's style.

6. Fitzgerald, "Introduction," 28.

capture the spare style of her stories and its kinship with biblical Hebrew. In his introductory essay to the posthumously published O'Connor short story collection, *Everything That Rises Must Converge*, Fitzgerald notes that despite O'Connor's displeasure the word ascesis "seems to me a good one for the peculiar discipline of the O'Connor style. How much has been refrained from, and how much else has been cut out and thrown away, in order that the bald narrative sentences should present just what they present and in just this order!"[7]

Kallistos Ware, in his essay "The Way of the Ascetics: Negative or Affirmative," argues that in figures like St. Antony we see a pattern that results from ascetic practices: "silence gives place to speech, seclusion leads him to involvement."[8] Ware emphasizes that asceticism rightly practiced does not lead to interminable isolation and self-flagellation, but to transformation both in the inner life of the ascetic and their outer labor in the world. He distinguishes what he calls a "natural" from an "unnatural asceticism" arguing that if asceticism is not practiced with moderation, it can lead to "either explicitly or implicitly a distinct hatred for God's creation."[9] Ultimately, Ware argues, natural and creation-affirming asceticism should be understood "as transfiguration rather than mortification." He continues, "*askesis* is universal in its scope—not an élite enterprise but a vocation for all. It is not a curious aberration, distorting our personhood, but it reveals to us our own true nature.... Without asceticism none of us is authentically human."[10] This understanding of asceticism as a universal practice for everyone to become who they truly are is one that shows up perennially in O'Connor's fiction and, as I argue in this book, extends through her spare style into the life of her readers. I use the term "stylistic asceticism" to draw together O'Connor's bare-bones style with the broader theological conviction that ascesis, in practices like fasting, self-denial, moderation, and prayer, plays a central role in becoming truly human.

In O'Connor's fiction, readers are met with a skeletal style most frequently in pivotal scenes that infer the possibility of divine disclosure. Like the ascetics who journeyed from the rabble of the city to the wilderness to find God and confront their demons, O'Connor's lynchpin moments of grace offered deny readers the opulence of narrative comment, descriptive

7. Fitzgerald, "Introduction," 28–29.
8. Ware, "Way of the Ascetics," 5.
9. Ware, "Way of the Ascetics," 9–10.
10. Ware, "Way of the Ascetics," 13.

landscaping, or sufficient dénouement to understand the impact of these revelations. Instead, O'Connor's bare climactic scenes and narrative silence invites readers to participate—to put themselves at-risk—in these often grotesque moments of response to divine revelation. O'Connor chooses to render grace in this way precisely because of her own creation-affirming conviction about the discreet and enigmatic ways God works in the world.

Parataxis and the Difficulty of Reading

The literary term "parataxis" characterizes the bare style of O'Connor's fiction. Rather than hypotactically—deriving from the Greek *hypo* "below" and *taxis* "arrangement"—narrating events where subordinate clauses modify the main clause, O'Connor's fiction paratactically—the Greek *para* "side-by-side" contrasts to *hypo* "below"—unfolds events without frequent modifying clauses.

Both O'Connor's fiction and biblical Hebrew narrative employ parataxis for narrating the fierce climaxes of their stories. Parataxis is characterized by its spare form of storytelling, which unfolds without overt description or explanations of motive and cause. It entails gapped narration that links independent clauses together without obvious causal connection. The hypotactic style of "telling rather than showing," by contrast, makes subordinate clauses and phrases fall below the main sentence-line to explain such causal links.[11] The heightened textual silence in paratactic narration requires readers to infer unspoken connections within the gaps.[12] Narrative

---

11. In *Understanding Fiction*, Cleanth Brooks Jr. and Robert Penn Warren distinguish "telling" from "rendering" characters as the former features "direct presentation . . . with rather flat and typical characters" while the latter employs indirect characterization, so as to renders characters "humanly credible" (Brooks and Warren, *Understanding Fiction*, 169–70). Using O'Connor's "A Good Man Is Hard to Find" as an example, Brooks and Warren emphasize that rendering (showing) rather than telling makes even such perverse of characters as the Misfit relate to the broader reading audience, showing even the most out-of-bound characters of story have "a large human significance" (170). The best way to render a character, the authors of *Understanding Fiction* note, is through dialogue, noting that "the use of speech is a rich resource for dramatic presentation" (171). Yet the artistic rendering of these characters must retain their own integrity: "An obvious test of fiction then is that the motives and actions of its characters are rendered coherent. It is the glory of fiction that the great artists have been able to render coherent so many strange and out-of-the-way, often apparently self-contradictory, examples of human nature" (173).

12. Such terms as "gapped," "spare," "lean," and "skeletal" will serve as synonyms for the paratactic means of storytelling that lacks abundant causal connections and narrative detail.

critic Meir Sternberg notes that when "the narrative become[s] an obstacle course . . . reading turns into a drama of understanding—conflict between inferences, seesawing, reversal, discovery, and all. The only knowledge perfectly acquired is the knowledge of our limitations."[13] Paratactic narration pushes readers toward a confrontation with their own interpretive limits through such dynamic interactions with the text.

Though Flannery O'Connor had no knowledge of biblical Hebrew and drew no direct influence from its style of narration, the presence of paratactic narration in the stories of both Flannery O'Connor and biblical Hebrew offers a particular kind of reading experience that combines a paratactic style with a theological conviction that wounds can bless.[14] This paradoxical result of a wounding blessing can be seen clearly in two climactic moments: in the Genesis narration of Jacob's wrestling with the angel-man and in Hazel Motes's self-blinding in O'Connor's *Wise Blood*.

As Ralph C. Wood astutely observes, grace sits at the center of O'Connor's fiction: "The conviction that the ultimate issue of our lives depends on our own reception or rejection of God's grace is the central premise of Flannery O'Connor's work."[15] O'Connor powerfully narrates her protagonists' reception or rejection of grace. For characters and readers alike, such violence-laden moments of redemption reflect the strange theological truth that grace can feel more like a tyrant than a healer. As O'Connor herself noted, "human nature vigorously resists grace because grace changes us and the change is painful" (HB, 307). O'Connor makes a similar judgment elsewhere: "This notion that grace is healing omits the fact that before it heals, it cuts with the sword Christ said he came to bring" (CW, 411). Thus do O'Connor's stories and certain biblical Hebrew narratives confront readers with the terrifying grace of God through the violent action of redemption.

To recognize the similarities in narrative style requires a knowledge not only of the themes and literary devices evident in English translations of the Bible, but also an awareness of a key feature of Old Testament narrative that is available only in the Hebrew text: the *wayyiqtol*. The *wayyiqtol*

---

13. Sternberg, *Poetics of Biblical Narrative*, 47.

14. Her library indicates unsurprisingly that she read from the Douay-Rheims translation of the Bible, based off of the Vulgate (Kinney, *Flannery O'Connor's Library*, 38–39), §§87–92. Though, just as unsurprising would be O'Connor's familiarity with KJV.

15. Wood, *Comedy of Redemption*, 90.

is a grammatical feature in biblical Hebrew storytelling that functions similarly to the English language's use of punctuation or conjunctions like "and," "but," and "now." But, unlike English's abundant choices for punctuation and conjunctions, biblical Hebrew narrative most frequently uses this *one* literary device to signal the connection of one clause to another in a variety of ways. The *wayyiqtol* effects a gapped narration that requires readers to infer meaning from narrative absence. I demonstrate that in the climactic moments of O'Connor stories and Hebrew narrative pericopes—paratactically narrated moments of what Williams calls "reality in the light of God"—the storytellers make a similar use of a gapped narrative style.[16] While she was unaware of the minutiae of Hebrew syntax, O'Connor's stories are full of stark sentences that, as she confessed, make her characters' "fictional qualities lean away from typical social patterns, toward mystery and the unexpected" (MM, 40). O'Connor's plain sentences become most jarring when they describe grotesque characters performing outrageous but unexplained deeds. As in biblical Hebrew narrative, readers are forced to fill in the explanatory gap for themselves, so as to stress the mysterious and unexpected quality of divine action and human response. In O'Connor's fiction and many biblical Hebrew stories, readers encounter meaning and significance precisely by means of a peculiar narrative style, as the *how* undergirds and enables the *what*.

A Note on Methodology

This book engages across disciplines—from literature to biblical studies, philosophy to theology—in order to illustrate the theological significance and impact of O'Connor's spare style. Narrative criticism serves as the lens through which I link the gapped narrative style that O'Connor's fiction shares with Hebrew narrative. This work is neither an exposition of biblical criticism nor theological construction, but rather a theological interpretation of Flannery O'Connor's narrative style that is illumined by the similar stylistic effect found in Hebrew narrative.

---

16. Throughout this work, I argue for similarity, not sameness, in style. The narrative styles found in biblical Hebrew narrative and O'Connor's fiction do not function at all times in exactly the same. Nor I am arguing that the parataxis found in these two narrative types is unique. Instead, I am drawing out the effect of spare narrative style and the conviction that wounds can bless to produce a kind of stylistic asceticism.

INTRODUCTION

Background

Since the second half of the twentieth-century, the distinctive features of biblical Hebrew narrative have received increased attention.[17] Notably, Robert Alter's influential *The Art of Biblical Narrative* emphasizes the importance of attending to the style of Hebrew narrative, particularly in the use of direct speech and narrative silence. Alter argues that the narrator's choice to forego omniscient knowledge while relying heavily on direct speech constitutes a theological choice because narrative style serves a mediatory role between God and readers.[18] In a later work, *Pen of Iron: American Prose and the King James Bible,* Alter contends that many modern translations of the Bible often abandon the King James Version's superb reflection of Hebraic parataxis.[19] Parataxis, Alter argues, leaves open causal connections in the narratives so that they "swarm with possibilities."[20] Moreover, Sternberg identifies the same paratactic style as a non-didactic means of biblical storytelling that pushes readers towards their own limits and avoids sentimentally moralistic readings of the texts.[21]

While the influence of the Old Testament on O'Connor's fiction is well-attested in O'Connor criticism, discussions of their similarities in style are either absent entirely or lack a robust understanding of the poetics of Old Testament narrative. By employing such a poetics, I share Sternberg's claim that to speak of a poetics of biblical narrative is to focus on narrative as communication and not simply a "listing of so-called forms and devices and configuration," for "our primary business as readers is to make purposive sense of it, so as to explain the *what's* and the *how's* in terms of the *why's* of communication."[22] Sternberg's biblical poetics attends to the form of storytelling to elucidate potential meaning from a story.

---

17. Significant works on biblical narrative and biblical poetics more broadly include: Sternberg, *Poetics of Biblical Narrative*; Berlin, *Poetics and Interpretation of Biblical Narrative*; Rimmon-Kenan, *Narrative Fiction*; Fishbane, *Biblical Text and Texture*; Bar-Efrat, *Narrative Art in the Bible*; Alter, *Art of Biblical Narrative*.

18. Alter, *Art of Biblical Narrative*, 155–57.

19. Alter, *Pen of Iron*, 41.

20. Alter, *Pen of Iron*, 134. Alter identifies the paratactic style in Hebrew narrative's employment of the *wayyiqtol*, which he identifies as the *waw*-consecutive. Chapter 3 offers a more detailed analysis of the use of terms *wayyiqtol* and *waw*-consecutive.

21. Sternberg, *Poetics of Biblical Narrative*, 37–47.

22. Sternberg, *Poetics of Biblical Narrative*, 2, 1.

The commonplace comparison between O'Connor's fiction and the Old Testament is grounded in O'Connor's own insistence that prophetic vision is a function of the imagination, for it allows the writer to have an uncanny discernment of divine mercy as it is often veiled within horrifically violent events. O'Connor writes of the expansive and imaginative function of prophetic vision in a 1959 letter to Cecil Dawkins: "According to St. Thomas, prophetic vision is not a matter of seeing clearly, but of seeing what is distant, hidden. The Church's vision is prophetic vision; it is always widening the view" (HB, 365) She also links her use of the concrete and grotesque with the expanding vision of the prophet, for "[t]he prophet is a realist of distances, and it is this kind of realism that you find in the best modern instances of the grotesque" (MM, 44).

Jordan Cofer's 2014 work, *The Gospel According to Flannery O'Connor: Examining the Role of the Bible in Flannery O'Connor's Fiction*, is one of the few full-length studies of the connection between O'Connor and the Old Testament.[23] He asserts that O'Connor adopts the unrelenting directness of Old Testament prophets: "O'Connor was *shouting* to have her message heard, as her religious and artistic ambitions intersected within these *startling* figures found in her fiction."[24] Yet, Cofer turns O'Connor's work into fictional illustrations of theological convictions that could just as well have been stated discursively, quite apart from their inextricable twining of meaning and manner. Cofer not only overlooks the stylistic similarities between O'Connor's fiction and certain Hebrew narratives, he misses their shared underlying premise—namely, that divine destruction is meant to enable human restoration.

O'Connor's overall narrative style leaves some critics wanting. Among the more severe critics of Flannery O'Connor's writing style, Joann Halleran McMullen argues that O'Connor's "show, don't tell" narrative approach leaves readers ill-equipped to connect the meaning in the stories to Christian belief. This lack of telling in O'Connor's fiction, McMullen contends,

---

23. Cofer, *Gospel According to O'Connor*. In this work, Cofer argues that O'Connor makes use of Scripture in three ways: 1) retelling biblical stories; 2) illustrating redemption through violence; and 3) startling readers by allowing them to feel the full impact of redemption.

Michaels's *Passing by the Dragon* focuses similarly on the biblical motifs in O'Connor stories, citing examples of biblical themes present in many of O'Connor's stories. May's *The Pruning Word* argues that O'Connor's stories function like parables in the way they interpret and render judgment on readers—but by suggesting apt analogies rather than employing startling narrative methods.

24. Cofer, *Gospel According to O'Connor*, 5, italics his.

risks leading readers astray from her intended meaning: "readers are often compelled into a non-Catholic, and yes, sometimes even anti-Catholic reading of her fiction."[25] McMullen bemoans that O'Connor's aim to draw readers towards the mystery of the Incarnation often fails. Readers must be coached to navigate O'Connor's "stylistic techniques of annihilation" to avoid an anti-Catholic misreading:[26]

> By keeping her characters largely unspecified, and by focusing on ambiguous or neutral pronoun references or indefinite noun referents such as 'the girl,' O'Connor disengages herself from her characters, who are theologically important only as instruments through which God works. This stylistic technique seems to defeat her intense personal desire to deliver an audience antagonistic to a loving, caring, Catholic God into the religious society she feels they have rejected. Despite her detailed glosses, her language guides her readers away from her theological designs. The reader might rightly ask where is the linguistic message reinforcing the Christian directive 'do unto others' or love of thy sister/brother, or that even the least of us is loved by God."[27]

One of the most prominent examples of what McMullen describes as O'Connor's annihilating techniques is her use of spare and direct sentences: "O'Connor's sentence structure throughout her fiction often follows the same predictable pattern of beginning with subject-verb sentence constructions with simple declarative sentences most prevalent. While O'Connor does employ complex sentences in her fiction simple sentences by far predominate."[28] This simplicity in form places substantial demands on readers to discern (or not) the divine Mystery present within the spare narrative. McMullen summarizes her work as paradoxically holding together O'Connor's religious convictions and her refusal to turn art into a proposition.[29] Yet McMullen neglects the fact that the seemingly oppositional

---

25. McMullen, *Writing Against God*, 8.
26. McMullen, *Writing Against God*, 9.
27. McMullen, *Writing Against God*, 17. In chapter 3, I explore the key features of biblical poetics, including characterization. As in O'Connor's stories, biblical Hebrew narrative leaves abundant room for inference regarding the key characteristics of the figures in the story. Whereas McMullen deems this spare quality as detrimental, I argue its benefit as a means of the often-painful work of grace in readers.
28. McMullen, *Writing Against God*, 10.
29. McMullen, *Writing Against God*, 141.

relationship between theological didacticism and narrative presentation allows readers a wide net when interpreting O'Connor's stories.

In a scathing review, Sally Fitzgerald—O'Connor's longtime friend and editor of O'Connor's posthumous works and letters—pinpoints the danger of speaking of O'Connor's theological beliefs and narrative style as standing in opposition to one another as a sort of cheap and sentimental game to trip up readers:

> McMullen's inquest would reduce a unique literary legacy to a mere literary curiosity, the product of a mean-spirited writer's solitary game, its contents of no real interest to the reader, except possibly as a demonstration of an immense but fundamentally wasted writing talent; or if not that, the sad spectacle of that talent, however great, revealed as having lacked a governing intelligence able to put it to its owner's intended use, and therefore inadvertently directed to the service of a diametrically opposed purpose. Given such a choice of mounts, this reviewer proposes to walk.[30]

Fitzgerald thus refuses to accept McMullen's premise that O'Connor sought to make a sentimental game of her fiction. In the spirit of Fitzgerald, my proposal in this book is rather the opposite of McMullen's, despite our shared recognition of O'Connor's distinctive story-telling: O'Connor's spare literary style makes significant interpretive demands of the reader, which fittingly narrates the human encounter with God.

Sarah Gordon, in *Flannery O'Connor: The Obedient Imagination*, attributes the spare and extreme form of O'Connor's style to her aim to write like a man because she was artistically dominated by her patriarchal Catholicism.[31] O'Connor, S. Gordon notes, "seems as imbued with the threat of the female, of those 'scribbling women' decried by Hawthorne, as her male predecessors and model." S. Gordon continues, "This stance reveals at least an unconscious decision that, I believe, accounts for the disturbing quality of O'Connor's fiction—that is to say, the toughness of the narrative style and subject matter and the boldness of vision."[32] S. Gordon blames O'Connor's obedience (possibly unconscious) to the male-dominated Roman Catholic Church as the cause of her bare narrative

---

30. Fitzgerald, "McMullen's Choice," 528.

31. In this work, I will use the shortened name "S. Gordon" when discussing her work in order to avoid confusing Sarah Gordon with Caroline Gordon, O'Connor's writing mentor.

32. S. Gordon, *Obedient Imagination*, 29–30.

style. S. Gordon's gendered interpretation of O'Connor's paratactic style of narration problematizes rather than celebrates it, as if hypotactic style were somehow "feminine."

In contrast, Frederick Asals's *Flannery O'Connor: The Imagination of Extremity* lauds O'Connor's bold writing style.[33] Asals emphasizes the stylistic extremes that O'Connor employs to push her characters towards all or nothing responses to God's demands on them. Asals notes that the "very leanness" of O'Connor's two novels, when set against the "heftier works" of many of her contemporaries, demonstrates O'Connor's "deliberate limitation of form."[34] Her "sharply economical style," Asals argues, conveys "bright but bare images" that produce a dramatic effect,[35] as her spare syntax intensifies the focus and impact of her characters and their actions.[36]

Further illumnating O'Connor's distinctive writing voice, Donald Hardy offers extensive attention to the technical qualities of O'Connor's style.[37] He compares the linguistic patterns found in O'Connor's fiction to the Brown general fiction corpus, a database created in 1967, compiling selections of current American English so as to provide a basis for lexical computational analysis. Hardy employs these computational statistics to identify the essential features of O'Connor's fiction, emphasizing the frequent use of independent clauses, including a heavy reliance on coordinate conjunctions. Hardy also highlights O'Connor's above average use of negation (e.g., "not" and "-n't") as well as her use of gerundive complements (e.g., "seeing," "knowing"). Hardy thus confirms the unique quality of O'Connor's style, but he does not link it to her theological vision.

---

33. Asals, *Imagination of Extremity*.

34. Asals, *Imagination of Extremity*, 160.

35. Asals, *Imagination of Extremity*, 20. Asals goes on to note that in *Wise Blood* we find a maturing of her narrative style over her earliest unpublished prose, for the novel has "a greater economy of notation, a flatter, sharper rhythm, and an expansion in suggestiveness" (21).

36. Asals identifies the force of O'Connor's style in the "dynamics of opposition" within the human person, as seen in St. Augustine's *Confessions*, noting that "the essential cast of her imagination was far more Augustinian than Thomistic" (Asals, *Imagination of Extremity*, 200). In St. Thomas, Asals recognizes a traditional form of Catholic humanism with a faith-reason synthesis rather than opposition and paradox marks the human person. Asals surmises that because O'Connor's location was within the Protestant South, Augustine—a figure prominent in both Catholic and Protestant tradition—played a more central role in O'Connor's character formation and expression than Thomas Aquinas (Asals, *Imagination of Extremity*, 201).

37. Hardy, *Narrating Knowledge in Flannery O'Connor's Fiction*.

I offer this survey to demonstrate that no one has thus far offered a robust theological articulation of O'Connor's style and its impact on readers. I aim to do just that by relating O'Connor's spare style to biblical Hebrew narrative's paratactic narration through its use of the *wayyiqtol*. In this book, I demonstrate that the two narrative styles undergird a basic theological conviction shared by the ancient biblical narrators and the modern fiction writer alike: stories that fittingly narrate encounters with the divine require substantial readerly involvement in discerning the subtlety of skeletal narration. The gapped narrative style, with its ambiguous and abrupt qualities, invites readers to plumb the depths of meaning within a story, confronting not only the characters but themselves in their encounter with the grace which, as O'Connor famously said, must wound before it can heal.

Book Overview

In Chapter 1, "A Style Too Demanding? Caroline Gordon, the New Criticism, and Flannery O'Connor's *Wise Blood*," I explore the relationship between O'Connor and Caroline Gordon, her writing mentor, to illuminate how Gordon's expectations for O'Connor's writing style were met and thwarted throughout O'Connor's writing career. This exploration primarily centers on the feedback Gordon offers to O'Connor on drafts of her first novel, *Wise Blood*. While one can never get inside the mind of another, my exploration will raise the central question of intention regarding O'Connor's temperamental reception of Gordon's advice: why did O'Connor accept some, but not all of Gordon's recommended changes? Notably, Gordon's repeated advice not to place such harsh demands on readers with O'Connor's skeletal narration. Despite Gordon's ongoing insistence that O'Connor add more substance to her skeletal stories, O'Connor's never strays too far from the lean style of storytelling found in *Wise Blood*. O'Connor's refusal to make her style easier on her readers results in an ascetic quality to her storytelling.

Chapter 2, "Flannery O'Connor's Grotesque as Moments of Excess," connects O'Connor's artistry and theology in order demonstrate the relationship between the manner in which a story is told and the muddled allusions to divine mystery therein. I begin with Jacques Maritain's Thomistic theological aesthetics and end with Rowan Williams's exploration of the wounding involved in knowledge of God. Tying these two sections together is an examination of the function of O'Connor's constant recourse to situations of extreme, even grotesque, violence. The relationship between

INTRODUCTION

wounding and blessing, disruption and revelation, ugliness and beauty emerges through an investigation of how we glimpse the divine in quotidian life. Recognizing the connection between a story's form and meaning establishes the groundwork for my argument that O'Connor's style effects a distressing response in her readers akin to the excessive moments in her stories. The ascetic demands on readers invites them into a readerly suffering that serves as its own kind of spiritual discipline.

In Chapter 3, "On Stories Sparely Wrought," I attend to the paratactic style in biblical Hebrew narrative and O'Connor's fiction. In so doing, I draw out the demands that spare narration places on readers. Notably in this chapter, I resource the scholarship of biblical narrative criticism to elucidate O'Connor's distinctive narrative style, focusing on the functions of characterization, pacing, and, most significantly, the *wayyiqtol*. This work of this chapter lays the groundwork for the side-by-side readings of the patriarch Jacob in Gen 32 and *Wise Blood*'s Hazel Motes in the next chapter.

In Chapter 4, "Genesis 32 and *Wise Blood*: The Wounded Victor and the Blinded Convert," I establish how reading biblical Hebrew narrative alongside O'Connor's fiction illuminates the style and force of O'Connor's storytelling. In this chapter, I demonstrate the significance of the climactic moment in *Wise Blood* by attending to its narrative pacing and gaps. I explore how Haze's narrated conversion shares thematic and stylistic features with a much older story: Jacob's night-time wrestling with a mysterious man in Gen 32:22–32, as he receives the new name Israel. I will not argue that O'Connor's depiction of Haze's conversion placed the account of Gen 32 in its background, nor even that it plays an essential role in understanding the events of *Wise Blood*. Instead, I will draw out the similarities in paratactic style through the presence and transposition of the *wayyiqtol* to signal an underlying theological conviction concerning a fitting narration of divine self-disclosure in human activity.

I turn from the world of fiction to that of readers in Chapter 5, "Reading Spare Stories," as I illustrate the ascetic of O'Connor's skeletal stories. The work of the preceding chapters comes together in an exploration of the ways that O'Connor's paratactic narration of reality illumined by God draws readers into their own terrifying and potentially wounding encounters with divine grace. To demonstrate this wounding effect on readers, I first outline a phenomenological account of the act of reading through the work of Wolfgang Iser. In this section, I emphasize the necessarily participatory nature of readers to infer a story's meaning. I articulate the vulnerability and entanglement of readers in the reading event, which includes the recognition that different styles of narrative make different degrees and sorts of demands on readers. I then turn to an analogue of the vulnerability of reading found in the act of prayer as drawn out by Jean-Louis Chrétien. Chrétien articulates prayer as a wounding event, paralleling it to the wounding and blessed outcome of Jacob's wrestling with a divine visitor on the banks of the Jabbok. My exploration of the analogue of a wounding reading to a wounding prayer culminates in St. Bonaventure's account of St. Francis receiving the stigmata—where the mystical seraphic vision pierces St. Francis's heart and flesh. Sharing an affinity with St. Francis's reception of the stigmata, a certain kind of reading event can make readers vulnerable to their own wounding event as spare narrative style invites them into a posture of prayer.

In Chapter 6, "Blessed Wounds of Reading: 'The River,' 'The Enduring Chill,' 'Parker's Back,'" I turn to three of O'Connor's short stories to illustrate the way O'Connor's spare narration invites readers into their own blessed and wounding reading event. Each story illustrates one of three reading wounds: wounds that humiliate, wounds that implicate, and wounds that overflow with love. "The River," arguably one of O'Connor's most beautiful and sorrowful stories, leaves readers with the conflicting feelings of a good and tragic end with boy Bevel's once-and-for-all baptism in order to find the Kingdom of God. This tension creates an awareness of the limits of a reader's interpretive reach and generates a humbling, even humiliating effect. "The Enduring Chill," with prideful and intellectual Asbury made a fool, reveals the way a story can implicate us in our own folly and arrogance. Finally, "Parker's Back," one of O'Connor's most beloved stories, demonstrates the power of Christ's stigmatizing love to overflow, both within the story and without in the lives of readers.

Finally, in the concluding chapter "Stylistic Asceticism," I weave together the strands of earlier chapter to reinforce that the demands placed on readers of O'Connor's spare narration share a kinship with the self-denying practices found in asceticism. Stories sparely wrought invite readers into confronting themselves as they are confronted with reality illumined by God. I close with a reflection on the ways the narrations of the crippled victor Jacob and of the blinded convert Haze present protagonists who know well the effect of blessed wounds. This blessed wounding extends out from the narrative art itself and puts readers at risk of their own wrangling and transformation. Analogous to the artist laboring over her work, readers engage these sparsely narrated stories as an event—a participation of readers with the text that requires their creativity and vulnerability to produce a credible interpretation of the story.

In summation, this book deals with Flannery O'Connor's ascetically narrated stories, with their syntactic parallel to biblical Hebrew narrative, as stories concerning (often uninvited and unwelcome) divine grace breaking into the created order of things. To narrate grace effectively and credibly is difficult. An examination of the spare style of these narratives of grace reveals the role style plays in meaning. Grace hypotactically rendered runs the risk of saying too much about an event veiled in mystery. Paratactic narration demonstrates how silence and sparse detail, opens up meaning rather than shutting it down. O'Connor's employment of spare style, notably in narrating transformative grace, resists demands to render grace clearly and explicitly. Therein, spare narration fittingly renders the terrifying and splendid moments when God illumines our reality.

Excursus: Attending to the Language of the "Violence" of Redemption

Language of wounding and violence in discussing God's revelation and redemption invites criticism that is worthy of pause and consideration. The most well-represented critical position against Christian language of redemptive violence—centrally located in the discussion of the atonement—is found within feminist criticism. The critique and resistance to Christian language of the atonement by feminist critics are extensive, and therefore only a cursory evaluation can be provided here.

Anna Fisk's *Sex, Sin and Our Selves: Encounters in Feminist Theology and Contemporary Women's Literature* provides a helpful overview of feminist critiques of the traditional Christian position of redemptive and violent suffering exemplified on the cross—a position that this chapter has partially explored.[38] The atonement theory of penal substitution stands at the center of feminist critique. Penal substitution is most readily identified with the Reformers but can be found in nascent form in the medieval theologian Anselm of Canterbury in his Christological treatise *Cur Deus Homo* ("Why God Became Man"). The central idea of penal substitution is that Christ was punished for humanity's sins against God: Christ vicariously received the judgment of the Father and atoned for sins that were not his own. Fisk refers

---

38. Fisk, *Sex, Sin, and Our Selves*, 104–33.

to penal substitution as "the most blunt-edged version of Christian atonement theology," which many feminist critics regard as not only condoning violence against the innocent but also sacralizing it.[39]

Further, the creative work of feminist theologians who see in Christ's suffering a solidarity with the suffering of the female body illustrates how the violence against Christ becomes sexual violence when the sufferer's body is female rather than male.[40] Violence against women in any age—undoubtedly including first-century Judea—is most often found in domestic violence and sexual assault. In summarizing this work, Elizabeth Bettenhausen encapsulates the re-gendering work of Christ's suffering by asking: "Would women ever imagine forming a religion around the rape of women?"[41] To which Fisk fiercely responds: "'of course not: that would be horrendous.'"[42]

Fisk pushes back against these criticisms not because they are unfounded, but because they too simplistically reflect on the suffering of Christ and the suffering of bodies, including female bodies. Fisk autobiographically reflects on how her own wounds, now scars, brought about through self-mutilation: they "testify to the truth obvious to the point of banality: that suffering exists."[43] Fisk raises the concern that while feminist critics want to reject the valorization of violence with regard to the Crucifixion, in their zeal they fail to deal realistically with the world and the bodies that inhabit it. In their idealism of how the world should be, Fisk argues that these critics fall into nearly gnostic anti-body tendencies: "[J]

---

39. Fisk, *Sex, Sin, and Our Selves*, 104. Fisk draws on the often-referenced essay "For God So Loved the World?" by Joanne Carlson Brown and Rebecca Parker to illustrate the critique: "[a]t the center of Western Christianity is the story of the cross, which claims God the Father required death of his Son to save the world. We believe this theological claim sanctifies violence" (Brown and Parker, "For God So Loved the World," 26).

A further critique of making Christ's suffering a model for the Christian life is found in Asian-Feminist Sharon Bong's concern over "'violence of abstraction'" which pathologizes violence (e.g., women as inherently weak because they are the most common recipients of violence). This danger is found in "romanticizing and appropriating the narrative of subjected positions." To avoid this danger, Bong argues must involve narrating bodies that receive violence as capable of resistance and, more broadly, making the systemic sin of the violence point towards transformation in the world (Bong, "Suffering Christ and the Asian Body," 359, 340).

40. Fisk, *Sex, Sin, and Our Selves*, 106. A summary of these reimagined accounts are found in the Foreword to *Christianity, Patriarchy and Abuse*.

41. Bettenhausen, "Foreword," xi.

42. Fisk, *Sex, Sin, and Our Selves*, 106.

43. Fisk, *Sex, Sin, and Our Selves*, 108.

ust as the ontological reality of the suffering body is eschewed in favor of an idealized, erotic body, so is the possibility of representing human, embodied suffering as in any way divine. Yet, arguably, throughout the world and throughout history, pain and suffering is not a distortion of human bodily experience: it is *constitutive* of it."[44] Fisk worries that "a theology that refuses the representation of the wounded, suffering body because it falls short of the feminist ideal of embodiment... is unable to honor how things actually *are*."[45] This worry brings us to Fisk's central critique of the critics who want to reject any veneration of the suffering body of Christ: "the feminist deconstruction of the soteriological aspects of Christian theology ... [are] a detriment of a real engagement with the complex and painful realities of the world."[46] Namely, "theology would do better to attend to how things are, rather than how we want them to be."[47] Christ's suffering can be seen not as an idealization of violence but as a truthful representation of the way of the world, a world that crucified Love.[48]

The criticism Fisk identifies and to which she responds does not capture the full range of dangers in speaking of blessing and wounding in tandem. As a further example, Rosemary Radford Ruether identifies the problematic gendered dichotomy that captures much of the Christian tradition (and continues in many circles presently) in which pride and anger serve as the pinnacle of vice and, as remedy, humility and self-denial capture the center of virtue. While the truths of these claims may arguably be correct, the patriarchy has twisted these virtues and vices to the detriment of women in many Christian communities. Humility has been perversely twisted into a tool to subjugate women by insisting that it is virtuous for the

44. Fisk, *Sex, Sin, and Our Selves*, 113, italics hers.
45. Fisk, *Sex, Sin, and Our Selves*, 113, italics hers.
46. Fisk, *Sex, Sin, and Our Selves*, 104.
47. Fisk, *Sex, Sin, and Our Selves*, 104.
48. In *Resurrecting Wounds: Living in the Afterlife of Trauma*, Shelly Rambo makes a similar response to feminists who wish to dismiss the salvific significance of Christ's suffering: "in turning away from interpreting the cross redemptively, there is a danger in not theologizing suffering at all, in avoiding any moves to narrate human suffering by way of the Christian story" (Rambo, *Resurrecting Wounds*, 6). Later in her work, Rambo draws out her critique of "feminist theology that flees from wounds" because it fails to take note of the distinctive character of Christ's transfiguring wounds: "The movement through death, through pain, is not problematic in itself, but it needs to be reinscribed in Christian understanding. The reinscription via the scar envisions shared flesh with marks. In its marking, it is also transfigured.... The memory of suffering is not there naked and exposed; it is protected, covered, and witnessed" (69).

women not to hold herself in high esteem. Virtue is twisted in these communities, often under the Isaianic label of living as "'suffering servants' by accepting male abuse and exploitation."[49] The virtue of humility becomes perverted into a patriarchal tool of oppression.

I do not expect that my presentation of the relationship between wounding and blessing will fully satisfy those who worry that allegedly redemptive violence perpetuates broader systems of violence, particularly against women. Explanation of the action of wounding related to blessing might help clarify, if not entirely placate, critics who are rightfully wary of the claim that God acts violently in the work of redemption. There are two central ways of interpreting the act of a wounding blessing: first, as an act of trespass, harm, and violent force; or, second, as an act of purgative healing and painful medicine. The interchange of wounding and blessing—exemplified in Rowan Williams focus on a wound of knowledge—fits within the latter characterization of the action of a wounding blessing as purgative. This kind of wounding is a movement of dispossession rather than violent possession. In discussing the work of praise in the Judeo-Christian tradition, Williams comments: "the action of praise necessarily involves evoking a moment of dispossession, a death, in order to bring the *novum* of God into focus."[50] The imagery of baptism—death of the self, life in Christ—captures this dispossessing effect.[51]

49. Ruether, *Sexism and God Talk*, 186.
50. Williams, *On Christian Theology*, 10.
51. I realize that my distinction between force and dispossession does not cover the range of criticisms leveled against the language of wounding related to human encounter with the divine. One of the most recent and arguably best criticisms of the language of a reordered desire that causes a dispossessing wound—as articulated in Williams—is found in "Chapter Three: Speaking 'Father' Rightly: Kenotic Reformation into Sonship in Sarah Coakley" in Tonstad's *God and Difference*. Tonstad highlights Coakley's emphasis on "dependence on God as vulnerability," which leads to a collapse of finitude and sin when discussing the purgation necessary for union with God (Tonstad, *God and Difference*, 99). Tonstad sees in Coakley's proposal in *God, Sexuality, and the Self* human union with God as both a rejection of finitude and a continual power of the patriarchy: "There is no place for the human being in the trinity unless she willfully and deliberately evacuates herself and becomes ontologically identical with the incarnate Son in the process. The infusion of divinity into the contemplative paradoxically elevates her too highly while reinforcing the figuration of the God-creation relationship in hierarchically and heterosexually gendered terms" (Tonstad, *God and Difference*, 107). Tonstad's critiques leaves us at an impasse. Tonstad's desire to reject the language of ascent that appears in the early Christian tradition and continues in some strands of medieval and modern thought because of the kenotic action exemplified in Christ and imitated by the Christian leaves those, like Coakley and Williams, who appeal to tradition without much ground

INTRODUCTION

Fisk's realist argument for using Christ's suffering as a point of solidarity because suffering exists in the world (even if we object to it) aligns well with the writers I have discussed. O'Connor remarks in a letter to fellow writer Andrew Lytle that her decision to depict grace violently rests on the evil present in the world: "grace can be violent or would have to be [so, in order] to compete with the kind of evil I can make concrete" (CW, 1121). Her comment here both reflects the reality of evil in the world and her ability to render grace within the world. In the very next sentence, O'Connor recognizes that the use of force might not always be the best way to depict grace: "At the same time, I keep seeing Elias [a variation of Elijah, used in the Douay-Rheims Catholic Bible] in the cave, waiting to hear the voice of the Lord in the thunder and lighting and wind, and only hearing it finally in the gentle breeze, and I feel I'll have to be able to do that sooner or later, or anyway keep trying (CW, 1121). O'Connor echoes the feminist concern about the danger of abstracting violence. To speak of a wounding blessing is not to argue that all blessings must wound, or at least wound in such a violent way as to create Jacob's life-long limp. Instead, speaking of the relationship of wounding and blessing brings to the fore the uncomfortable and unsentimental work of rightly ordering our desire to its proper end. The sometimes violent struggle inherent in such work is a symptom, not the source or center, of reality illumined by God.

---

to stand on. This specific problem points to the broader tension between Christian theology and feminist criticism. While wrestling within this place of tension is important, ultimately one claim—inadvertently or intentionally—takes priority over the other.

Chapter 1

A Style Too Demanding?

Caroline Gordon, the New Criticism, and
Flannery O'Connor's *Wise Blood*

Introduction

AT THE START OF a friendship that would last through Flannery O'Connor's tragically short life, acclaimed novelist and literary critic Caroline Gordon writes a nine-page letter to O'Connor regarding the draft-form of *Wise Blood*.[1] Gordon praises O'Connor for her current draft: "I admire tremendously the hard core of dramatic action in this book. I certainly wouldn't want to soften it up."[2] The remainder of the letter entails a number of recommendations to improve the flow and clarity of *Wise Blood*: "I think that the whole book would gain by not being so stripped, so bare, by surrounding the core of action with some contrasting material."[3] Gordon jests that the bare quality of O'Connor's draft runs "the danger of making excessive demands of readers. He is not very bright you know, and the most intelligent person, when he is reading fiction, switches his intellect off and—if the author does what he is trying to do—listens like a three or thirteen year old child."[4] Gordon identifies *Wise Blood*'s crucial scene, where Hazel Motes is pulled over by the police officer, as a place that O'Connor moves too quickly in a way that minimizes the impact of the episode on readers. The final form of *Wise Blood* indicates that O'Connor

---

1. This letter is found in Fitzgerald, "Master Class," 831–46.
2. Fitzgerald, "Master Class," 832.
3. Fitzgerald, "Master Class," 833.
4. Fitzgerald, "Master Class," 834.

heeded Gordon's advice but only to a certain degree, for O'Connor still demands a lot—some might say too much—of readers in the novel's final events that conclude with Hazel's self-blinding.

In this chapter, I explore the relationship between Gordon and O'Connor to elucidate how Gordon's expectations for O'Connor's writing style were both met and thwarted throughout O'Connor's writing career. While one can never get inside the mind of another, my exploration raises the central question of intention regarding O'Connor's temperamental reception of Gordon's advice: why did O'Connor accept some but not all of Gordon's recommended changes?

My exploration begins with a brief look at Caroline Gordon's narrative style in her most famous story "Old Red" to place the narrative style between master and student in stark relief. I then move to an overview of the contours and influence of New Criticism—Gordon being one of its strongest advocates—on O'Connor. I continue by attending to the mentoring relationship that began in the revisions of O'Connor's first major publication and ended with O'Connor's untimely death. Finally, I turn to a closer reading of the correspondence between Gordon and O'Connor in the drafting of *Wise Blood* that typifies the extent to which O'Connor followed her writing mentor's advice. Through both wide and narrow examinations of their relationship, the contours of O'Connor's particular style of storytelling—which at times frustrated and confounded Gordon—will be drawn out. Summarily, despite Gordon's ongoing insistence that O'Connor add more substance to her spare stories, O'Connor's stories never stray too far from the lean style of storytelling found in *Wise Blood*.[5]

---

5. While I could make judgments about Gordon's theological or philosophical impulse for recommending the radical changes and therein argue for Gordon's deficient theological imagination when confronted with the imaginative and theological artistry of O'Connor, I am avoiding this line of argumentation altogether. My concern in this chapter is to establish O'Connor's distinctive and willful spare style. It also must be said that O'Connor took the majority of Gordon's advice and her stories are better for it. To pit Gordon against O'Connor undercuts their important mentoring relationship. Gordon herself recognized the genius and originality of O'Connor's work and saw her advice as an offering, not a mandate, for O'Connor's consideration: "I feel like a fool when I criticise your stories. I think you are a genius.... I might as well come out with it. I also think you are one of the most original writers now practising. It really is presumptuous for me to offer you suggestions. But you have asked for them and since you have more talent and more humility than most of the young people who ask for my criticism I shall just set forth my notions as they come into my head" (Flanagan, *Letters*, 144). In 2018, Christine Flanagan edited a collection of mostly unpublished correspondence between Gordon and O'Connor, from which I am gratefully citing in this chapter. Flanagan notes in the

Caroline Gordon's "Old Red"

Gordon's fiction is known for its use of symbol. The function of symbolism in her fiction, as one critic comments, "moves *toward* abstraction rather than proceeds from it."[6] O'Connor notes that Gordon's use of symbol in "Old Red" served as an introduction to "what I could be expected to do with a symbol" (HB, 200).

The employment of symbol in "Old Red" revolves around the story's namesake: a fox named Old Red.[7] The aged protagonist Aleck Maury recalls his first sighting of Old Red:

> An image had risen in his memory, an image that was familiar but came to him infrequently of late and that only in moments of elation: the wide field in front of his uncle's house.... They would be waiting there in that broad plain when they had the first sight of the fox. On that little rise by the river, loping steadily, not yet alarmed. The sun would glint on his bright coat, on his quick turning head as he dove into the dark woods.[8]

At the story's close, the elderly Maury again recalls Old Red:

> He ran slowly, past the big boulder, past the blasted pine to where the shadow of the Pinnacle Rock was black across the path. He ran on and the shadow swayed and rose to meet him. Its cool touch was on his tongue, his heaving flanks. He had slipped in under it. He was sitting down, panting, in black dark, on moist earth while the hounds' baying filled the valley and reverberated on the mountainside.[9]

In both of these reflections on the fox, Aleck Maury returns to the present: in the first instance his memories of exhilarating hunts shift to his present walk along the riverbank with his fishing rod, and in the second instance the movement from the memory of Old Red resting his well-worked body on cool rock to the old man lying in bed imagining his deceased wife. The

---

collection's introduction that while the perennial debate around Gordon's influence on O'Connor continue, "[w]hatever scholars conclude about her influence, Gordon's admiration for O'Connor's work was genuine.... O'Connor was equally appreciative" (Flanagan, *Letters*, 14). I echo this sentiment.

6. Landess, *Short Fiction of Caroline Gordon*, 2, italics his.
7. Gordon, *Old Red*.
8. Gordon, *Old Red*, 134.
9. Gordon, *Old Red*, 146.

vibrant and striking images of Old Red reverberate against Maury, a feeble man who now takes up fishing rather than the hunt and lies awake at night groaning in pain and remembering days gone by.

Gordon's narration of Maury's recollection of the fox evidences her artistry in symbolic description. O'Connor praises Gordon's ability to introduce readers to "a complete world" where "the meaning comes from the things themselves and not her imposing anything. Right when you finish reading, you don't think you've read anything, but the more you think about it the more it grows" (HB, 187). O'Connor is not alone in this assessment. One review of "Old Red" describes her world-making skill as a kind of "telling" by making a subtle "showing" of "selected details that form the basis of realistic fiction."[10] Gordon's fiction thus extends from the concrete to the abstract as her narrative Gordon's literary style works "from the inner reality outward."[11]

The majority of the story narrates the interior life of Aleck Maury, playing out his memories of the past and his feelings about the present as he lies in bed at night. The interiority of Gordon's story contrasts starkly with O'Connor's focus on the action of her characters that rarely offers glimpses into their interior thoughts and feelings. Gordon's interior world is filled with rich description—as seen in Maury's description of the fox sightings—while O'Connor's spare style leaves readers with ample interpretive work to fill-in a scene. That is, Gordon's hypotactic style, when set alongside O'Connor's paratactic narrative style, reveals the essential difference between Gordon and O'Connor.

This statement is not critical assessment of the *quality* of Gordon's work in comparison to O'Connor's fiction. Instead, this brief look at "Old Red" reveals the disparate styles of the two authors. O'Connor welcomed Gordon's advice yet never fully adopted the interior-focused and luxurious narrative style found in "Old Red." As the remainder of the chapter shows, the relationship between O'Connor and Gordon was always tense: O'Connor the student sought to learn from her teacher but, at times, remained unwilling to flesh out scenes that Gordon recommended as guides to the reader. As a result, O'Connor never ceases to make tremendous interpretive demands on the reader.

---

10. Wiggins, "Caroline Gordon: 'Old Red,'" 67.
11. Wiggins, "Caroline Gordon: "Old Red," 68.

New Criticism, Gordon, and O'Connor

In *Flannery O'Connor, Walker Percy, and the Aesthetic of Revelation*, John D. Sykes Jr. explores O'Connor's relationship with New Criticism, the dominant interpretive method in mid-twentieth century America.[12] Sykes introduces Caroline Gordon as a striking influence on O'Connor, as well as fellow contemporary southern writer, Walker Percy:

> Along with her husband, Allen Tate, Gordon represented three allegiances that help us place O'Connor and Percy in context: she was closely committed to a theory of literature we may broadly call New Critical, she was a self-conscious Roman Catholic and she was a southerner. Although Percy's philosophical interest in language theory and his inclination toward the novel of ideas would lead him away from New Critical ideas, O'Connor seems to have resonated deeply with the older writer's [i.e., Gordon's] views on the nature of fiction. And this New Critical bent was to have consequences for her fiction.[13]

Sykes identifies the influence of New Criticism on O'Connor as beginning prior to her relationship with Gordon during her graduate studies at the University of Iowa in 1945: "Although as a whole the Iowa's Writer's Workshop was a hardly a New Critical bootcamp . . . clearly the atmosphere was permeated with the attitudes and the personalities of the movement."[14] New Criticism is centered on showing over telling within narrative, an idea which Sykes identifies in Gordon's advice to O'Connor again and again: "'Don't state, render!'"[15] Sykes recognizes this New Critical emphasis on rendering as one of the two poles of O'Connor's fiction, the other being Catholic dogma.[16] Sykes states the tension between these two poles succinctly: "She [O'Connor] believed she had something of great importance to say to an audience who greatly needed to hear it, yet she was committed to a poetics that prized ambiguity."[17] O'Connor's literary identity encapsulates two distinct influences: the New Critical prizing of ambiguity and the prophetic voice of the Catholic faith in the modern world.

---

12. Sykes, *Aesthetic of Revelation*, 9–38.
13. Sykes, *Aesthetic of Revelation*, 10.
14. Sykes, *Aesthetic of Revelation*, 11.
15. Sykes, *Aesthetic of Revelation*, 17.
16. Sykes, *Aesthetic of Revelation*, 17.
17. Sykes, *Aesthetic of Revelation*, 19.

Sarah Gordon comments on how these two poles—the New Critical and theological—reveal O'Connor's struggle to find her authorial voice in drafting of *Wise Blood*: "a work deeply influenced by O'Connor's reading in the moderns, her assimilation of the New Criticism, and the emergence of a stringent Catholicism as the bedrock of her fiction"[18] S. Gordon's dismissive notion of the stringency of O'Connor's religion prompts her negative conclusion that O'Connor forced her fiction to fall in line with the patriarchy of the Roman Catholic Church.[19] Even so, S. Gordon helpfully points out that the many drafts of *Wise Blood* disclose the "painstaking process of the novel's creation and the author's groping for subject matter consonant with her Christian vision and with the stylistic demands of the New Criticism."[20] While the extent to which one can distinguish between O'Connor's Christian vision and New Criticism's literary style is rather more complicated than S. Gordon presents, identifying O'Connor as both Catholic and New Critic reinforces Sykes's overall assessment.

An Outline of New Criticism

To understand the atmosphere of New Criticism requires a quick overview of its rise and central tenets.[21] New Critics are characterized by a concern for close and careful reading of texts where the concern is primarily with the text itself, rather than attempting to get behind or around the text. This form of criticism arose in direct response to a scientifically-oriented academy that some identified as failing to engage imaginatively with primary texts.[22] As one author notes, "This [failure of attention to the text] is where the New Critics came in: they managed persuasively to trace the contours of a text-centered approach, giving substance to the phrase 'the text itself' and demonstrating in action the interpretive tools the study of

---

18. S. Gordon, *Obedient Imagination*, 89.

19. This critique of the Roman Catholic Church's patriarchal influence serves as the central theme for S. Gordon's feminist reading of O'Connor's fiction in *Obedient Imagination*.

20. S. Gordon, *Obedient Imagination*, 89.

21. I follow Sykes's lead when he notes that "New Criticism itself is better understood as a *collection of attitudes and orientations* than as a critical system" (Sykes, *Aesthetic of Revelation*, 12, italics added).

22. Cain, "Literary Criticism," 505.

the text required."[23] Pedagogically, the concern to return to the text itself enabled teachers to empower their students to engage and interpret texts from the outset of their studies without requiring the acquisition of laborious pre-reading strategies.[24] A prime example of this concern for students to approach literature directly is seen in Cleanth Brooks and Robert Penn Warren's *Understanding Fiction*, which, first published in 1943, served as a text in one of O'Connor's 1945 classes at the Iowa's Writers Workshop.[25] In the book's preface entitled "Letter to the Teacher," the authors lay out their central and quintessential New Critical claim:

> This book is based on the belief that the student can best be brought to an appreciation of the more broadly human values implicit in fiction by a course of study which aims at the close analytical and interpretive reading of concrete examples. It seems to us that the student may best come to understand a given piece of fiction by understanding the functions of the various elements which go to make up fiction and by understanding their relationships to each other in the whole construct.[26]

New Criticism certainly did not ignore formalist concerns for structure and textual patterns, but it returned the delight of reading to the classroom, enabling students to be drawn into the text without being bogged down by background ideology, historiography, and so on.[27] The central aim was to imbue students with an appreciation of the irreducible quality of fiction, whose meaning cannot be encapsulated in an abstract propositions.

The appendix to *Understanding Fiction* offers insight into how New Criticism translates into judgments about good and less good artistry. While there is "no single, special technique or formula for writing good fiction," it

---

23. Cain, "Literary Criticism," 505.

24. Cain, "Literary Criticism," 544.

25. Sykes, *Aesthetic of Revelation*, 11.

26. Brooks and Warren, *Understanding Fiction*, xiii–xiv.

27. Despite the great benefit wrought by New Criticism's concern with a return to the text itself, it suffered from a lack of concern for authorial intention. Cain notes that the New Critics either downplayed or even ignored the plight of and discrimination against African Americans and women (Cain, "Literary Criticism," 547–58). Thus did the "fiercest opposition" to New Critics arise during the heightened social awareness of the 1960s and 70s: "They [social protestors] declared that pious talk about aesthetic values and reverence for close reading of literature cloaked anti-human institutional realities and prevented students from striving to end the evils of the world outside the academy" (560).

must authentically represent human experience.[28] Narratival unity remains central to the artistic rendering of what is distinctively human:

> A good writer knows in his very bones that fiction involves not the mere exploiting of a bag of tricks, but the careful study of the possible relationships among the numerous elements which go to make up a piece of fiction. He knows that characterization, setting and atmosphere, plot, style, tone, symbolism, theme, and various other elements must be functionally related to each other to create a real unity—a unity in which every part bears an expressive relation to the other parts.[29]

Brooks and Warren proceed to lay out ten central features to which writers must attend in order to achieve a "real unity" of story to their readers:

1. how a story begins, including vital background information;
2. sufficient descriptive rendering of setting and scene;
3. story's mood;
4. right sort and amount of character and setting description;
5. key illuminating moments;
6. a decisive climactic moment;
7. narrative tension building towards illuminating moment;
8. clear trajectory of interest guiding readers to central conflict;
9. sufficient denouement; and
10. portrayal of characters dynamically as a "complex of potentialities for action."[30]

In addition, there are six non-organizational elements that compromise good fiction:

1. creating interest and curiosity in readers;
2. making clear the central character whose fate is at stake;
3. maintaining consistent and clear narratival point of view;
4. creating a necessary distance created between readers and characters;

---

28. Brooks and Warren, *Understanding Fiction*, 644.
29. Brooks and Warren, *Understanding Fiction*, 645.
30. Brooks and Warren, *Understanding Fiction*, 646–57, quote from 656.

5. finding an appropriate story length; and

6. the pacing of a story as it employs narrative action and summary.[31]

Brooks and Warren make repeated use of Gordon's most famous short story, "Old Red," as an exemplary case of good storytelling. As we will see later in this chapter, their concern for readers plays a principal role in Gordon's recurring critiques of O'Connor's narrative style. Namely, Gordon's advice to O'Connor on *Wise Blood* reflects the New Critic's points of concern regarding the coherence of the story.

S. Gordon offers a hypothesized psychological account of O'Connor's attraction to the New Critics: "O'Connor's shy and self-conscious demeanor may well have been drawn to the emphasis in the New Criticism on the necessary impersonality of the work of art and the need for the writer to erase herself from the work."[32] While there is no demonstrable evidence for such psychologizing, S. Gordon is correct to say that the New Critical desire to let the art stand apart from the artist as it represents itself maps onto her Thomistic view of art, as expressed in her essays:[33] "Art is a word that immediately scares people off, as being a little too grand. But all I mean by art is writing something that is valuable in itself and that works in itself. . . . St. Thomas said that the artist is concerned with the good of that which is made" (MM, 65). For New Critics and Thomists alike, the story itself is the locus point of meaning-making, as O'Connor repeatedly emphasizes: "The meaning of fiction is not abstract meaning but experienced meaning, and the purpose of making statements about the meaning of a story is only to help you experience that meaning more fully" (MM, 96). Such experienced meaning depends, in turn, on *how* a story should be told and thus on the question of style. Examining the mentoring a relationship between Gordon and O'Connor illumines the distinctively spare character of O'Connor's storytelling as the student at times rejects the advice of her mentor, a quintessential New Critic.

---

31. Brooks and Warren, *Understanding Fiction*, 657–67.

32. S. Gordon, *Obedient Imagination*, 85.

33. Most notably in "The Nature and Aim of Fiction" and "Writing Short Stories" in MM.

A STYLE TOO DEMANDING?
Gordon and O'Connor's Writing Mentorship

Gordon and O'Connor's friendship began when Robert Fitzgerald sent along a copy of the *Wise Blood* draft to Caroline Gordon in 1951. Gordon's response, which the next section more closely examines, launched a mentoring friendship that would last through to O'Connor's final completed story before her death, "Parker's Back." The timing for the handoff of O'Connor's writing from Fitzgerald to Gordon just so happened to mark the nascent moment of O'Connor's professional writing career, which comprises two novels—*Wise Blood* (1952) and *The Violent Bear It Away* (1960)—and two collections of short stories—*A Good Man Is Hard to Find* (1955) and *Everything that Rises Must Converge* (posthumously published in 1965).

Even before their writing mentorship began, Gordon influenced O'Connor's literary imagination. In a 1957 letter to Betty Hester, O'Connor comments that Gordon's short story "Old Red" (1934) "introduced me to what I could be expected to do with a symbol and I sat down and wrote the first story I published ['The Geranium' (1946)]" (HB, 200). Yet S. Gordon maintains that the similarity between the two stories extends beyond the use of symbol: "I believe that 'The Geranium' resembles 'Old Red' in other significant ways that O'Connor does not acknowledge. Although the tone and thematic concerns of the stories are markedly different, both 'Old Red' and 'The Geranium' have, as background, father-daughter relationships that leave much to be desired."[34] While both share in the father-daughter relationships and in use of third-person-limited point of view, the tenor of the stories is ultimately different, as O'Connor's story is marked by "sharp, vivid images and strong, often monosyllabic verbs, [which] signal the O'Connor style that is to come."[35] Caroline Gordon's ongoing influence is evident in many of O'Connor's letters, including one letter to an English professor wherein O'Connor shares her mentor's warning against the dangers of the omniscient narrator (CW, 923) and in another letter to Betty Hester commending the unifying effect of the right use of point of view (HB, 157).

Gordon received a draft of everything O'Connor wrote from *Wise Blood* forward, and just as O'Connor's gratitude lasted throughout their friendship, so did Gordon's frustration with O'Connor's limiting narrative viewpoint. In one letter, Gordon describes the importance of point of view with the imagery of an imprisoned reader:

---

34. S. Gordon, *Obedient Imagination*, 71–72.
35. S. Gordon, *Obedient Imagination*, 76.

> I think of [POV] this way: The reader is, as it were, a prisoner, seated on a stool so low that he cannot see out of the window. Therefore he sees of the human scene only what he sees reflected in the eyes of the figure at the window. At first glance this would seem to restrict what he see: he will see only what is reflected in a pair of eyes. But when you stop to think of it that is all anybody can see ordinarily: what he sees through his own eyes. If he sees through his own eyes what is reflected in another pair of eyes he will see twice as much as the next man, who is looking only through his own eyes sees. Here is a great mystery of the craft. I can't explain it. I merely try to tell you how it seems to me.[36]

For Gordon, the job of the narrator is to provide the reader with "another pair of eyes" to see with a double vision available through storytelling. Because Gordon identifies this double vision as the essential quality of writing and reading, she holds O'Connor to a high standard of narration. Gordon wants to provide the imprisoned reader ample information to see for herself by means of the narrator's vision. This reflective narrative vision involves both the panoramic and the scenic. Gordon identifies O'Connor as mastering the scenic—which is precisely what makes O'Connor's stories at once formidable and believable—but needing to develop more of the panoramic viewpoint that unveils the circumambient scene surrounding the central action. Hence, Gordon's insistent call for O'Connor to add landscaping to the narrative action.

In one of Gordon's last letters before O'Connor's death in 1964, Gordon offers her persistent critique against a too limiting point of view in "Parker's Back." Gordon advises O'Connor to add a "panoramic opening" so as to set the scene for Parker's obsession with tattoos—a suggestion to which O'Connor complied—and to change the title to something like "Under Every Green Tree" in order to open up the allegorical level of the story—a proposal O'Connor did not adopt.[37] Where Gordon wanted O'Connor to open up her scenes to a wider view of landscape and deeper insight into characters inner-lives, O'Connor appears to have received and amended her stories according to Gordon's advice only to a certain degree. This partial adoption of Gordon's critique appears again and again throughout their friendship.[38]

36. Flanagan, *Letters*, 66.
37. Flanagan, *Letters*, 214.
38. The examples are too abundant to cover in detail here, but consider the following as a sampling. On "A Circle in the Fire," Gordon suggests that O'Connor provides readers

A prime example of the tension between Gordon's concern for opening up a scene and O'Connor's narrowly-focused point of view is evident in her most famous and also one of her more straightforwardly-told stories, "A Good Man Is Hard to Find." One of O'Connor's most troubling recourses to spare storytelling is found in this story when she narrates "[a]nd the grandmother's head cleared for an instant" to indicate a change in the grandmother (CW, 152). Following this opaque line, the grandmother speaks to the Misfit, "Why you're one of my babies. You're one of my own children" (CW, 152). While the grandmother's moment of clarity and utterance to the Misfit could signal a conversion moment wherein the grandmother's words function as a confession, they could just as well evidence an attempt to manipulate the convict into sparing her life. The Misfit's response, on the other hand, is clear: he reacts to the grandmother's affection with her execution.

Gordon's playful frustration with O'Connor's style is on display in an undated 1953 letter regarding a working draft of the story: "I told you some months ago that I thought your stories suffered from too narrow a focus. I also told you that the omniscient narrator does not speak colloquially—but here you are, at it again."[39] Gordon comments that the

---

a "helping hand" on why the two women's hats stand in opposition—one stiff and the other out of shape (Flanagan, *Letters*, 82). O'Connor does not make the change. On "A Later Encounter with the Enemy," Gordon suggests that O'Connor bulk up the description of the old man seeing his family history flash before his eyes as death comes for him (Flanagan, *Letters*, 89–90). The published version of the scene provides vivid descriptions of his wife, son, and mother (CW, 261). On "The Displaced Person," Gordon points again to "the chief weakness in [O'Connor's] work: the tendency to use too restricted a viewpoint at crucial moments," especially the scene where Mrs. Shortley stands in the field and receives a vision. Gordon recommends that in this scene—and scenes like it—O'Connor shift from the limited point of view of the character to a broader view: "to soar above the conflict, to view it as if through the eyes of an eagle" (Flanagan, *Letters*, 87). In the published version, there is no sign of an eagle-eyed view of this scene (CW, 301). On "The Enduring Chill," Gordon encourages O'Connor to take on elevated speech in the climactic close of the story when Asbury is assaulted by the whirlwind-like power of the Holy Spirit. Gordon comments: "Every time I read your last sentence in your story I balk. I balk on the phrase 'with ice instead of fire.' . . . You cannot say that the HG is coming with ice instead of fire. The phrase is colloquial. . . . Couldn't you say 'enveloped in ice instead of flames'?" (Flanagan, *Letters*, 155). In the published version, we find an affinity with Gordon's advice: "emblazoned in ice instead of fire" (CW, 572). In that same story, Gordon insists that O'Connor rework the initial scene when Asbury steps off the train, so that the sun plays a central role in the landscape because it functions antiphonally in the story at its start and end. In the published version, the opening scene reflects Gordon's recommendation in full (CW, 547).

39. Flanagan, *Letters*, 58.

story does not possess the "proper dimension" with the narrator speaking as commonly as he does, emphasizing that O'Connor's inability to master the omniscient narrator's voice is a "major fault" in her work.[40] Gordon worries that O'Connor's "terrific, unremitting, almost unbearable effort to achieve intensity" contributes to a less than authoritative narrative voice.[41] Regarding the narrow focus of O'Connor's narration, Gordon points to the moment the grandmother hears the gunshots that signal her son and grandson have been killed in the woods: "just after the two pistol shots we need to know how the road, the woods look after these shots were fired."[42] In the published edition, Gordon's insistence on the need for the scene's landscaping were met, though possibly not to the extent Gordon hoped; it reads: "There was a pistol shot from the woods, followed closely by another. Then silence. She could hear the wind move through the tree tops like a long satisfied insuck of breath" (CW, 149).

Gordon's critique of O'Connor's limited and spare style of storytelling never fully subsided. Markedly, Gordon's great lament of O'Connor's fiction is arguably one of the central characteristics of her storytelling: spare narration. The final comments and revisions of *Wise Blood* demonstrate the consistent strain between Gordon and O'Connor concerning how a story is told. Without discounting O'Connor's great admiration and gratitude to be mentored by Gordon, O'Connor's editorial choices demonstrate the ongoing tension between Gordon's concern with the panoramic view and O'Connor's stubborn insistence on keeping her stories straight and spare in order to have her characters and readers confront realities that a more complex style—while seeming to clarify—would have actually obscured.

Caroline Gordon and Wise Blood

Caroline Gordon's critique that O'Connor demands too much of readers involves narrative pacing: "It takes much longer to take things in than we realize. In our effort to keep the action from lagging we hurry readers over crucial moments. But anything that is very exciting can't be taken hurriedly."[43] While she makes a number of suggestions for slowing down scenes, Gordon highlights three pivotal moments in *Wise Blood* "where a

---

40. Flanagan, *Letters*, 58.
41. Flanagan, *Letters*, 58.
42. Flanagan, *Letters*, 60.
43. Fitzgerald, "Master Class," 834.

few strokes might make a lot of difference": 1) the discourse on Enoch's "wise blood;" 2) Hazel, Sabbath, and Enoch's meeting in the boarding house; and 3) the scene with Hazel and the patrolman.[44] By comparing these three scenes in an earlier undated draft—which the matching page numbers in Gordon's letter and the archived material suggest was most likely the 1951 draft Gordon reviewed—to the final published edition of *Wise Blood*, I will demonstrate the extent to which O'Connor acted on the advice of her writing mentor.[45] The focused attention in this chapter on the ways O'Connor both did and did not heed her mentor's counsel lays the groundwork for the later examination (ch. 5) of the theological fruit of O'Connor's distinctive literary style. This exploration attends to O'Connor's deliberate choices in narrating her stories, a deliberation that sometimes flouts the advice of her writing mentor for whom she had the utmost respect.

Before moving to the three central scenes Gordon highlights, a brief summary of some of the minor suggestions Gordon made and O'Connor's revisions based on these suggestions is in order. Gordon offers a number of notes on the early chapters of *Wise Blood*, including expanding the description of the Taulkinham train station's bathroom stall and providing a more rounded characterization of the taxi driver. On the bathroom stall, Gordon remarks, "I need to see the inside of that toilet. The scene would be much more real if we could see what it was like before you begin telling us of his situation: 'He had no place to go,' for instance. The fact that you haven't set your stage properly, haven't showed us what the little room looked like, takes away from the drama of this scene, which otherwise would be one of your best"[46] Regarding the taxi driver, Gordon reiterates the New Critical motto: a character "must be rendered. That is, the reader must be given enough details to enable him to visualize the man. . . . One gives a character like this a different kind of attention from the kind one gives important

---

44. Fitzgerald, "Master Class," 837.

45. Flannery O'Connor Collection, Special Collections, Ina Dillard Russell Library, Georgia College, Milledgeville, GA, 149a. O'Connor signals that she is reworking a draft under the advised comments returned from Gordon, among others: "Bob Giroux and Mrs. Tate [Caroline Gordon] made some suggestions for improving my book and I have been working on these and have by now about come up with another draft of it, of which I will have one copy—readable but with a good many inked-in corrections—I hope in a few weeks" (CW, 889). The archived 1951 draft contains O'Connor's promised well-marked changes.

46. Fitzgerald, "Master Class," 839.

characters. Nevertheless, one must give him his due."⁴⁷ Commenting on Hazel's exchange with the taxi driver, Gordon also offers a crucial judgment concerning dialogue: "It is dangerous, I think to have a character emit more than three sentences in one speech. If he does you get an unlifelike effect. If he has to say more than that you ought to dramatize the fact that he is making quite a long speech. . . . Speeches need air around them—a liberal use of white space improves almost any dialogue."⁴⁸

In both matters, O'Connor faithfully heeds Gordon's advice. But regarding the more pivotal scenes, O'Connor most often refuses to soften her unflinching gaze. Such directness is required by her prophetic vision, "seeing near things with their extensions of meaning and thus of *seeing far things close up*" (MM, 44, italics added). This denial of Gordon's insistence on the need for air to breathe paradoxically opens up rather than closes down all that stands around and outside the sparely narrated scene. Hence my insistence on qualifying the widespread notion that O'Connor unwaveringly submitted to her mentor's advice.⁴⁹

Enoch's "Wise Blood"

The fifth chapter of *Wise Blood* contains a clear example of O'Connor's sidestepping of Gordon's recommendation. Gordon critiques this chapter because O'Connor provides too much narrative *telling* in place of *showing*:

> This is the only part of the book where you rely on statement rather than rendition. I *think* it is because you are uncomfortably aware of the difficulty of putting over Enoch's conviction that he has 'wise blood.' (It's a hellishly difficult problem!) I don't think you handle

---

47. Fitzgerald, "Master Class," 839–40.
48. Fitzgerald, "Master Class," 840.
49. Often the relationship between Gordon and O'Connor is caricatured as O'Connor taking all of Gordon's advice in full. As a quintessential example, Moran in *Creating Flannery O'Connor: Her Critics, Her Publishers, Her Readers* remarks in passing that O'Connor trusted Gordon's instincts "absolutely" (cf. Moran, *Creating Flannery O'Connor*, 19). John D. Sykes Jr. emphasizes Gordon's influence as a New Critic on O'Connor to an extent that potentially runs the risk of overstating the case. Sykes attributes some of O'Connor's non-New Critic moves in her early work to "immaturity." Continuing, "She simply had not yet developed her skills to Caroline Gordon's level." Cf. Sykes, *Aesthetic of Revelation*, 19. I want to argue that O'Connor's divergences from Gordon's advice and style—which show up at times in both her early and later writings ("A View of the Woods" as a prime non-New Critic example in the latter)—demonstrates O'Connor's own crafting of her stories in a way that heeds the advice of her writing mentor without simply falling in line.

it quite right. You rather give your show away beforehand. That is, you tell us what Enoch did every day before you show him in the act of doing it. If you sum up what is going to happen before it happens the reader is not interested in it when it does happen.... But suppose you had prepared a little for your wise blood in previous chapters, say when Enoch and Haze first meet... suppose Enoch let drop a few words to the effect that he, too, has a secret power. Maybe several times.[50]

Gordon suggests two means of strengthening the content of this chapter. First, she dissuades O'Connor from first announcing that Enoch's daily ritual is to walk through the city zoo after work, before narrating Haze's joining Enoch in his disturbing ritualistic journey through the zoo. Second, she encourages O'Connor to leave some hints for readers earlier in the novel to prepare them for Enoch's declaration that he has wise blood.[51] In both cases, Gordon intends these suggested revisions to clarify and emphasize the dramatic action of the chapter.

Notably, O'Connor amends her draft minimally in light of Gordon's broad critique. O'Connor leaves the description of Enoch's daily practice as-is in the final version of her draft, seemingly ignoring Gordon's recommended changes. The only change made to this chapter from the 1951 draft to the published edition comes in the introductory paragraph. On the 1951 draft, O'Connor adds a handwritten note—likely made after reading Gordon's recommendation—in an earlier chapter where Haze and Enoch have a verbal exchange after the initial run-in with Asa and Sabbath Hawks: "'I got wise blood like my daddy,' he said. I know a heap of thing you don't know and you'll probably need me!"[52] In the published edition, this amendment is split up so that it appears in two different iterations. The first appears in the same dialogue between Haze and Enoch, when Enoch tries to provoke Haze, "'You act like you think you got wiser blood than anybody else, he said, but you ain't! I'm the one has it. Not you. *Me*'" (CW, 33, italics original). The second appears in the opening lines of Chapter 5: "That morning Enoch Emery knew when he woke up that today the person he

50. Fitzgerald, "Master Class," 836–37, italics hers.

51. O'Connor references Enoch's wise blood nine times in this chapter of *Wise Blood* (CW, 44, 45 [twice], 49 [twice], 51, 54, 55, 57).

52. Flannery O'Connor Collection, Special Collections, Ina Dillard Russell Library, Georgia College, Milledgeville, GA, 149b, 36). Copyright 1951 Flannery O'Connor. Reprinted by permission of the Mary Flannery O'Connor Charitable Trust via Harold Matson-Ben Camardi, Inc. All rights reserved.

could show it [the shrunken mummy] to was going to come. He knew by his blood. He had wise blood like his daddy" (CW, 44). These additions are the only changes O'Connor made regarding Gordon's recommendations. While it is not entirely clear why O'Connor chooses to keep her description of Enoch's daily ritual as-is, without amply preparing the reader for it or to drop hints that Enoch believes he has wise blood, it is clear that O'Connor's priorities are not the same as Gordon's. Namely, O'Connor does not share Gordon's concern that the readers may be uninterested or unprepared for the unveiling of Enoch's claim to have wise blood.

The Meeting of Haze, Enoch, and Sabbath[53]

After her general statements on the *Wise Blood* draft, Gordon notes that there are "one or two devices used by many novelists that I think you would find helpful:"[54] a creative use of landscape description to draw out the inner-life of characters and breaking up fast-paced scenes with descriptions.[55] The former device, Gordon advises, could aid in the scene of Haze, Enoch, and Sabbath's meeting at the boarding house, while the latter could enhance the climactic scene just before Haze's self-blinding.

Gordon notes that though O'Connor often uses a scenic landscape to reflect the mood of the characters, O'Connor would "get a much more dramatic effect by having it [the landscape] contrast with them."[56] Using the scene between Haze, Sabbath, and Enoch at the boardinghouse as an

---

53. There is a bit of confusion working backward from the published version here because when Gordon summarizes her more expansive notes she refers to "the scene where Haze and Sabbath and Enoch first meet" (cf. Gordon, "Master Class," 837). The true *first* meeting of the three comes near the beginning of the novel in the scene with the potato peeler salesmen (CW, 20–22). While this technically serves as the first meeting, the scene Gordon refers to here comes much later in *Wise Blood* when Haze, Sabbath, and Enoch meet at Haze's boarding house, a blow-up that ends with Haze throwing the "new jesus" shrunken mummy out the fire-escape window (CW, 106–7). By referencing her earlier comments about changes that should be made to the scene, Gordon clearly is referencing the latter rather than initial meeting because she describes each of the three characters trying to respond the best they could to their own emotions in the moment. The true first meeting sparked none of the emotional depth that would require a careful rendering on O'Connor's part, whereas the latter scene does depict all three characters in emotional turmoil.

54. Fitzgerald, "Master Class," 833.

55. Fitzgerald, "Master Class," 835.

56. Fitzgerald, "Master Class," 834.

example, Gordon suggests the use of the landscape to contrast the mood of the scene: "If the night sky were beautiful, if the night were lyrical the sordid roles the characters have to play would seem even more sordid."[57] The turmoil between the divergent agendas of the three characters centered in the scene on the shrunken mummy might be contrasted with a tranquil evening landscape. Instead of heeding Gordon's advice for the scene and the landscape to stand in stark relief, O'Connor has a storm mirror Haze's mood when he opens the fire escape to dispose of the ravaged shrunken mummy: "The rain blew in his face and he jumped back and stood, with a cautious look, as if he were bracing himself for a blow" (CW, 106).[58] O'Connor thus keeps the external scene as dark and charged as the explosive atmosphere within the boardinghouse.

Gordon goes on to note that while O'Connor does well by focusing in on the character, it might be with too intense a gaze:

> [H]ere are three young people trying to do as best they can what they feel they ought to do. Sabbath wants to get married. Enoch want to live a normal human life. Haze, who is a poet and a prophet, wants to live his life out on a higher level. You convey that admirably, I think, by emphasizing his fierce dedication to his ideals. But the scene itself is too meagre for my taste. Your spotlight is focussed too relentlessly on the three characters.[59]

O'Connor's spotlight remains harshly in place in the published version. She maintains her severe gaze on an intense scene, refusing to draw the reader away from the encounter that turns out to contain the makings of Hazel's attempted escape from Taulkinham and all that he has wrecked there.

Haze and the Patrolman

Gordon notes a troubling hastiness in O'Connor's narration of Haze's encounter with the police officer. The climactic event that follows this incident underscores the decisive character of Haze's encounter here on the road. Gordon provides several recommendations for improving the draft form of this scene, including a desire to see described Haze's facial expression as he peers over the embankment after the officer pushes Haze's car

---

57. Fitzgerald, "Master Class," 834.

58. In fact, O'Connor makes four other references to the rain in the space of a page and a half (CW, 106–7).

59. Fitzgerald, "Master Class," 834.

over the edge.⁶⁰ Gordon writes, "I want to know how Haze's face looked then."⁶¹ O'Connor heeded her mentor's advice by adding: "His face seemed to reflect the entire distance that extended from his eyes to the blank gray sky that went on, depth after depth, into space" (CW, 118).⁶²

Notice, though, that O'Connor offers a description of "how Haze's face looked then," but in an indirect way. Readers are not told precisely how his face looked, but rather how it appeared to have the look of something else. O'Connor depicts the distance before Haze as reflecting off his face and in so doing provides a nearly opaque descriptor of his face in that moment. O'Connor could have applied Gordon's advice in a more straightforward manner by describing Haze's emotional response either through description of his face non-metaphorically or through internal dialogue. A straightforward description of Haze's moment of conversion would have pummeled readers instead of allowing them to infer a mystical experience that gains credibility through the readers' engagement with the text.⁶³ In addition to the metaphorical description of Haze's face reflecting the landscape before him, O'Connor returns to Haze's face once more, following his exchange with the officer: "His face didn't change and he didn't turn it toward the patrolman. It seemed to be concentrated on space" (CW, 118).

When considering the changes O'Connor made to this vital scene and the ways she adopted and resisted Gordon's advice, a brief consideration of O'Connor's convictions about how divine grace works in the created world illumines O'Connor's stylistic choices in Haze's moment of conversion. In an April 4, 1958 letter to Betty Hester ("A."), O'Connor writes about the narration of conversion in fiction: "It seems to me that all good stories

---

60. Gordon also writes that she wants to know how the officer's face looked when he questions Hazel after pushing the Essex over the edge of the embankment (Fitzgerald, "Master Class," 835).

61. Fitzgerald, "Master Class," 835.

62. The 1951 draft includes a handwritten note reflecting Haze's face and eyes just after the description of him looking out over the embankment that alludes to O'Connor's first run-through of adopting Gordon's advice (cf. Flannery O'Connor Collection, Special Collections, Ina Dillard Russell Library, Georgia College, Milledgeville, GA, 149g, 36).

63. Ralph Wood demonstrates the interpretive opportunity in O'Connor's addition: "Looking away from himself for the first time, he beholds the infinite space—'depth after depth' (CW, 118)—of the sky. The firmament is not cold and frightening, as Pascal found it at night, but alive with a burning mercy, a purging peace. And having preached the counter-gospel that nothing is true but one's own body and place, Motes must work out his salvation precisely there, by mutilating the flesh that he had once deified . . . (Wood, *Christ-Haunted South*, 169).

are about conversion, about a character changing. . . . The action of grace changes a character. Grace can't be experienced in itself" (CW, 1067). Because it's always mediated, supernatural grace must be narrated indirectly, "in a story all you can do with grace is to show it is changing the character" (CW, 1067). These are what Rowan Williams identifies as "moments of excess," where grace is revealed by its effects (see ch. 2).

O'Connor confessed that most of her readers do not "know what grace is and don't recognize it when they see it." Thus do her stories of conversion—of supernatural grace radically altering human life—often appear "hard, hopeless, brutal, etc" (CW, 1067). Without the hard work of unveiling the grace that enables Haze Motes's post-conversion actions of asceticism, his self-blinding appears brutal rather than redemptive. This difficulty in narrating the action of grace demonstrates the tension between Gordon's advice and O'Connor's own storytelling. Gordon advises O'Connor that "[t]he minute we are unable to visualize it [the action] we quit believing it," and yet the most profound moments of grace in O'Connor's stories can only be recognized indirectly.[64] Because grace resides in the realm of the supernatural, the supra-rational, its narration requires a different kind of visibility—an excessive moment that directs the reader to something hinted at the margins of a scene.

Throughout her extensive comments on the 1951 draft of *Wise Blood*, Gordon recommends additional scenic details to make the interpretive task easier on readers. In three central scenes, including the climactic scene of Haze's transformation, O'Connor made only minor changes in the face of her mentor's major critiques. These minimal changes result in a final version that is spare, difficult, and intense in its central scenes and makes significant demands on readers. While we cannot get inside the mind of O'Connor, the published version of *Wise Blood* suggests her intentional choice to retain the unrelenting gaze on the central moments that leads to Hazel Mote's conversion.

Conclusion

An examination of Gordon's comments and O'Connor's amendment in *Wise Blood* and a wider look at Gordon and O'Connor's writing mentorship draws attention to the particularity of O'Connor's style of storytelling. Throughout her writing career, O'Connor maintains a consistent resistance

---

64. Fitzgerald, "Master Class," 835.

to painting scenes with too vividly-landscaped brushstrokes or too complicated syntax. Her skill in writing develops in the course of her all-too-brief career, but O'Connor never strays from bold and bare narrative that often leaves readers just as confounded: from Hazel Motes dead in the back of a patrol car in her first published novel to Obadiah Elihue Parker weeping like a baby at her final completed story's close. Despite her profound respect for Caroline Gordon, O'Connor prefers readerly consternation to authorial explanation. Thus does she quietly resist Gordon's repeated pleas for her to abandon a simple and seemingly obtuse style of narration.

As we have seen throughout this chapter, O'Connor refuses to provide readers with what some might consider sufficient information to read her stories well. O'Connor resists a more hypotactic rendering of *Wise Blood*'s central scenes. Instead, she renders the central moments paratactically, offering a spare narration rooted in the concrete world and capturing the divine workings of grace only indirectly. In the next chapter, I turn to the theological dimension of O'Connor's stories through her use of the grotesque. In these moments, we find excessive moments where grace is made possible through narrative implication in lieu of overt description.

Chapter 2

Flannery O'Connor's Grotesque as Moments of Excess

Introduction

Come, O Thou traveler unknown,
Whom still I hold, but cannot see;
My company before is gone,
And I am left alone with Thee.
With Thee all night I mean to stay,
And wrestle till the break of day.[1]

THE HYMNIST CHARLES WESLEY reflects on the wounding and blessing of the patriarch Jacob as he wrestles with the angel-man at the banks of the Jabbok river. This event is one of the earliest and most enduring images of the relationship between God's simultaneous wound and gift of a blessing. The image of a blessed wound— found initially in the prose of the Hebraic text and then with a long legacy in the literary realm—captures the seemingly paradoxical relationship between God and humanity as one that builds up even as it tears down.

In this chapter, I explore this relationship between wounding and blessing by first turning to the impact on Flannery O'Connor of Thomistic aesthetics, by way of Jacques Maritain. This aesthetic sensibility serves as an interpretive key for understanding the use of the grotesque in O'Connor's fiction: it opens up the possibility of divine action in the created world. I then return to the image of Jacob's wrestling event and how this story in the biblical witness speaks to the profound relationship between wounding

---

1. Charles Wesley, "Come, O Thou Traveler Unknown" (1742).

and blessing, as seen in the work of Jean-Louis Chrétien and Rowan Williams. O'Connor's use of the grotesque in her art credibly witnesses to the paradoxical and difficulty rendered action of grace in the world.

Art as Transcendental Realism

In *Grace and Necessity: Reflections on Art and Love*, Rowan Williams examines the opaque poetry of Welsh poet David Jones and the sparsely narrated fiction of Flannery O'Connor. Williams links these two artists together through the Thomistic understanding of art in Jacques Maritain's *Art and Scholasticism*.[2] Williams identifies Maritain's major influence on the work of Jones and O'Connor with two central claims: the insistence on the integrity of the art itself and the rootedness of the artistic work in ordinary life. Maritain argues that the artist employs her observations of the world in order to reveal what is already there in a new way that opens to the transcendent. As Williams summarizes, the artwork is "inescapably a claim about reality."[3] This claim stands on its own merit without need for a mediatory voice of the author between the art and its participant. One who engages with a work of art—be it visual, literary, or performance-based—encounters a work that possesses its own integrity to communicate freely without a slavish adherence to the intentions of its creator.[4]

O'Connor spoke frequently about the influence of Maritain's *Art and Scholasticism* on her art and thought, which makes it worth examination in its own right.[5] In *Art and Scholasticism*, Maritain outlines Thomas Aquinas's identification of art as a virtue of the practical intellect. Maritain distinguishes

---

2. Maritain, *Art and Scholasticism*.

3. Williams, *Grace and Necessity*, 16.

4. Hans-Georg Gadamer echoes Maritain's insistence on the integrity of the artwork in the first part of *Truth and Method* when discussing the play offered by a work of art: "When we speak of play in reference to the experience of art, this means neither the orientation nor even the state of mind of the creator or of those enjoying the work of art, nor the freedom of a subjectivity engaged in play, but the mode of being of the work of art itself" (Gadamer, *Truth and Method*, 102). Both Maritain and Gadamer insist on the ability of the work of art to communicate with its participants. Gadamer goes further than Maritain in insisting that it is not until play is exercised on a work of art that the work itself becomes wholly itself: "[the being of art] is part of the *event of being that occurs in presentation*, and belong essentially to play as play" (Gadamer, *Truth and Method*, 115, italics original).

5. See: HB, 28, 105, 107, 144, 157, 166, 216, 218, 221, 231, 259, 274, and 417. O'Connor also references Maritain's wife, Raïssa in a January 1956 letter (HB, 125–26).

between speculative and practical knowledge through their transcendental *teloi*: speculative knowledge finds its perfect end in Truth, while practical knowledge finds its perfect end in Goodness and Beauty. Further, practical knowledge is divided into two parts by their respective ends: the practical order of action (*agibile*) ends in Goodness while the practical order of making (*factible*) ends in Beauty.[6] The distinction between the making and the use of a thing delineates the aesthetic and the practical orders. The practical order of action yields right moral behavior by displaying and directing an agent's will. The practical order of making, by contrast, is a "productive action," the result being a self-sufficient product measured by its own criteria and standing apart from its maker and her intentions.[7]

Possibly the easiest way to characterize the practical order of making is to consider the craftsman.[8] The craft produced reveals the work of a skilled or faulty craftsman, not the other way around, that is, the craftsman's success is measured by the thing produced and not the will or good intentions of the maker. A chair is deemed a good chair for its durability and comfort, not its maker's temperament. Maritain summarizes: "So Making is ordered to such-and-such a definite end, separate and self-sufficient, not to the common end of human life [this would be Goodness, the aim of the practical order of action]; and it relates to the peculiar good or perfection not of the man making, but of the work made."[9] The work itself is the aim and concern of the practical order of making. Thus, art belongs to this practical order of inherent excellences.

Aquinas, Maritain, O'Connor, and Williams all recognize the centrality of the claim that art is an intellectual virtue of the practical order of making. The aim of the artist is to produce a work that stands on its own aesthetic merits, which Flannery O'Connor aptly summarizes when talking about the final form of a story: "A story is a way to say something that can't be said any other way, and it takes every word in the story to say what the meaning is. You tell a story because a statement would be inadequate.

---

6. Maritain, *Art and Scholasticism*, 5–6.

7. Maritain, *Art and Scholasticism*, 5.

8. While craftsmanship and the fine arts both belong to the practical order, Natalie Carnes helpfully delineates between Maritain's view of 'useful arts' and 'fine art' by pointing to fine arts as ordered toward the transcendental beautiful in a way that craftsmanship is not, though the latter can possess beautiful features: "It is an intelligibility born of creative intuition that animates artistic making, and it grants the fine arts a special—and more important—kind of beauty than crafts" (Carnes, *Beauty*, 37).

9. Maritain, *Art and Scholasticism*, 6.

When anybody asks what a story is about, the only proper thing is to tell him to read the story" (MM, 96). O'Connor's insistence on the integrity of the work of art extends into her letters when explaining to her spiritual director, Fr. McCown, the danger of turning fiction into propaganda: "The novel is an art form and when you use it for anything else you pervert it . . . it has no utilitarian end. If you do manage to use it successfully for social, religious, or other purposes it is because you make it art first" (HB, 156–57). A story speaks to its readers on its own terms. A story communicates what a slogan or proposition cannot.

The artist possesses the virtue (i.e., *habitus* of art) to perceive the beautiful in the world. Maritain employs the Scholastic language of *connaturality* to explain how the artist sensuously and intuitively finds pleasure in the beautiful apprehended in the created world.[10] He emphasizes that beauty represents an entirely different kind of knowledge than what is found in abstract thinking: "So, although the beautiful is in close dependence upon what is metaphysically true, in the sense that every splendour of intelligibility in things presupposes some degree of conformity with that Intelligence which is the cause of things, the beautiful nevertheless is not a kind of truth, but a kind of good."[11] Essential to this point on *connaturality* is the recognition that the same metaphysical reality—the Transcendentals of Truth, Goodness, and Beauty—grounds all knowledge available to the rational human, just as different kinds of recognition reveal different properties of metaphysical realities.

Helpfully, Maritain points to the perception of beauty as being more like the "ecstasy of love" than, say, empirical scientific investigation.[12] To perceive beauty in the natural world is to "touch being itself, a likeness of God, an absolute, all that enables and makes the joy of life: we enter the realm of the spirit."[13] Thus it makes sense that the ensouled animal, the human person, is the only creature capable of re-forming the particular data of the physical world into a new thing wherein the spiritual can be freshly perceived in the physical world:

> The human artist or poet whose mind is not, like the Divine Mind, the cause of things, cannot draw this form complete out of his

10. Maritain, *Art and Scholasticism*, 19. For more on O'Connor and the conception of *habitus*, see: Mears Bruner, "Artistic *Habitus*" in *Subversive Gospel*, 108–38.
11. Maritain, *Art and Scholasticism*, 21.
12. Maritain, *Art and Scholasticism*, 22.
13. Maritain, *Art and Scholasticism*, 26.

creative spirit: he goes and gathers it first and foremost in the vast treasure of creating things, of sensitive nature as the world of souls, and of the interior world of his own soul. From this point of view he is first and foremost a man who sees more deeply than other men and discovers in reality spiritual radiations, which others are unable to discern. But to make these radiations shine out in his work and so to be truly docile and faithful to the visible Spirit at play in things, he can, and indeed he must to some extent, deform, reconstruct and transfigure the material appearance of nature.[14]

The artist is a scavenger searching out the visible world, looking for opportunities to reform the familiar so as to unveil something hidden from common view. The transcendental property of beauty plays an essential role in Maritain's understanding of art, for the self-sufficiency of the art made—not its maker's intention—is the locus of Beauty where ultimate things can be perceived in the temporal created work.

In her essays on the writing of fiction, collected in *Mystery and Manners* (MM), O'Connor explores the relationship between the observations the artist makes about everyday life and the awareness of the transcendent within the created world. O'Connor characterizes as "manners" those customary, well-established patterns of speech and action that offer concreteness and believability to fiction. Only by working within the givens of local speech and action does the artist have any chance of discerning transcendent meaning within them. In an address at a Southern writer's workshop, O'Connor critiques the participants' short stories for failing to capture the "manners" of the characters in their stories: "You get the manners from the texture of existence that surrounds you. The great advantage of being a Southern writer is that we don't have to go anywhere to look for manners; bad or good, we've got them in abundance. . . . And yet here are six stories by Southerners in which almost no use is made of the gifts of the region" (MM, 103–4). The fact that these stories could just as well be set in Pittsburgh as Atlanta makes them artistically unremarkable and literally incredible. For a story to possess the possibility of opening to the mystery of the transcendent, it first requires that the writer attend to the manners of her particular place and time—the "texture" to be perceived in the quotidian world. If not, the story fails the artistic test of locating ultimate meaning within the local and regional. Manners and mystery are fatally separated, causing the work to collapse on itself in mere self-reflection.

14. Maritain, *Art and Scholasticism*, 48–49.

Of course, the danger of a story not taking flight can run an opposite but equally damaging outcome with an excess of manners, as in what was once called "local color" fiction.[15] O'Connor surmises that workshop participants avoided regional parlance because other Southern writers have overemployed the manners of the region: "There is nothing worse than the writer who doesn't *use* the gifts of the region, but wallows in them. Everything becomes so Southern that it's sickening, so local that it is unintelligible, so literally produced that it conveys nothing" (MM, 104, italics original). Just as the abstraction of a story from its local texture makes a story unbelievable, so does the excessive use of the regional flavor. The writer as an artist must gather, in Maritain's language, sharp perceptions of the world so as to imagine something new and credible; this process involves both keen observation and a creative use of it.

Rowan Williams uses the language of "superabundance" to describe how beauty does not serve in an oppositional but rather complementary relationship with truth. "The delight of the subject is in the recognition of what Aquinas called *splendor formae*, 'splendour of form', a sense of the work achieved as giving itself to the observer in an 'overflow' of presence."[16] Art as a subject *communicates* to the observer. Here we find Maritain's insistence that art opens onto transcendence by pointing the observer not to some new world but to the world that-is in order to reveal something before unseen, i.e., a trace of the transcendental Beauty that grounds and orders the created world in all its splendor of form. O'Connor echoes this idea of revealing what is hidden in the created order when discussing the prophetic vision of the writer: "The writer learns, perhaps more quickly than the reader, to be humble in the face of what-is. What-is is all he has to do with; and he will realize eventually that fiction can transcend its limitations only by staying within them" (MM, 146).

---

15. The phenomenon of "local color" fiction arose in the late nineteenth-century and can be seen in the writing of the frontier West and, most prevalently, in the South (cf. Ewell et al., *Southern Local Color*, xiv).

16. Williams, *Grace and Necessity*, 13. Williams writes: "This object is there *for me*, for my delight; but it is so because it is not there *solely* for me, not designed so as to fit my specifications for being pleased." Williams here notes that Maritain's enthusiasm in emphasizing "the gratuity of the artwork, its disinterested characters" may overstate his case and obscure his real argument (Williams, *Grace and Necessity*, 13–14). Maritain's larger argument, more evident in his later work *Creative Intuition in Art*, speaks of the relationship of the artwork to the metaphysical reality that the artwork's overflow reflects. Williams worries that Maritain's early emphasis on the beauty that overflows from an artwork may downplay its link to metaphysical truth.

Art opens up to the transcendent by embracing, rather than resisting, the limited yet creative viewpoint of the artist.

Maritain understands art as inherently logical (i.e., realistic): "It [every work of art] must be steeped in logic; not in the pseudo-logic of clear ideas, not in the logic of knowledge and demonstration, but in the working logic of every day, eternally mysterious and disturbing, the logic of structure of the living thing, and the intimate geometry of nature."[17] Williams labels Maritain's logical understanding of art as "transcendental realism."[18] Art points the observer to the world as it really is, Williams declares, in a way that illuminates the mysterious and perplexing quality of quotidian life. Art both reveals the infinite and humbles the finite.

In his 1952 A. W. Mellon Lectures in the Fine Arts, Maritain speaks of the perception of beauty in art as a creative intuition.[19] In one of his lectures, entitled "Poetry and Beauty," Maritain distinguishes between beauty before "the eyes of God" and the eyes of human beings.[20] Because humans intuit the beautiful through their intellect and senses in tandem, human perception is limited by the enfleshment that is the human person—limited by residing in a particular time and occupying a particular space. Omniperception is available only to God, so human perception is inherently limited in vision and judgments of the beautiful. Maritain identifies this distinction between limited and limitless access to beauty respectively as aesthetic and transcendent Beauty.[21] By designating human creative intuition of the beautiful as restricted to the "realm of aesthetic beauty," Maritain avoids collapsing transcendental Beauty into the immanent confines of human recognition and representation without undercutting the possibility for human access to the perfect form of Beauty.[22]

The categories of ugly and beautiful belong only to the creaturely realm of aesthetic beauty because the designation "ugly" belongs to the effect of privation on Being: ugly things "are things deprived in some respect of due proportion, radiance, or integrity, but in which Being still abounds,

---

17. Williams, *Grace and Necessity*, 21; Maritain, *Art and Scholasticism*, 41.
18. Williams, *Grace and Necessity*, 21.
19. Maritain, *Creative Intuition*. In this work, Maritain focuses more specifically on poetry.
20. Maritain, *Creative Intuition*, 125.
21. Maritain, *Creative Intuition*, 125.
22. Maritain, *Creative Intuition*, 125.

and which keep on pleasing the sight to that extent."[23] Only through the senses can privation be recognized as having the status of some-thing rather than no-thing. God as pure intellect sees at once all that-is and deems it as good (and thus also beautiful). Because human beings are limited in their perception of beauty and cannot see all things all at once, they are left to make judgments of beauty with what is before them through the cooperation of the senses and the intellect.

O'Connor identifies the strange play between the beautiful and the ugly most readily in her preface to *A Memoir of Mary Ann* (CW, 822–31). Mary Ann was a child with an inoperable tumor that caused a sizable deformation across one side of her face. She spent most her short life living with the Dominican Nuns of our Lady of Perpetual Help at their Free Cancer Home in Atlanta, Georgia. O'Connor describes the girl's photo, which she received when asked to help the Sisters tell the story of Mary Ann: "It showed a little girl in her first Communion dress and veil. She was sitting on a bench, bolding something I could not make out. Her small face was straight and bright on one side. The other side was protuberant, the eye was damaged, the nose and mouth crowded slightly out of place" (CW, 823). O'Connor's exposure to the life of this little girl with a missing eye and disfigured face transformed how she understood the relationship between good and evil, the beautiful and the grotesque. While we readily recognize evil as grotesque, as ugly, "[f]ew have stared at [the good] long enough to accept that fact that its face too is grotesque, that in us the good is something under construction. . . . When we look into the face of the good, we are liable to see a face like Mary Ann's, full of promise." (CW, 830). If one gazes upon the face of the grotesque with honesty, that is, without, as O'Connor says, "a cliché or a smoothing down that will soften their real look," one might be surprised to find beauty and goodness (CW, 830); one might see a face, like Mary Ann's, which is on its way to perfection.[24]

The gift of art for Maritain is its ability to expand the limited human perception of the beautiful through a movement from aesthetic beauty into

---

23. Maritain, *Creative Intuition*, 126.

24. O'Connor artistically renders this image of the good within the grotesque in "A Temple of the Holy Ghost." After hearing her cousins describe an intersex person they saw in a circus tent, the twelve-year old girl protagonist imagines the intersex person leading a congregation in a litany affirming that all people are temples of the Holy Ghost: "'God made me thisaway and I don't dispute hit[sic] . . . God done this to me and I praise Him'" (CW, 207). In her innocence and ability to really look, the child saw what her cousins could not: beauty in the unusual.

transcendent reality: "art struggles to surmount the distinction between aesthetic beauty and transcendental beauty and to absorb aesthetic beauty in transcendental beauty."[25] Art increases human perception of the beautiful, enabling even the ugly to open onto the transcendent. This idea appeals to O'Connor, who underlines the following in her own copy of Maritain's *Creative Intuition:* "[art] draws beauty from ugly things and monsters, it tries to overcome the division between beautiful and ugly by absorbing ugliness in a superior species of beauty, and by transferring us *beyond* the (aesthetic) beautiful and ugly."[26] Art transforms our vision, but this transformation is not instantaneous or complete.

As finite creatures, our perception of transcendent beauty cannot be deemed perfect—whole and complete—in the same way that transcendental beauty is perfect. Maritain identifies imperfect human perception as "a certain sacred weakness" and the "kind of imperfection through which infinity wounds the finite."[27] The quintessential image for Maritain of this sacred wounding is Jacob's limp after his wrestling with the angel. He derives it from Thomas's *Summa* where Aquinas cites a homily by Gregory the Great:

> After contemplation Jacob halted with one foot, "because we need to grow weak in the love of the world ere we wax strong in the love of God," as Gregory says (Hom. xiv in Ezech.). "Thus when we have known the sweetness of God, we have one foot sound while the other halts; since every one who halts on one foot leans only on that foot which is sound."[28]

Rowan Williams identifies this wounding-blessing effect as an "artistic moment of truth" where "the artist has to decide whether the end of the process is unavoidable tragic frustration—or a contemplative orientation towards what is never going to be contained, the world in the eyes of God."[29] These moments of revealing human fallibility through art can go the way of either comedy or tragedy, with both options truthfully speaking about

---

25. Maritain, *Creative Intuition*, 126.

26. Maritain, *Creative Intuition*, 126, italics his; Kinney, *Flannery O'Connor's Library*, 20–21, §27.

27. Maritain, *Creative Intuition*, 128.

28. Aquinas, *Summa Theologica* 2a2ae 180, 5 ad. 4. Maritain points to this quote in *Creative Intuition*, 128.

29. Williams, *Grace and Necessity*, 21.

the kataphatic and apophatic dimensions of knowing God.³⁰ The wounding effect Maritain emphasizes can be understood as a kind of humility, even a humiliation. Art illuminates our limits by offering glimpses of the transcendent that disclose meaning while making clear what we do not know. While this *could* result in disappointment or even despair in the illumined viewer, it can also function as revelation.

Williams finds one of the key insights of Maritain's Thomistic aesthetic in the recognition that "art in one sense 'dispossesses' us of our habitual perception and restores to reality a dimension that necessarily escapes our conceptuality and our control. *It makes the world strange.*"³¹ Art unsettles our preconceptions, not because it points to some vague "beyond," but rather because it points viewers back to the world itself—the world readily available to us—with fresh insight.

This dispossessing and estranging effect of art is an inconvenience, even a disruption. Williams observes that the artist's discernment in making "present the underlying structures and relations apprehended may involve a degree of imaginative violence to surface harmonies."³² Quickly protecting his claim of the need for "imaginative violence" as a glorification or boorish rendering of "shock and awe," Williams notes "the deliberate cultivation of what jars is as much folly, artistically, as the deliberate striving for beauty. The issue is always and only about the integrity of the work. The artist first listens and looks for the pulse or the rhythm that is not evident; but she cannot do any sort of job if she refuses to work with such pulses."³³

---

30. In *The Tragic Imagination*, Williams notes how sometimes what tragedy can communicate is that some things simply cannot be communicated, thus pointing to the unspeakable: "The business of tragedy is neither to tell us that the world is more bearable than it is nor to insist that it is 'absolutely' unbearable. It is a more problematic and unsettling matter than any such generalization, in that it shows us how *some* pain can be spoken of and understood, 'humanized', and some cannot, because the words are not yet there and, so far as we can know, may never be" (Williams, *Tragic Imagination*, 41).

31. Williams, *Grace and Necessity*, 37, italics added.

32. Williams, *Grace and Necessity*, 26.

33. Williams, *Grace and Necessity*, 26–27. In a March 7, 1958 *Commonweal* review of O'Connor's work, William Etsy accused O'Connor of belonging to the "cult of the Gratuitous Grotesque" (Etsy, "In America," 588). Etsy takes aim at "Good Country People," concluding that "[a]ll of these overingenious horrifics are presumably meant to speak to us of the Essential Nature of Our Time" but end up devolving into "clever gimmicks" (Etsy, "In America," 588). As will be discussed in the next section, O'Connor is never flippant in her use of the grotesque, but employs it as a means of catching the attention of a complacent audience. Still, Etsy demonstrates that the line between "imaginative violence" and "shock and awe"—despite the careful intention and attention of the

The artist creates through careful attention to reality—the what-is—to produce art that disrupts the status quo, not disruption for disruption's sake but for the integrity of the work of art. The work functions as a communicating subject with something to say—not simply as a utilitarian tool to sooth sweetly, shock grotesquely, or entertain pornographically.

Flannery O'Connor's Moments of Excess

In a letter to Eileen Hall, editor of the book review page of *The Bulletin*, the diocesan newspaper to which O'Connor submitted many reviews, O'Connor makes some of her most revealing statements about fiction writing (CW, 987–89). In this particular letter, O'Connor responds to Hall's concerns about "scandalizing the 'little ones'" through the grotesque aspects of her fiction. Using a startling biblical example, O'Connor asks, "If a novelist wrote a book about Abraham passing his wife off as his sister—which he did—and allowing her to be taken over by those who wanted her for their lustful purposes—which he did to save his skin—how many Catholics would not be scandalized at the behavior of Abraham?" (CW, 987). The answer, of course, is that few would *not* be scandalized. O'Connor continues, "The fact is that in order not to be scandalized, one has to have *a whole view of things*, which not many of us have" (CW, 987, italics added). Such an encompassing view of Scripture includes the morally suspect stories alongside the overtly virtuous ones. For a reader to be surprised by Scripture's inclusion of the story of Abraham's deceptive claim—that Sarah is his sister to assure his own (and not his wife's) safety—requires a lack of familiarity with the disobedience and moral depravity found even in the most faithful figures of Scripture. When O'Connor asks how many Catholics would not be scandalized by this story, she is implicating fellow Catholics who have not grappled with their own sacred text. To be shocked by O'Connor's fiction is to be similarly scandalized by the sacred text. Both the Scriptural witness and O'Connor's storytelling truthfully speak to the particularities of the human condition—the scandalous and offensive alongside the upright and edifying.

The integrity of the fiction writer, O'Connor continues in her letter to Hall, is found in making available the whole of human experience to the artist, since "[f]iction is supposed to represent life" (CW, 988).

---

author—ultimately is drawn by the reader. Of course, judgments can just as well be made about the quality of the reader as the quality of the work.

The fiction writer shows the reader reality through the art of *representation*: "The fiction writer doesn't state, he shows, renders" (CW, 988).[34] O'Connor's insistence on the artist making use of her everyday observations echoes Maritain's claim that the artist perceives more deeply than others the transcendent trace in the created world. For both O'Connor and Maritain, the subject of art reveals the transcendent through the sensual character of the created world. Re-imagining the world through story-telling produces "a concrete expression of mystery—mystery that is lived" (CW, 988). O'Connor's artistry is found in showing—often through absence and negation rather than presence and affirmation—the hidden realities of good and evil, thus glimpsing the infinite through the finite.[35] Her fictional representations provide opportunities for readers to discern for themselves the unfathomable mystery of life.

Rowan Williams insists that O'Connor's Catholic faith adds to rather than subtracts from her artistic vision:

> Doing justice to the visible world is reflecting the love of God for it, the fact that this world is worth dying for in God's eyes. The tightrope that the Catholic writer must walk is to forget or ignore nothing of the visually, morally, humanly, sordid world, making nothing easy for the reader, while doing so in the name of a radical conviction that sees the world being interrupted and transfigured by revelation. The event that disrupts and questions and changes the world is precisely what obliges the artist not to try and recreate it from scratch. Irony is going to be unavoidable in this exercise.[36]

---

34. Here in this proclamation of rendering not stating we sense Caroline Gordon's influence on O'Connor's aesthetics. In *The Edge of Words*, Rowan Williams similarly understands the work of representation (rather than description) when defining 'representation' as "a way of speaking that may variously be said to seek to embody, translate, make present or re-form what is perceived" (Williams, *Edge of Words*, 22).

35. Again in *The Edge of Words*, Williams picks up this connection between negation and revelation when he uses the idea of silence as a sort of indirect referent, an awareness of a gap in understanding (Williams, *Edge of Words*, 157).

36. Williams, *Grace and Necessity*, 99–100. Likely the best example of the counter-argument to Catholic faith as opening up O'Connor's artistic vision is found in Brinkmeyer's *The Art and Vision of Flannery O'Connor*. Using M. Bakhtin's monologic versus dialogic perspectives, Brinkmeyer argues that ultimately O'Connor's stories display the tension between her faith and artistic vision (23). The dialogical exchange found in the stories resides in the underlying conversation—Bakhtin's second story—between the story's characters and its narrator. Brinkmeyer identifies O'Connor's narrative voice as representing the faithful Catholic voice where the narrator takes a "sanctified position" that is "severely challenged" by the characters, resulting in a deconstruction of the

Here, Williams makes three important claims about the relationship between O'Connor's faith and her fiction. First, O'Connor's mandate to make use of the created world by artistically re-shaping it so as to reveal something previously unseen takes on extra importance because it is *this* world that God loved enough to die for it. Second, and further, this world's worth is demonstrated not only in the humiliating act of the Son on the cross but in the entire Incarnation event. In his self-emptying, the Son took on materiality with all its contingency, including dying a human death. The Incarnation does not allow O'Connor to ignore or make less important the features of creaturely existence, for these are the very things Christ took on himself. The Incarnation event and the Eucharistic event, which extends the Christ event into the life of the Church, creates a non-negotiable challenge for the Catholic artist, as Williams comments later in his lecture: "The uncompromising specificity of the dogma of the Incarnation and the action of the Mass again becomes a key to the artist's task: the infinite cannot be *directly* apprehended, so we must take appearance seriously; it is the *infinite* that is being apprehended, so we must take appearance seriously enough to read its concealments and stratagems."[37] As the body of Christ integrates the natural with the supernatural—with the Real Presence mediating that integration in the life of the Church—so does the artist mediate between these two realms by drawing out the particular and beautiful in the created world and discerning the mystery of God in it.

Third, O'Connor's use of irony—of making the world strange in her fiction—functions as a vital tool for unveiling the supernatural realities that ground and enliven the created world. Part of what this means is that O'Connor's job is not to "tidy up the data" of the world but instead to make plausible "humanity's relation to God."[38] The grotesque aspect of O'Connor's fiction serves as the crux of relating a disordered world to its perfect Creator.

---

narrator's omniscient voice and revealing the dangerous quality not only of O'Connor's freakish characters but of the authoritative stance of the narrator (66). O'Connor's fiction, Brinkmeyer argues, functions as a means of self-reflection by the author rather than creating a work of art that stands on its own and challenges the assumptions of readers. Sarah Gordon finds that Brinkmeyer's contention creates strawmen of both Catholicism and fundamentalism (S. Gordon, *Obedient Imagination,* 43). In addition, she points out that O'Connor herself gives no indication that she struggled with her Catholic faith but saw herself as presenting a clear Catholic vision of the world. This leads Gordon to make the opposite mistake from Brinkmeyer's, claiming that O'Connor is a monological rather than a dialogical writer (S. Gordon, *Obedient Imagination,* 44).

37. Williams, *Grace and Necessity,* 103.
38. Williams, *Grace and Necessity,* 96.

Rather than defaulting to the assumption of God's absence or some configuration of a "god of the gaps," O'Connor is "always taking for granted that God is possible—thinkable or accessible or even manifest—in the most grotesque and empty or cruel faith."[39] O'Connor's use of the unusual, paradoxical, and ironic in her fiction enables her to address directly the underbelly of the human situation without sacrificing her Holy Saturday conviction that there is nothing and nowhere that God, in his love, will not endure.

In her essay "Some Aspects of the Grotesque in Fiction," O'Connor explains how her fiction bends towards the distorted and grotesque because of her belief in the mysterious qualities in the created world that point to something ultimate: "Fiction begins where human knowledge begins—with the senses—and every fiction writer is bound by this fundamental aspect of his medium. I do believe, however, that that kind of writer I am describing will use the concrete in a more drastic way. His way will be much more obviously the way of distortion" (MM, 42). The irony involved in making God's grace evident through aspects of the grotesque—the cruel, the violent, the disfigured—forces the reader to pay attention to where and how God might show up in a way that avoids the two great blasphemies of storytelling for O'Connor: pornography and sentimentality.[40] Irony protects the grotesque aspect from utilizing violence for its glorification (this would be pornographic), and the grotesque protects the act of supernatural grace from becoming cheap and thin (this would be sentimental).[41] The Misfit's sneering declaration that the grandmother might have been a good woman if someone had been there to shoot her every day of her life exemplifies the use of irony to avoid both sentimentality and pornography. Whatever her final spiritual state may be, the grandmother is no saccharine saint or obviously damned soul.

In *The Grotesque in Art and Literature* (*Das Groteskes: seine Gestaltung in Malerei und Dichtung*)—one of the most readily referenced works on the

---

39. Williams, *Grace and Necessity*, 100.

40. O'Connor writes in her aforementioned letter to Eileen Hall: "The two worst sins of bad taste in fiction are pornography and sentimentality. One is too much sex and the other too much sentiment. You have to have enough of either to prove your point but no more "(CW, 988).

41. Williams helpfully clarifies the language of supernatural action in O'Connor's fiction to avoid any gnostic or superstitious sentiment: "The 'supernatural' here does not of course mean the paranormal, but the action of God, perceived as it touches the human condition in ways that open up a radically 'other' depth in things" (Williams, *Grace and Necessity*, 102).

grotesque in the broader investigation of the grotesque in literature—Wolfgang Kayser identifies the difficulty of using the designation "grotesque" because it so easily becomes "one of those quickly cheapened terms."[42] This cheapening occurs because, while the term conveys an emotional weight, it fails to speak to its specific character which distinguishes the grotesque from other indefinite terms like strange or incredible. Kayser's work presents the transformation of the language of the grotesque from its Italian roots during the Renaissance era to its use in the twentieth century, demonstrating how the word began as an ornamental caricature (e.g., gargoyles) and morphed into the clashing dissonance between the familiar and the strange, where the standard rules do not apply.[43] Kayser ends his work with a chapter entitled "An Attempt to Define the Nature of the Grotesque," wherein he summarizes: "THE GROTESQUE IS THE ESTRANGED WORLD."[44] Unlike a fairy tale, whose world operates by different rules than the familiar, the grotesque estranges those things that *should be* familiar to us with "[s]uddenness and surprise," thus producing "a situation that is filled with ominous tension."[45] The effect of grotesque estrangement disorients the spectator or reader. Kayser observes the way that humor functions within a grotesque work, commenting that "THE GROTESQUE IS A PLAY WITH THE ABSURD."[46] In making the world strange or incredible, the grotesque aspect of art unsettles its participant by challenging and confounding the kinds of significance that is supposedly fixed and stable.

Williams characterizes O'Connor's lynchpin scenes of the grotesque as "moments of excess."[47] The language of excess is similar to Williams's earlier

---

42. Kayser, *Grotesque*, 17.

43. Kayser, *Grotesque*, 17. Kayser goes on to trace the etymological root of the term "grotesque" beginning in its Italian root *grotta* (cave) with *la grotessca* used during the Italian Renaissance to refer to features of a world at odds with the familiar, one where distinctions like inanimate and animate objects collapses. The term extends into Germany in the sixteenth century to designate "the monstrous fusion of human and nonhuman elements" (Kayser, *Grotesque*, 24).

44. Kayser, *Grotesque*, 184. All capitalization is original.

45. Kayser, *Grotesque*, 184.

46. Kayser, *Grotesque*, 187.

47. Williams uses language of excess throughout his discussion of O'Connor in *Grace and Necessity*. See p. 105 (on actualization of grace in finite world), p. 113 (on O'Connor's excessive characters), p. 117 (on grace as an excess), p. 131 (on O'Connor's artistry in identifying moments of excess as tragic or comic), and p. 155 (on Balthasar's discussion of the sacred in the world).

The different approaches to O'Connor's use of the grotesque would easily fill volumes.

use of superabundance to name that moment of overflow described by Maritain as the opening of aesthetic beauty to transcendent beauty, enabling Aquinas's "splendor of form" to shine through. But, while the language of superabundance suggests a magnificent moment of revelation, O'Connor's moments of excess take on a disruptive and often macabre appearance during "a moment when the irony is most intense; it is not that the finite rises without interruption to a degree of sublimity but that the actuality of grace is uncovered in the moment of excess—which may be in a deliberately intensified gracelessness—without doing violence to the narrative surface."[48] Moments of excess reveal grace through drastic action without bringing into question the integrity of the story. Timothy J. Basselin, in his work on O'Connor and disability, highlights that "In contrast to modernity's dealing with imperfections, God's mercy is never sentimental . . . grace or the possibility for grace arrives only through the experience of grotesque limitations; mercy is forged in the fires of suffering."[49] It is precisely this avoidance of sentimentality that renders her stories credible.

A 2002 annotated reference guide to Flannery O'Connor's fiction cites hundreds of works related to O'Connor's conception of and indebtedness to others' use and depictions of the grotesque in her fiction (Scott, *Flannery O'Connor: An Annotated Reference Guide*, 998–99). I would wager that number has grown by at least another hundred since 2002, with master's theses, doctoral dissertations, journal articles, and full-length publications addressing the use of the grotesque in O'Connor's fiction.

To capture the range of judgments around her use of the grotesque, consider Carol Shloss's comments about the grotesque in O'Connor as displaying a certain Christian arrogance in comparison to Williams's designation of the grotesque as moments of excess. Shloss writes that though grotesque events are readily identifiable in O'Connor's fiction, knowing how to interpret those events often leaves readers confused. This confusion "undercuts a reader's potentially sympathetic identification with horrible experience by ironic or humorous rendering, suggesting implicitly that the categories which normally apply to our world view are no longer applicable" (Shloss, *Dark Comedies*, 38–39). Shloss finds fault with O'Connor's grotesque scenes because of O'Connor's own Catholic assumptions. Shloss argues that, contrary to O'Connor's insistence that her Catholic vision makes what is eschatologically normal freakish in the present world, comes off as arrogance rather than insight (Shloss, *Dark Comedies*, 40–41).

48. Williams, *Grace and Necessity*, 104. Williams uses "A Good Man Is Hard to Find" to illustrate his point. If the dialogue between the Misfit and the grandmother had ended with an embrace of the Misfit rather than three bullets in the grandmother's chest, the narrative would have ended as a feel-good story rather than a revelation of grace: "It is a risk-charged incident, veering towards sentimentality, then brutally pulled back" (Williams, *Grace and Necessity*, 107). The story needs the radical turn from recognition to repulsion in order to be a believable moment of excessive grace by the grandmother and excessive rejection by the Misfit.

49. Basselin, *Theology of Disabled Humanity*, 2.

The moments of excess as revelations of grace in O'Connor's fiction are dangerous and unpredictable. Far from being sentimentalized, grace appears to the characters of O'Connor's stories more often as a threat, even "as a death sentence," than as hopeful or salvific.[50] Williams highlights the tragic and violent dimensions of grace in her stories as an honest grappling with the non-deterministic choices that grace offers: "O'Connor is insisting on a perception of grace that is *not* necessarily the introduction of a meaning or even an absolution. . . . Grace is an excess that *may* make for significance or forgiveness, but needn't. Yet without the breakthrough to the level of hunger and 'futureless' passion, there is no forgiveness."[51] The grotesque nature of these moments of excess protects characters and readers alike from any illusions about the grace revealed. Like the news of the birth of Christ, the revelation of the infinite within the finite can appear to be a threat as often as a gift.

Insightfully, Williams articulates how O'Connor's fiction evokes the world infused with the reality of God without recourse to a convenient invoking of divine presence: "When hunger is faced without illusion, in the way she argues only a believer can face it, what the artist achieves is exactly the representation of what Maritain calls the 'woundedness' of the world in its entirety. Without the evocation (not invocation) of God in these narratives, the scope of the human actuality would be denied or reduced."[52] O'Connor's identity as a fiction writer who is also a Catholic enables her to take in the world through her senses and reason, and to freely represent those perceptions in her art because it is God, not the world or O'Connor, that does the work of redemption. Further, it is *this* world, in all its eccentricities and deformities, wherein God acts. Williams's emphasis on O'Connor's evocation rather than invocation of God speaks truthfully to what it means for human perception of the uncreated within the created world.

If O'Connor were to insert narratival comments that overtly announce the intervention of divine grace, the work of art as representation would undercut its own aim and insert the artist into the communicating work that belongs to the art, not its maker. As Williams rightly states, "Explanation is reduction; it is trying to contain another in your own identity."[53] Thus, O'Connor refuses to invoke supernatural grace explicitly

---

50. Williams, *Grace and Necessity*, 114.
51. Williams, *Grace and Necessity*, 117, italics his.
52. Williams, *Grace and Necessity*, 120.
53. Williams, *Grace and Necessity*, 120.

in her fiction. The outcome of O'Connor's choice as an artist to render rather than state leaves meaning unstable. This instability is another version of O'Connor's comment to Eileen Hall that grace can be made believable by honestly representing the world as it-is, not as we think it should be. As evidenced in the last chapter, O'Connor's refusal to explain comes up against continual criticism from Caroline Gordon that readers might be left with insufficient evidence to make any kind of confident judgment about the stories. For Williams, by contrast, such instability and insufficiency are essential ingredients for any convincing relation between humanity and the God whose ways are not our ways.[54]

To summarize: The presence of the grotesque in O'Connor's fiction artistically renders the wounding effect of creaturely encounters with supernatural grace. O'Connor narrates grace with a realistic vision that understands grace as being deemed a call to death as much as a gift of new life. The grotesque as moments of excess disrupts patterns of radical autonomy or morality-driven piety, setting the scene for characters to accept or reject the invitation of grace. These scenes play out in a complex fashion where violence and redemption are often so entangled that they are hard to distinguish precisely because O'Connor seeks to represent reality as it-is in her fiction. O'Connor confidently renders the possibility of grace through the lens of her Catholic faith, which gives her the wide view of the world in relation to God.[55] O'Connor's fictional rendering of encounters with grace succeed because she creates evocative scenes that signal to attentive readers the possibility of what is invisible—goodness, truth, beauty, transcendence, God—within the visible realm. O'Connor's grotesque storytelling offers a vision wherein, like Jacob after wrestling the angel, characters and readers readily limp along, affirming that paradoxical claim that "to live is Christ and to die is gain" (Phil 1:21).

54. Williams, *Grace and Necessity*, 117–18.

55. There is debate about the influence and impact of O'Connor's Catholicism on her fiction. Marshall Bruce Gentry points to four schools of thought regarding the relationship between O'Connor faith and storytelling: 1) complete denial of any theological authorial intention; 2) an overtly orthodox Catholic vision, which is evidenced in her fiction; 3) a harsh dogmatic Catholic vision, which is evident in her fiction; and 4) question O'Connor's Catholic faith entirely, possibly arguing for a demonic vision evident in her fiction (Gentry, *Religion of the Grotesque*, 3). Gentry notes that the first option was in vogue during the early years of O'Connor criticism, but by the time of his writing in the mid-1980's had fallen out of fashion (Gentry, *Religion of the Grotesque*, 3). The third option is evident in Brinkmeyer's *Art and Vision of Flannery O'Connor*, discussed earlier. My position clearly belongs in the second camp as I affirm the centrality of O'Connor's confident and robust Catholic faith.

Wounding and Blessing

Jacob's wrestling with the angel and subsequent limp captures the enigmatic quality of the divine coming into contact with the human. When St. Thomas writes that "when we have known the sweetness of God, we have one foot sound while the other halts," he captures the peculiar quality of encountering the divine: moments of grace, of revelation, produce a grounding limp more often than angelic flight. Why does a limp, rather than flight, encapsulate encounters with the divine? In this section, I explore the connection between blessing and wounding through the writing of Jean-Louis Chrétien and Rowan Williams. The link between invitations of grace with receptions in humiliation, plays a central role for both thinkers. Just as O'Connor's fiction disrupts quotidian life to gift characters and readers with new sight, so too do understanding and narrating grace produce a disruptive effect alongside the gift of a new thing.

Chrétien helpfully complicates the language of victory and defeat in his essay "How to Wrestle with the Invisible," where he employs the motif of Jacob's wrestling with the angel to illustrate his point.[56] Chrétien begins his exploration with the claim that "[t]here are victories that weigh heavily and overpower. There are also defeats that revive, where new, unlooked-for strengths spring forth suddenly from the wounds received."[57] Success can weaken rather than energize one's resolve, and failures can enliven rather than diminish one's determination. Chrétien points to Rilke's "The Beholder" (*Der Schauende*) to express the ultimate image of defeat that strengthens the one defeated after pondering the damage done to trees after a fierce storm:

> How small that is, with which we wrestle,
> what wrestles with us, how immense . . .
> What we triumph over is the Small,
> and the success itself makes us petty.
> The Eternal and Unexampled
> *will* not be bent by us.[58]

56. Chrétien, *Hand to Hand*, 1–17.
57. Chrétien, *Hand to Hand*, 1.
58. Translated by Chrétien (see Chrétien, *Hand to Hand*, 1–2), italics original; original German:
*Wie ist das klein, womit wir ringen,
was mit uns ringt, wie ist das groß . . .
Was wir besiegen, ist das Kleine,*

Rilke's poem moves from the image of the battered tree to the biblical image of Jacob's wrestling in this stanza. With the same suddenness that the storm assaults the tree, so too does the angel appear to Jacob in the middle of the night:

> Whomever this Angel overcame
> (who so often declined the fight),
> *he* walks erect and justified
> and great out of that hard hand
> which, as if sculpting, nestled round him.
> Winning does not tempt him.
> His growth is: to be the deeply defeated
> by ever greater things.[59]

Rilke defines Jacob's growth precisely in his defeat. The profundity of this claim expands in Rilke's parenthetical note that Jacob had up to this point avoided conflict by cutting corners and running away from the consequences of his deception.

Chrétien uses Rilke's poetic rendering of Jacob's blessed defeat to differentiate two different kinds of wounds. On the one hand are wounds that scab and heal over. These wounds serve to remind the receiver of their past defeat. On the other hand are wounds that "*must* not heal."[60] Notice Chrétien's imperative claim: these kinds of wounds cannot be permitted to heal. These wounds must not heal because "they are the sources of our loving intimacy with our highest task, the one we have received, impossibly,

---

> *und der Erfolg selbst macht uns klein.*
> *Das Ewige und Ungemeine*
> *will nicht von uns gebogen sein.*

59. Translated by Chrétien (see Chrétien, *Hand to Hand*, 2), italics original; original German:

> *Wen dieser Engel überwand,*
> *welcher so oft auf Kampf verzichtet,*
> *der geht gerecht und aufgerichtet*
> *und groß aus jener harten Hand,*
> *die sich, wie formend, an ihn schmiegte.*
> *Die Siege laden ihn nicht ein.*
> *Sein Wachstum ist: der Tiefbesiegte*
> *von immer Größerem zu sein.*

60. Chrétien, *Hand to Hand*, 2, italics added.

without having sought it."⁶¹ This type of wound does not turn into a scar that from time-to-time might make the receiver recall something that happened long ago; instead the wound itself is the means of the message the wound imparts: revelatory grace.

Chrétien locates Jacob as the eponym of this second kind of wounding where, together with his wounding, also came a new name: "Eponym of the highest struggle, he is thus in addition the eponym of the name lost and found, the eponym of changes of name insofar as this struggle left nothing of his existence intact, neither body nor identity, insofar then as the event of the intimate confrontation is also the advent of the unforeseen and new intimacy."⁶² Jacob's living wound, his limp, cannot be separated from the blessing of the new name. Jacob needed to experience a displacement—the literal paralleling the figurative—in order to enter into a new and unforeseen blessing.⁶³

Chrétien's claim that God blesses via wounding runs contrary to the erroneous, yet prevalent conception that God's blessing is synonymous with favor, physical and emotional security, even financial prosperity. Wounding, not prosperity, aptly characterizes the experience of God's revelation and blessing both in Scripture—as we have seen in Jacob's blessing and limping—and in the history of Christian spirituality. In *The Wound of Knowledge: Christian Spirituality from the New Testament to Saint John of the Cross*, Rowan Williams examines the seemingly paradoxical characterization of knowledge and revelation of God as wounding from the New Testament witness through writings of the sixteenth-century Spanish mystics, Teresa of Ávila and John of the Cross.⁶⁴ Williams delves into the work by examining the "strangeness of the ground of belief" that pushes

---

61. Chrétien, *Hand to Hand*, 2.

62. Chrétien, *Hand to Hand*, 2–3.

63. The dialectic relationship between activity and receptivity plays a central role in Chrétien's large religious phenomenological account. In *La Voix Nue: Phénoménologie de la Promesse*, Chrétien grounds phenomenology of the promise in the fact that even at a person's first breaths she is already in a position of receptivity and response, cf. Chrétien, *La Voix Nue*, 7. The naked voice is the voice of the *Parousia*, which no person, at no point in his or her life, is capable of receiving in its fullness. These encounters leave wounds, but these wounds, like Jacobs's, open up rather than shut down fulfillment of the promise. Chétien likens these kinds of wounds to the wounds of Christ, which do not disappear after the resurrection (cf. Chrétien, *La Voix Nue*, 31). The glorified body retains the blessed wounds, with the fullness of glory radiating out of those wounds.

64. Williams, *Wound of Knowledge*.

against any tidy account of the Christian faith.[65] What characterizes the saints whom the church holds up as exemplars in faith is their willingness to surrender to poverty, humiliation, even death because of their Christian conviction. What lies at the center of their faith? The radical claim that God works in history, and because of that fact Christians cannot but reinterpret all of history—including their own—in light of divine activity. Williams emphasizes how Christian spirituality cannot escape the materiality, the this-worldliness, of life: "If the heart of 'meaning' is a human story, a story of growth, conflict, and death, every human story with all its oddity and ambivalence, becomes open to interpretation in terms of God's saving work."[66] Escapism from this world is a non-option for the Christian because it is into this world that God became man.

Christian spirituality, then, is not a private and internal activity but rather a public and embodied one. The goal of the Christian life is not to enter a disembodied Nirvana, but experience *shalom* in its proper sense of completeness and perfection: "'Spirituality' becomes far more than a science of interpreting exceptional private experiences; it must now touch every area of human experience.... And the goal of human life becomes not enlightenment but wholeness—an acceptance of this complicated and muddled bundles of experiences as a possible theatre for God's creative work."[67] The event of the Incarnation affirms embodied life with all its entanglements and limits.

God's action in history precedes the Incarnation as evidenced in the older Testament. Part of the muddled character of God's work in history lies in the difficulty of understanding how the workings of God in ancient Israel connect with the new thing brought about by Jesus Christ. Williams emphasizes that the often problematic relationship and incorporation of the old law within the new confirms the witness of the Incarnation wherein God takes to himself all the ambiguities and limits of earthly life: "If God is to be seen at work here [the relationship between the God of the Jewish people and the God of the Christian people], he is indeed a strange God, a hidden God, who does not uncover his will in a straight line of development, but enters into a world of confusion and ambiguity and works in contradictions— the new covenant which both fulfills, and radically alters the old."[68] While

65. Williams, *Wound of Knowledge*, 11.
66. Williams, *Wound of Knowledge*, 12.
67. Williams, *Wound of Knowledge*, 12.
68. Williams, *Wound of Knowledge*, 14.

Williams's recognition of confusion does not appease concerns and critiques of potential supersessionism, even nascent anti-Semitism, his affirmation of God as strange and hidden goes a long way in explaining the difficulty of understanding God's working in history as a straight progressive line from the genesis of the world up to the present age.

A central aspect of understanding the wounding effect of encounters with God comes through examining precisely what occurs when the human person is confronted with the divine; namely, all idols are exposed in stark relief. These idols, of course, can be found in many things, but arguably the most common human proclivity for idolatry is the distorted view of the self.[69] The self-autonomous and self-sufficient person faces a definitive threat when confronted with the divine. As Williams aptly summarizes, "Because it is menacing and painful to be confronted with the knowledge that our constructions of controlled senses are liable to self-emptying, we readily turn to violence against the bearers of such knowledge."[70] Glimpses of divine grace can unsettle delusions of control, making grace manifest as menace rather than a gift.

O'Connor recognizes not only the intrusive nature of grace, but also the diminished understanding of grace as both a real and often an unwelcome presence in modern life: "Our age not only does not have a sharp eye for the almost imperceptible intrusions of grace, it no longer has much feeling for the nature of the violences which precede and follow them" (MM, 112).[71] O'Connor's stories play up the startling effect of grace precisely because of our own forgetfulness and domestication of it. In one of O'Connor's most famous lines, she contends that the work of the writer who is also a Christian is to alert the impaired modern readers to their need for redemption: "to the hard of hearing you shout, and for the almost blind you draw large and startling figures" (CW, 806). Grace must be rendered

---

69. Sarah Coakley helpfully describes this distortion of the self as rooted in perverted desire, with a distorted longing for possession, coercion, and control rather than submission to the will and desires of God (Coakley, *God, Sexuality, and the Self*, 15).

70. Williams, *Wound of Knowledge*, 17.

71. O'Connor also touches on the modern person's confusion of grace with something more pithy and ultimately dangerous in her preface to *A Memoir of Mary Ann*: "One of the tendencies of our age is to use the suffering of children to discredit the goodness of God, and once you have discredited his goodness, you are done with Him. . . . In the absence of this faith now, we govern by tenderness. It is a tenderness which, long since cut off from the person of Christ, is wrapped in theory. When tenderness is detached from the source of tenderness, its logical outcome is terror. It ends in forced labor camps and in the fumes of the gas chamber" (CW, 831).

both strangely obvious and strangely indispensable for the modern person. The violence that precedes and/or follows grace shakes the characters and readers out of any delusional conceptions about what we confront when grace reveals itself in the world.[72]

Grace demands a response. Williams characterizes this response as a moment of "acknowledgment of God as God who is present in and works in human failure and helplessness—so much so that it can be said he 'forces' people into a decision to acknowledge or not to acknowledge their failure."[73] In moments of grace, the recipient must respond to the gift of grace with a "yea" or a "nay." Grace enables the possibility for the participant to respond; grace is not an act of coercion, but instead one of cooperation or refusal. In effect, graced moments corner a person into choosing one path or another, to reject or receive what the graced moment communicates: "reality in the light of God." For the person to receive the "new thing" that Christ offers is to accept and invite the undoing that precedes remaking.

Williams takes up the Pauline conviction that to understand our redemption requires attention to being like Christ, in his life, his death, and his resurrection. Christ as incarnate Lord places suffering at the center of the obedient life. Obedience, rather than self-determination, characterizes the Christian life. For the Christian to become like Christ involves an "unselfing," a displacing of our desire to control those around us and results in making room for the other, both the neighbor and God.[74] Here, Williams stresses that to *know* God in disruptive moments of grace signals an experiential sharing in the divine life rather than conceptual mastery, a "conformity to God," rather than "a subject's conceptual grasp of an object."[75] To know God is to surrender the desire for control. This release of control captures at least in part the wounding effect of blessing. Accepting the gift of grace—participation in the divine life—demands that we lay down all the weapons of the ego: control, mastery, winning.

---

72. Note well, I am discussing violence here in the context of O'Connor's storytelling. I am not arguing that God's grace is literally violent. O'Connor artistically renders the dispossessing effect of grace in her fiction with often violent scenes to catch the reader's attention.

73. Williams, *Grace and Necessity*, 16.

74. Williams, *Grace and Necessity*, 23. Williams discusses the idea of unselfing in relation to otherness and dispossession in his essay "Hegel and The Gods of Postmodernity" (Williams, *Wrestling with Angels*, 25–34).

75. Williams, *Grace and Necessity*, 23.

The incarnate life of Christ demonstrates the inherent choice to submit or resist of recognition of divine grace. This Christoform condition offers people the freedom to choose submission or rejection, surrender or control, discipleship or self-mastery. Christ's life shows both the possibility and consequences of freely choosing the way of submission. Ultimately, to choose the way of submission—of saying "yea" in acknowledgment of our own failure in the light of God—is a union of wills: "salvation is the encounter and union of these two wills, when human beings will to be what God wills them to be. And Christ, in this system, is preeminently the one in whom God's freedom and ours are perfectly expressed."[76]

The result of the union of wills is best characterized by Augustine's infamous autobiographical line in his *Confessions* Book I.1: "You have formed us for Yourself, and our hearts are restless until they rest in you." Rest characterizes the union of the human will with the divine will, but we should not understand this rest as easy or comfortable. The rest Augustine speaks of here is the result of a person's desire being directed towards its proper end; it is rightly ordered love. Williams emphasizes that in Augustine, as in the earlier Cappadocian Fathers, redirected desire characterizes the affirmative acknowledgement of the believer's failures in the light of God. Properly directed desire—the result of a conversion moment—does not instantaneously rectify the perversions and idolatries in a person's life. In fact, conversion's shifting of desire often unsettles a person's life even as she finds rest in God as the proper object of her desire: "The beauty of God . . . is the vison of an indescribable loveliness that calls our hearts out of darkness, breaking down the barriers of false love, right ordering those desire and impulses by which we live."[77] Human desire directed towards its proper end recasts everything that is capable of becoming idols. Strangely and yet logically, finding a resting place in God creates a restlessness in daily life. Only God and no other end—be it human striving, material possession, or any other created thing—can satisfy human desire. The Christian suffers in this process because the soul's journey to God through rightly directed desire remains constrained by the limits of fallenness and finitude.[78] Thus, a joyful suffering—evidenced

---

76. Williams, *Grace and Necessity*, 41.

77. Williams, *Grace and Necessity*, 85.

78. This movement of the soul's journey towards God through rightly-ordered desire is epitomized in medieval Christian works such as Bonaventure's *Itinerarium Mentis in Deum*, Dante's *Divine Comedy*, and Teresa of Ávila's *The Interior Castle*.

For more on the connection between desire and wounding framed by Gregory of Nyssa's theology, see "Bodies Luminous and Wounded: The Spirit Manifests the Beauty of the World" in Carnes, *Beauty*, 183–250.

in language of "purgation" through prayer, contemplation, and asceticism—disrupts and reorders the human will.

Williams illustrates that in Augustine's thought, desire is cultivated through both the appealing and the reprehensible: "the compulsion towards the love of God comes not only from the loveliness but also from the horror of the world."[79] The "hope for fulfillment of joy" encourages properly ordered desire along, but also hope "for the healing of the world's wounds."[80] Williams's Augustinian language of human desire's proper end as found both in the resplendent beauty and horrific wounds of the world echoes the discussion earlier in this chapter on the function of the ugly and the beautiful in Maritain's aesthetic. Just as art draws out beauty from ugly things, so also does a person whose desires have been rightly ordered see the possibility for new life in marred things. Hope recasts both the beautiful and the grotesque in the world.

Returning to Chrétien's image of Jacob, we may say that there are wounds that disrupt in order to usher in something new. Jacob's example is a religious, not a moral one: "he summons up for us not a law, but the paradox of faith."[81] Jacob's wounding is the violence of love, which can come as a shock, even as a violent storm. Chrétien describes the onslaught of violent love as the "irresistible power that raises us, and knocks us down, loses us, and finds us, in a dizzying whirlwind."[82] Encounters of this sort signal a defeat that opens that way to victory, a loss that brings in unforeseen new life.

Conclusion

In an early journal entry written after her father's death from lupus, O'Connor noted:

> The reality of death has come suddenly upon us and a consciousness of the power of God has broken our complacency like a bullet in the side. A sense of the dramatic, of the tragic, of the infinite, has descended upon us, filling us with grief, but even above grief, wonder. Our plans were so beautifully laid out—ready to be

---

79. Williams, *Grace and Necessity*, 88.
80. Williams, *Grace and Necessity*, 88.
81. Chrétien, *Hand to Hand*, 5.
82. Chrétien, *Hand to Hand*, 10.

carried to action when with magnificent certainty God laid them aside and said, 'You have forgotten—mine?'[83]

O'Connor's metaphor of "a bullet in the side" as a means of God's revelation imaginatively renders the possibility of wounds that bless—in this case, as her father's death disrupts the projected arc of her life. Even from these early years of her life, O'Connor does not shy away from the unsettling and painful work of redemption. The antagonist we frequently find in O'Connor's stories—bullish, glaring, and belligerent—can be best understand not as the enemy of the good, but the enemies of our own invention: our pride, apathy, independence, and self-assurance.

---

83. Fitzgerald, "Rooms with a View," 17. Sally Fitzgerald, reflecting on this passage, surmises that this entry is not only a reflection on her father but a foreshadowing of her own suffering with lupus ten years later.

Chapter 3

On Stories Sparely Wrought

Introduction

ONE OF THE BEST known descriptions of biblical Hebrew narrative outside of biblical studies comes by way of Erich Auerbach's *Mimesis: The Representation of Reality in Western Literature*.[1] In the opening chapter "Odysseus' Scar," Auerbach distinguishes between Homeric and Hebraic epic narratives. Auerbach uses a scene in the *Odyssey*, when Odysseus's nursemaid recognizes him in his later years after she touches his scar, to reflect on the epic's style of narration: "the syntactical connection between part and part is perfectly clear, no contour is blurred. There is also room and time for orderly, perfectly well-articulated, uniformly illuminated descriptions of implements, ministrations, and gestures; even in the dramatic moment of recognition."[2] In the Homeric epic "men and things stand out in a realm where everything is visible," and because everything is visible readers are not troubled with a concern for the unspoken backdrop.[3] Auerbach contrasts this entirely foregrounded narrative with "an equally ancient and equally epic style from a different world of forms" recognizable in Abraham's binding of Isaac (Gen 22).[4] Whereas the scene of recognition with Odysseus's scar foregrounds all information readers

---

1. Auerbach, *Mimesis*. Originally published in 1953.
2. Auerbach, *Mimesis*, 3. Auerbach summarizes the whole of the Homeric epic similar to this particular scene: "the basic impulse of the Homeric style: to represent phenomenon in a fully externalized form, visible and palpable in all their parts, and completely fixed in their spatial and temporal relations" (cf. Auerbach, *Mimesis*, 6).
3. Auerbach, *Mimesis*, 3.
4. Auerbach, *Mimesis*, 8.

need to assess the full picture of the scene, the Hebraic binding scene sparingly narrates the events:

> [I]f we conceive of Abraham in the foreground, where it might be possible to picture him as prostrate or kneeling or bowing with outspread arms or gazing upward, God is not there too: Abraham's words and gestures are directed toward the depths of the picture or upward, but in any case the undetermined, dark place from which the voice comes to him is not in the foreground.[5]

Auerbach sets the Homeric style of foregrounding over against biblical Hebrew narrative drawing readers into the ambiguous depths of an unnarrated background in order to identify the significance of the narrated events.[6] Here in two ancient styles of narrating epics—one Greek, the other Hebraic—two radically different styles of narration confront us. While the broad strokes he uses to distinguish between the Homeric and biblical epic narratives may overstate the case at times, Auerbach pinpoints the distinctive style of Hebrew biblical narrative decades before the height of narrative criticism of the Bible and robust development of biblical poetics.[7]

The way a story is told both opens up and limits its interpretive possibilities. As Michael Fishbane notes at the start of *Biblical Text and Texture: A Literary Reading of Selected Texts*: "Form is inseparable from

---

5. Auerbach, *Mimesis*, 9.

6. In the case of Gen 22, Auerbach notes that the great moment of tension—when Isaac asks where the animal is for the sacrifice and Abraham ambiguously responds—readers must infer the tension: "everything remains unexpressed" (cf. Auerbach, *Mimesis*, 11).

7. An easy example of Auerbach's argumentative deficiencies regarding Old Testament narrative is his use of the "Elohist" as the narrator and promotion of the narrator's ideology, most notably that these religious stories "involves an absolute claim to be historical truth" (cf. Auerbach, *Mimesis*, 14). Auerbach continues the language of absolutizing by arguing that readers must subject their own realities to the dogmatic claims that make-up the background—concealed meaning—of the narrative (Auerbach, *Mimesis*, 15). While Auerbach is right to note that religious convictions root the texts and provide for a deeper reading, his language actually flattens the possibility for interpretive play by restricting the range of interpretation to an authoritarian ideology. There are many reasons this is unconvincing, including the fact that with the slow-death of the source author (i.e., Jahwist, Elohist, Priestly, Deuteronomist), trying to assert any universal and authoritative Old Testament theology becomes quite the task. In addition, as we will see in this chapter, the minimal foregrounded material offers readers interpretive exploration that is not restricted to submitting to some external reality that imposes a particular religious structure of reality, but opens up a number of levels of inference and investigation that include but are not limited to religious claims concerning the cosmos.

content, such that every textual formulation of an event constructs a unique literary reality; to imagine a different formulation of it would be to construct a different reality."[8] In this chapter, I present a bird's eye view of the function and impact of biblical Hebrew narrative style, known as biblical poetics. My purpose for occupying an entire chapter with the topic of biblical poetics is simple: to offer an outline of how biblical Hebrew stories are told, which sets the groundwork for illuminating O'Connor's spare style through the transposition of the *wayyiqtol* onto the climactic scene of *Wise Blood* in the next chapter.

As was seen earlier, O'Connor's spare form persisted throughout her writing career, despite Caroline Gordon's continual advice to make fewer demands on readers. Biblical Hebrew narrative makes similar demands on readers. I begin the chapter with a definition of biblical poetics that underscores the unique artistry of storytelling found in the Hebrew narrative. Identifying the artistry of biblical narrative includes the need to attend to the issue of historicity by asking the question of the relationship between artistic representation and historical event. Following my introduction to the field of biblical poetics, I turn to the particular style of biblical Hebrew narrative: parataxis. An essential element of the artistry of biblical narrative is the dramatic action offered to readers between the bare-bones "truth" of a story and the "whole truth"—only fully available at the divine level of omniscience, but available to readers as opportunities for exploration and inference. After demonstrating what Meier Sternberg identifies as the drama of reading found in biblical narrative, I unfold the definitive features of paratactic style in biblical Hebrew narrative, most notably evident in three vital areas for interpretive play through gap-filling: characterization, pacing, and the function of the *wayyiqtol*.[9] Vital for this survey of biblical poetics is the recognition that the stories we find in the Old Testament read very differently in their original language than in translation. While suggesting that something is lost in translation stands true of any translated text, I demonstrate in this chapter that much of the distinctive character of

---

8. Fishbane, *Biblical Text and Texture*, xi.

9. It should be noted that because the scope of my study is limited to biblical narrative, parallelism, a central feature of biblical poetry, will not be explored. While parallelism is distinctive to biblical Hebrew poetry and not to narrative, the function of parallelism strengthens my insistence that the artistry of biblical writers invites readers into profound interpretive play, which cannot be fully captured without attending to the Hebrew text.

Hebrew narrative—notably its paratactic style of narration—is often rendered unrecognizable when glossed in translation.

Defining Biblical Poetics

In *Poetics and Interpretation of Biblical Narrative*, Adele Berlin distinguishes between poetics and interpretation through a baking metaphor.[10] Poetics, Berlin argues, is like a cake recipe, concerned with how a text comes together to become what it distinctly is. Interpretation is the tasting, as it were, of the text where the concern is not with the mechanics of a recipe but the final product. While poetics and interpretation are symbiotically related, they remain distinct.[11] Berlin works backwards from the final product of the text through an inductive study to discover the literary devices at work that make-up the final product.[12] At the heart of Berlin's analysis lies the conviction that "[i]f we want to understand a biblical story, we must first take seriously the effort to learn how stories are told, specifically how biblical stories are told."[13] In seeking to understand the poetics of biblical narrative, Berlin insists that biblical stories are art and, like all art, requires a *relational* understanding of the work with the observer. Biblical narrative, as literary art, communicates through its poetics to a receptive reader who actively engages the text. Biblical narrative "suggests what it does not show" by means of literary devices such as characterization, repetition, variation, and point of view.[14]

---

10. Berlin, *Poetics and Interpretation*, 15.

11. Berlin, *Poetics and Interpretation*, 16. Berlin warns against the tendency to confuse an artistic choice for a pure historical sign of development. There are dangers in source and form criticism, where the assumption is not of a literary whole (i.e., final form), but rather a conviction that all incongruities (e.g., gaps, inconsistencies, repetition) indicate historical development: "To be sure, there are gaps, inconsistencies, retellings, and changes in vocabulary in biblical narrative, but these can be viewed as part of a literary technique and are not necessarily signs of different sources. The whole thrust of source criticism is toward the fragmenting of the narrative into sources, while, at the same time it ignores the rhetorical and poetic features which bind the narrative together" (cf. Berlin, *Poetics and Interpretation*, 121). We will see this same insistence echoed later in this chapter in the work of Meier Sternberg and Robert Alter.

12. In Berlin's work, her primary concerns are with characterization and point of view (cf. Berlin, *Poetics and Interpretation*, 20).

13. Berlin, *Poetics and Interpretation*, 21.

14. Berlin, *Poetics and Interpretation*, 139. Here, Berlin applauds Auerbach's distinction between the Homerian epic as it provides the reader everything they need to know

Undoubtedly the most influential work on the artistry of biblical Hebrew narrative is Robert Alter's *The Art of Biblical Narrative*.[15] While Berlin focuses on the "recipe" of literary devices that make-up the final narrative, Alter intentionally avoids an investigation of poetics apart from the practical task of reading the narratives themselves. In his emphasis on reading, Alter shares the New Critics' concern, discussed in the previous chapter, with the text itself. Alter identifies his method as diverging from the two opposing approaches that Berlin classifies as the distinct but symbiotic categories of poetics and interpretation. Poetics, Alter argues, exists apart from an interpretation in the realm of structuralism where a formal presentation of literary devices coheres only abstractly to the texts in their final form.[16] The opposing approach of interpretation focuses on the performance of a text on readers where interpretation resides *solely* in the response of readers to the text, which undercuts any possibility of a text as possessor of meaning.[17]

Alter bypasses these two opposing approaches—one he identifies in abstraction and the other in radical subjectivism—by modeling "a third approach, not really between these two alternatives but rather headed in another, more practical direction."[18] Alter identifies his approach as standing apart from formal poetics because he finds too much particularity in the stories themselves to impose a system without it ending in misrepresentation: "the actual operation of these tales are too manifold and too untidy to be contained in any symmetrical frame of formal taxonomies, neatly labeled categories, tables and charts, without distortion."[19] While avoiding abstraction of the text by a system of rules, Alter also aims to avoid making an individual's interpretation the sole authority of a text's meaning. Alter recognizes that he offers his own particular interpretations of the texts he evaluates but quickly adds that while a text has no singular meaning (e.g.,

---

to understand the story and Old Testament narrative where readers must infer background knowledge with only the bare minimum information about the narrative.

15. Alter, *Art of Biblical Narrative*.

16. An example of an approach that comes near the pure realm of structural is Ska's *Our Fathers Have Told Us*. While Ska provides helpful language to analyze biblical narrative, the work focuses more on the structural elements in narrative (time, plot, narration, point of view, etc.) than on the ways these features work in particular texts. This sort of analysis can offer the illusion of uniformity in the structure of biblical narrative that, as Alter argues, runs the danger of imposition rather than illumination in reading.

17. Alter, *Art of Biblical Narrative*, 178.

18. Alter, *Art of Biblical Narrative*, 178.

19. Alter, *Art of Biblical Narrative*, 178.

via the historical-critical method) readers must be attentive to the ways the stories tell themselves. The *way* a story is told provides "the range of intended meanings—theological, psychological, more, or whatever—of the biblical tale."[20] Alter's "third way" emphasizes the artistry found in the telling of a story—as reflected in the title of his work as the *art* of biblical narrative—similarly to Berlin's emphasis on the communicative act of a story with its readers. Unlike a more formal conception of poetics, the scholarship around biblical poetics stands strongly in a tradition that emphasizes the play between the inner-workings of how a story is told and the interpretive possibilities available to readers.

Because we are dealing with ancient stories that developed over a long period of time, an analysis of biblical narrative could focus on the curt style of narration as the result of a heavily redacted text that was put together piecemeal resulting in a semi-coherent whole.[21] While there is no doubt that the biblical Hebrew narratives as we have them are a result of textual transmission and redactions spanning generations, Alter warns against a modern critique of incoherency or lack of unity regarding these ancient stories: "[t]he biblical text may not be the whole cloth imagined by pre-modern Judeo-Christian tradition, but the confused textual patchwork that scholarship has often found to displace such earlier views may prove upon further scrutiny to be a purposeful pattern."[22] Within biblical narrative we find a coherent artistry that despite being foreign to our modern sensibilities conveys in its style a particular kind of reading experience. The subsequent discussion adheres to the conviction that the study of biblical poetics explores literary devices functioning in particular texts as artistic strokes that communicate meaning to readers.

---

20. Alter, *Art of Biblical Narrative*, 179.

21. For a visual representation of the piecemeal approach, Richard Elliot Friedman's *The Bible with Sources Revealed* color codes proposed sources for the books of the Pentateuch (Friedman, *Bible with Sources Revealed*). Friedman offers six source options, plus an additional "other" category: J (an early source making use of title "YAHWEH" origination in the Southern Kingdom), E (contemporary source to J originating in Northern Kingdom and making use of more generic name "Elohim"), RJE (later redactor of J and E produced after the fall of the Northern Kingdom to Assyria in eighth century BCE), P (priestly source from the fifth/sixth centuries offering alternate reading of history to J and E), D (includes "Dtn" for law code, "Dtr" for Deuteronomistic History, and two further revisions of this history in "Dtr1" and "Dtr 2"), and R (final redactor and compiler of the Pentateuch).

22. Alter, *Art of Biblical Narrative*, 133.

Viewing the biblical narrative as a united whole rather than a piecemeal collection of disjointed parts leads to the important discussion of the relationship between history and artistry in historical narrative. Berlin warns against the tendency to confuse an artistic choice for a pure historical sign of development. Source, form, and redaction criticisms, among others, ground their investigations in the assumption that incongruities (e.g., gaps, inconsistencies, repetition) indicate historical development rather than a literary whole (i.e., final form) whose discrepancies reflect an artistic choice. Berlin pushes back against the critical stance that historical development trumps artistry:

> To be sure, there are gaps, inconsistencies, retellings, and changes in vocabulary in biblical narrative, but these can be viewed as part of a literary technique and are not necessarily signs of different sources. The whole thrust of source criticism is toward the fragmenting of the narrative into sources, while, at the same time it ignores the rhetorical and poetic features which bind the narrative together.[23]

In short, biblical poetics privileges artistry over historical disassembling.

Emphasizing the artistry of biblical narrative over against critical diachronic methods raises the question: is biblical narrative history or fiction? Frequently, answers to this question that avoid the extremes of historical literalism on one end or fabrication on the other find themselves in a muddled middle. In *The Art of Biblical History*, V. Philips Long wrestles with the language of "fictionalized history" and "historicized fiction" that Alter uses in *The Art of Biblical Narrative*.[24] Long argues that while Alter recognizes some distinction between these two terms, he is not careful enough in distinguishing between them.[25] In both cases, the modifier fails to undercut the basic principle of the header word. "Historicized fiction" carries with it the assumption that at its core, the narrative is a fictionalized account with historical elements thrown in. Whereas, the term "fictionalized history" communicates the notion that, while embellished, the account remains a historical one of events that empirically occurred.

---

23. Berlin, *Poetics and Interpretation*, 121.

24. Long, *Art of Biblical History*, 61.

25. Long, *Art of Biblical History*, 61, cf. 14: "He [Alter] does show awareness of the distinction on occasion; see, e.g., *Art of Biblical Narrative*, pp. 25, 33–34, 41. But his lack of clarity on this important point still leaves him open to criticism."

Avoiding the confusion of these phrases altogether, Long adopts the language of "history-writing" or "historiography" to identify the type of stories in biblical narrative.[26] Historiography offers a means of identifying the artistry of biblical narrative without running the danger of over-emphasizing the fictional element, for historiography "might be fairly described as a kind of verbal representational art, with a visual type of representational art such as painting."[27] Long, himself a painter, recognizes that representational art—e.g., a landscape painting—suggests both a referent in the real-world and the imaginative strokes the artist makes. Central to this comparison is the observation that there is no clear delineation between the literal (i.e., historical/referential) and fictional (i.e., artistic/imaginative) works of art. The way representational artwork is judged as representation is by its context: "the difference between a narrative whose primary purpose is aesthetic is the degree to which the artist is constrained by the actualities of the subject matter."[28] Thus, Long reasons that real events constrain historical-writing found in biblical narrative, just as a landscape constrains the landscape painter.[29] These constraints provide boundaries for proper representation and show how the artist works within those bounds so as to display the artistry at work in history-writing.

Long acknowledges that not all of Scripture is literally and directly referential to historical events, but he also recognizes a "historical impulse" that "runs throughout the Bible, which, though not in every place and not always equally evident is nevertheless pervasive."[30] This historical impulse protects Long from falling into the polarities of claiming Scripture as either history or theology, propaganda or fantastical fiction. While Long does not eliminate the historical problem of delineating the historical elements from the fictional, his emphasis on the artistic representation of events rather than on an excavation for historical traces allows us to speak of the Bible as literature without jettisoning the historical impulse for the representation undergirding the whole of the text, if not in all its parts.

26. Long, *Art of Biblical History*, 58–87.
27. Long, *Art of Biblical History*, 63.
28. Long, *Art of Biblical History*, 68.
29. Long uses the example of comparing the historical accounts in Samuel–Kings to the Chronicler's summarizing: "In short, what the comparison of the two renderings of the dynastic promise illustrates is the extent to which historians may be creative in their presentations, while at the same time remaining constrained by the facts" (cf. Long, *Art of Biblical History*, 86).
30. Long, *Art of Biblical History*, 57.

The field of biblical poetics explores the distinctive features of biblical Hebrew narrative. Standing apart from the foundational convictions of traditional biblical criticisms, scholars of biblical poetics insist that artistry is the central principle for understanding biblical narrative. The narrative artistry found in biblical Hebrew narrative requires focused attention because of the particular kind of reading experience offered by the narrative.

Parataxis as Interpretive Play

In the analysis of fiction, scholars often identify two styles of storytelling summarily understood as parataxis and hypotaxis. This distinction is spoken of as the difference between showing (i.e., parataxis) and telling (i.e., hypotaxis). Auerbach's proposal sharply delineates between the two with the Homeric epic hypotactically telling readers all they need to know and Hebraic epic paratactically showing events. In *Analyzing Prose*, Richard A. Lanham distinguishes between the showing and telling models by examining the relationship between clauses:

> A style's characteristic manner of connecting its elements provides an easy way to recognize it. Whatever units a writer chooses to work with—phrases, clauses, or complete sentences—he or she must relate them equally or unequally. He or she can tell us how they are related —A *caused* B, B *came after* A—and thus subordinated one to the other, by cause, time or whatever, or can simply juxtapose them and leave the relationship up to us.[31]

In paratactic narration clauses are linked without causal connection and explicit judgments are absent. The central distinction here is between equal or unequal treatment among the prose units. The subordination of clauses indicates unequal treatment between "phrases, clauses, or complete sentences." While some narratives are more prone toward a paratactic or hypotactic style of narration, Wayne Booth warns against using the showing or telling distinction too definitively as the features of both showing and telling can appear in various degrees.[32] Booth prefers language of "various forms of telling in the service of various forms of showing" so as to

---

31. Lanham, *Analyzing Prose*, 29, italics his.

32. Booth, *Rhetoric of Fiction*, 16. Originally published in 1961. Booth uses the prose of medieval writer Giovanni Boccaccio as an example of an author who demonstrates varying degrees of showing and telling in his stories.

illustrate the stylistic play between paratactic and hypotactic storytelling.³³ Booth's warning protects the genre from generalities that fail to deal with the particularities of individual stories. I contend that one can safely assert that some stories are more paratactic than hypotactic—and vice versa—in tendencies of narrative style without falling into the danger of complete polarity between showing and telling. A strong case of this tendency towards paratactic style is found in biblical Hebrew narrative.

In his work *Poetics of Biblical Narrative*, Meier Sternberg emphasizes the perplexing character of Hebrew biblical narrative: "Far beyond the normal demands of interpretation and with no parallel in Oriental literature . . . the world and the meaning are always hypothetical, subject to change from one stage of the reading *process* to another, and irreducible to any formula."³⁴ Sternberg pushes back against Auerbach's formulaic proposal of distinguishing Homeric and Hebraic epics as one of foreground and background because the polemical differentiation minimizes and distracts from the artistry of biblical narrative.³⁵ The mimetic play between reality (i.e., the world) and representation (i.e., stories) creates an "obstacle course" for readers who must be taken up in the drama of reading to arrive at understanding.³⁶

Readers arrive at an understanding not only of the stories, but also of their own limits as readers.³⁷ Biblical narrative contains a tendency toward a dramatic rendering of the distance between God and the human realm. The disparity between the omniscient God and the finite human being creates an unambiguous picture of the world order: "God knows and controls

---

33. Booth, *Rhetoric of Fiction*, 16.

34. Sternberg, *Poetics*, 47, italics his.

35. Sternberg, *Poetics*, 232. Sternberg comments: "Even a cursory comparison of biblical narrative with Homeric epic . . . will reveal an unmistakable similarity in the management of sequence. It includes deformation of chronology, playing on the resultant gaps, baited traps and false impressions, rise and fall and yoking together of hypotheses, use of uncertainty for effects stretching from plot interest to intricate characterization. (To say nothing of related correspondences, whether the technique of repetition or the capacity for extended storytelling.) The Bible's art is on the whole richer and craftier, its surface incomparably less formulaic, its play more serious, its view of meaning and experience as a process built rather than incorporated into the composition. But *nothing like the famous antithesis drawn by Erich Auerbach between scriptural darkness and Homeric illumination has a leg to stand on*" (232, italics mine).

36. Sternberg, *Poetics*, 47.

37. Sternberg notes: "to make sense of the discourse is to gain a sense of being human" (cf. Sternberg, *Poetics*, 47).

all, and humans must learn their limitations, including the impossibility of fully comprehending God's ways with the world."[38] The narrator's omniscience within the narrative produces the overarching claims of an all-knowing God relating to an often ignorant and never fully enlightened humanity.[39] With all the play available to readers, the one non-negotiable framing principle is the epistemic limits of any and all readers. Alter similarly recognizes the central principle of human limits in the act of reading biblical narrative when he notes that "[f]iction fundamentally serves the biblical writers as an instrument of fine insight into these abiding perplexities of the human condition."[40]

Sternberg identifies the dynamic process of reading biblical narrative as "maneuvering between the truth and the whole truth."[41] While these stories can easily be misread, they cannot so easily be "counterread."[42] Sternberg suggests that biblical narrative possesses a readily available storyline within a well-established world held together by an overt theological system.[43] Even a deficient reader is able to read biblical narratives as coherent stories because of the information available on the surface without any recognition of the artistry of the text.[44] "Truth" identifies these readily available principles, where the narrator provides readers with reliable information. Here "reliable" does not necessarily suggest historical accuracy but instead the simple assumption that the narrator can be trusted in the telling of the story: "Historians may quarrel with his facts and others call them fiction; but in context his [narrations] remain accounts of the truth communicated on the highest authority."[45] A reliable narrator assures adequate information for readers to understand the basic plot development and interpretation of the story. The story must make sense for the narrator to be trustworthy.[46] In the case of Gen 32, the narrator provides enough

38. Sternberg, *Poetics*, 233.
39. Sternberg, *Poetics*, 184.
40. Alter, *Art of Biblical Narrative*, 176.
41. Sternberg, *Poetics*, 51.
42. Sternberg, *Poetics*, 50.
43. This echoes Auerbach's language of background in reading the Hebraic epic.
44. Sternberg, *Poetics*, 54.
45. Sternberg, *Poetics*, 51.
46. The reliable biblical narrator stands in contrast to the unreliable narrators found often in postmodern literature. Wayne Booth identifies the unreliable narrator as presenting convoluted narratives using irony rather than clarity as the guiding principle of literary excellence. As modern readers, we have grown accustomed to the labyrinthine

information for readers to understand Jacob wrestling from evening until dawn with a mysterious man, a tangle that ends with a wounded hip and a blessing in the form of Jacob's new name: "Israel."

While Sternberg argues that biblical narrative cannot be counterread, readers often read too much, too little, or even erroneously as they interpret the narratives. The narrator provides reliable information to arrive at the basic truth of a narrative, but this information can be aptly described as thin. Readers are not explicitly given information on characters' inner lives—motivations, emotions, virtues and vices—nor judgments of the events that transpired. The "whole truth" lies below the surface of the narrative and is only accessible to the reader by means of inference:

> [The narrator's] statements about the world—character, plot, the march of history—are rarely complete. . . . His *ex cathedra* judgments are valid as far as they go, but then they seldom go far below the surface of the narrative, where they find their qualification and shading. His reference to ends and means is conspicuous by its absence, but only to one alive to the novelty and intricacy of their working.[47]

Sternberg's distinction between the truth and the whole truth in biblical narrative invites readers to attend to the interpretive treasure available to attentive readings. The whole truth reveals opportunities for imaginative readings rather than shutting down opportunities for exploration. Gapped narration offers multivalent avenues into the text, thus providing readers with opportunities for the reader to infer further meaning or to make interpretive decisions that shut down further exploration. For Sternberg, exploration into certain gaps while resisting others contributes to the drama of reading.

The dynamic play between the truth and the whole truth results in a robust and coherent interpretation. This coherent reading should not be mistaken as the whole of the whole truth. Instead, the whole truth

---

convolutions of novelists such as Fielding and James: "we have looked for so long at foggy landscapes reflected in misty mirrors that we have come to *like* fog. Clarity and simplicity are suspect; irony reigns supreme. . . . Though no responsible critic has ever argued that all ambiguities resulting from irony are good ambiguities, it is astonishing to see how reluctant we have become to discriminate, to point to this or that particular difficulty, spring from irony and say, 'This is a fault.' After all, we say, it is only enemies of literature who ask that its effects be handed to the reader on a platter" (Booth, *Rhetoric of Fiction*, 372, italics his).

47. Sternberg, *Poetics*, 51–52.

functions as an opportunity for the reader to explore below the surface of the basic arc of the plot. To plumb the depths of the narrative does not end in a full excavation of all the content available for discovery within the gaps; rather, readers return to the surface with sufficient inferential knowledge for a more rich and lucid understanding of the narrative. The whole truth is available in full only to God and the narrator.

Like Berlin and Alter, Sternberg identifies a distinctive artistry in the narration of Old Testament stories arguing that Hebrew biblical narrative is "without precedent in literary history and unrivaled since."[48] Because of its peculiar mode of storytelling, Sternberg warns against opposing any one system of literary analysis onto the reading of biblical Hebrew narrative. The greatest danger of all, Sternberg warns, is the concern for "application" of a universal critical strategy without concern for the particularity of the text.[49]

Sternberg describes biblical narrative as "passing off its art for artlessness, its sequential linkages and suprasequential echoes for unadorned parataxis, its density of evocation for chronicle-like thinness and transparency."[50] Sternberg is not arguing that biblical narrative be understood categorically as primitive paratactic narration *par excellence*. Instead, the seemingly "unadorned parataxis" of biblical narrative possesses within its epistemic gaps and unsubordinated clauses a wealth of interpretive possibilities that weave an unspoken, yet rich overarching narrative through its seemingly simplistic narration.

The play between the truth and the whole truth that Sternberg presents as the drama of reading exists precisely because of the paratactic style. This play is available through the gaps within the narratives. Sternberg defines a gap as "a lack of information about the world—an event, motive, causal link, character trait, plot structure, law of probability—contrived by temporal displacement."[51] These gaps in the narrative create discontinuity within the narrative, which leads readers to do interpretive work to repair, as it were, the continuity in the narrative. Sternberg differentiates "gaps" from "blanks" through the test of relevancy: "to make distinctions between what was omitted for the sake of interest and what

---

48. Sternberg, *Poetics*, 53.
49. Sternberg, *Poetics*, 56–57.
50. Sternberg, *Poetics*, 53.
51. Sternberg, *Poetics*, 235.

was omitted for lack of interest."[52] Therefore, not all narrative silences are equal in terms of the available play between truth and whole truth. Blanks do not raise readerly curiosity in the same way as gaps, which invite further investigation by readers.

While differentiating between blanks and gaps, Sternberg admits the difficulty of clearly delineating between the two: "[i]n practice, however, the distinction turns out as problematic as it is inescapable, since it can appeal to no formal (and thus automatically applicable) marker."[53] Ultimately, readers judge a gap from a blank by the standard of relevancy: does it "heighten the reader's sense of suspension between the truth and the whole truth?"[54] As two case studies of differentiating gaps and blanks, consider two verses from the account of Jacob's nighttime wrestling. First, after describing Jacob and wrestling with a man until dawn, the narrative states in Gen 32:26: "And he saw that he was not able to prevail over him and he touched his hip socket and he dislocated Jacob's hip socket while wrestling with him." While the image of a wrestling bout lasting through the night and ending with a dislocated hip awakens the imagination, readers are less likely to wonder why the angel-man and Jacob were such an even match; e.g., the precise wrestling techniques of Jacob, the upper body strength of the mysterious angel-man. We can judge this lack of information as a blank because it does not offer readers play between the truth and the whole truth of the narrative. As a second case study, reflect on the dialogue between Jacob and his contender in Gen 32:29:

> And Jacob inquired: 'Please, tell me your name.'*
>
> And he [the angel-man] said 'Why is it that you ask for my name?'*
>
> And he blessed him there."[55]

Notice the two places where information is absent from the dialogue (signaled by asterisks): the angel-man does not offer his name in response to Jacob's question and Jacob does not respond to the motivation for asking for his name in the first place. How should these spaces of fissure be understood? Jacob's request for the angel-man's name sets up the subsequent question by the angel-man, but does the question heighten the curiosity

---

52. Sternberg, *Poetics*, 236.
53. Sternberg, *Poetics*, 236.
54. Sternberg, *Poetics*, 237.
55. Please note, all biblical translations are my own unless otherwise noted.

of the reader? In a way, yes: throughout the wrestling, we are not told with whom Jacob is wrestling and this leads to curiosity about the identity of the one with whom Jacob contends. In fact, the subsequent question by the angel-man regarding why Jacob wishes to know his name heightens the suspense of the previous unanswered question. These two questions without reply invite readers deeper into the story—who is this man contending with Jacob? The fact that these gaps are followed by the angel-man blessing Jacob and Jacob's proclamation of seeing God face-to-face invites further consideration of who this wrestler is: how (and why) does God wrestle with Jacob throughout the night?

Alter, building off of Sternberg's repeated insistence on the play between coherence and incoherence in biblical narrative, recognizes the indeterminacy provided by the gaps as a "technique of fiction" that leads readers to a "continual suspension of judgment, weighing of multiple possibilities, brooding over gaps in the information provided."[56] Midrashic exegesis serves as a fine example of embracing the brooding effect of artistically placed gaps in the narrative where gap-filling serves as an opportunity for intertextual reading across the entire Hebrew Scriptures.[57] With the assumption that God is the ultimate author of the text, these readers of Torah identify the gaps as an invitation to explore the baffling stumbling blocks in the text for these gaps are part of God's plan for telling ancient Israel's story.[58]

Understanding biblical Hebrew narrative as parataxis emphasizes the role of gaps in the act of reading. Gaps invite Sternberg's drama of reading, where curiosity and a need for coherence leads readers into various avenues of interpretive play. Three key features in biblical Hebrew narrative help to demonstrate this paratactic style and opportunity for gap-filling: characterization, pacing, and the function of the *wayyiqtol*.

---

56. Alter, *Art of Biblical Narrative*, 250.

57. See Boyarin, *Midrash*.

58. Boyarin comments, "God, the implied author of the narrative of the Torah, has willingly, as it were, encoded into His text the very kinds of dialogue that all of His epigones were destined willy-nilly to encode into theirs. As with all literature, so with the Torah, it is precisely the fault lines in the text, the gaps that its author has left, which enable reading . . . midrash enters into these interstices by exploring the ways in which the Bible can read itself" (cf. Boyarin, *Midrash*, 41).

Characterization

Characterization serves as a fitting entry-point into examination of the distinctive features of biblical narrative. The characters that populate ancient Israel's stories evidence their interior thoughts almost entirely through exterior actions. Readers are not often told about a character's inner life but rather have to rely on cues from dialogue or action to infer a character's personality, emotions, or motives. The lack of editorial information around a character's actions or direct discourse alerts modern readers to a distinctive feature of biblical Hebrew stories. Sternberg depicts the bare descriptions of characters as offering a "haunting portrait gallery" where stereotypical character-types fail to capture the unique quality of the central biblical characters.[59] Biblical figures tend not to act predictably nor fit particular motifs of the Hero, Victor, Villain, etc. For readers to build up a picture of the characteristics of an actor requires attention to all the information the narrative provides.

Jacob serves as a prime example of a character who appears as a sleazy salesman when he gains his brother's birthright with a bowl of stew (Gen 25:29–34); a momma's boy who fools his elderly father (Gen 27); a chosen one with whom God speaks in dreams (Gen 28:10–17); a romantic who works fourteen years for Rachel whom he loves (Gen 29:15–30); and a man who wrestles with God (Gen 32:23–33). Even within one narrative, Jacob takes on a number of different characteristics. A model of the need for close reading in order to attend to characterization is found when Jacob steals his brother Esau's blessing in Gen 27. While Jacob at first glance appears to be the "villain" of the narrative, willfully deceiving his father to attain his brother's blessing, a closer reading reveals a more profound picture of Rebekah than of Jacob, the ostensible central character of the pericope.

In an earlier chapter, readers are told that Isaac loved Esau because he liked the taste of game, but Rebekah loved Jacob (Gen 25:28). The narration in Gen 27 reminds the reader of this preferential tension, particularly in the descriptors provided in vv. 5–6 when the narration shifts from Isaac giving instruction to Esau to Rebekah's eavesdropping just outside of the scene: "Now, Rebekah overheard when *Isaac spoke to Esau, his son* . . . and *Rebekah said to Jacob, her son:* 'Behold! I heard your father speaking to *Esau, your brother* . . .'" In these two verses we are offered two sons, one son of Isaac and the other of Rebekah. The relationship between Rebekah

---

59. Sternberg, *Poetics*, 254.

and Esau is frigidly evidenced in her reference to Esau, never as her son, but as Jacob's brother. In the verses that precede and follow one son—addressed as "my son" (*bn*)—is directed by one parent to "go," "take," and "bring" in order "to bless" (vv. 3–4, 9). There are two competing intentions by mother and father for their favored sons. Rebekah's favoritism runs rampant in Gen. 27. The narrative tells us that Rebekah had been listening in on Isaac's instruction to Esau (v. 5a); Rebekah devises a plan for deception and instructs Jacob to follow her instructions exactly (vv. 7–10), and she even reassures Jacob when he worries that his father will realize the deception by promising that she will bear the responsibility if the plan goes awry (vv. 12–13). By attending closely to the narrative, Rebekah, not Jacob, is the agent of deception. Jacob, neither hero nor villain, is simply the obedient son who receives a stolen blessing.

Because the stories we find in the Old Testament are so brief and the means of sketching so spare, readers must attend to every detail offered by the narrator and signaled by the action of the characters. These narratives offer limited data for readers to imaginatively construct characters, but the scant amount of information does not mean that readers will be entirely unfamiliar with the strategies required for understanding another. Shimon Bar-Efrat describes the means of understanding narrated characteristics as "realistic" in that "[t]his approach resembles the one we adopt in real life, where we usually draw conclusions about people's personalities from what they say and do."[60] Readers come to know characters similarly to how people develop knowledge of others: via direct speech and indirect action. There are times when the narrator breaks into the scene as an omniscient narrator, but more often than not the narrators provide an unembellished account of the events, leaving inference and character judgment to readers. Readers of biblical narrative assume an inquisitive and attentive posture in order to make judgments and formulations regarding the characters within a story.

Biblical characters confound readers precisely because they do not fit into conventional roles. The greatest "heroes" of the Old Testament possess villainous characteristics at times: recall Noah's drunkenness (Gen 9:21), Abraham endangering Sarah out of self-protection (Gen 12:10–20; Gen 20:1–16), King David's coercive use of power to get Bathsheba into bed and betrothal (2 Sam 11), etc. Akin to real-life, readers are often not told what

---

60. Bar-Efrat, *Narrative Art*, 89.

to think about characters from an omniscient voice of judgment but rather must navigate characters through speech and action.

Pacing

The most familiar stories to modern readers link scenes within a story by a narrative bridge that temporally connects one scene to the next. These narrative bridges assist readers in recognizing the overt connection of one scene to another. Within biblical Hebrew narrative, compact scenes connect to one another conventionally through summary accounts that close a scene instead of narrative bridges clearly linking one story to the next. An example of this kind of summary is found at the close of Jacob's wrestling with the angel-man in Gen 32:33: "Because of this, the Israelites do not eat sinew of the hip, which is on the socket of the leg until this day for he struck the hip socket of Jacob in the sinew of the thigh." These summaries do not consistently occur, but when they do, they are most often brief.

With individual stories in biblical narrative most often unlinked by narrative bridges, the stories themselves are told in a style focused on showing rather than telling. Stories are narrated without commentary or bird's-eye observations and judgments. Bar-Efrat notes the effect produced by the vast majority of biblical stories narrated without outside comment: "there are very few instances in which time stops, and these are short and of little impact. This is what gives biblical narrative its characteristic dynamic nature and its almost incessant, rapid motion."[61] To understand the speed by which an episode is narrated, consider that the text of Jacob's wrestling with the angel-man that results in the patriarch's new name "Israel" (Gen 32: 23–33) fits easily within one-page of double-spaced text. In ten verses, one of which is narrative summary, arguably one of the most significant narrated events of ancient Israel's identity unfolds. The narrative time, in this case an all-night wrangling, stands in stark contrast to the narrated time. To produce such laconic effect entails biblical stories being told without much in the way of scenic description or interior life, as we have already seen. Dialogue between characters and simply described actions provide the outline of a narrative that must be filled-in by readers.

Generally, biblical narrative dedicates more narrative space to the events that lead up to a story's climactic moment than the climactic moment itself. Within the already curt narratives, the crux moment can come

---

61. Bar-Efrat, *Narrative Art*, 147.

and go so quickly that readers might not quite capture the moment *as* climax in their first reading. In the pericope of Jacob's wrestling, not even a full verse is dedicated to the climactic moment: "And he [the angel-man] blessed him [Jacob] there" (Gen 32:30c).

Bar-Efrat highlights the play in all narratives between the time it takes to narrate events—narrated time—and the time within the narrative in which events unfold—narrative time.[62] In biblical narrative, with such a contrast between narrated and narrative time, the rapidity of the unfolding of the narrative to readers creates a thrilling, even baffling reading experience. The play of internal and external times affects many dimensions of the reading experience: "[t]his twofold link with time has significant implications for the nature, possibilities and limitation of the narrative as well as for the way it is interpreted."[63] Because reading occurs through an unfolding of events—more like the experience of listening to music than the viewing of a work of art—narrators must sequentially present the story's actions to readers, allowing for withholding or even misleading readers of vital information.[64]

Returning to Alter's insistence that there is an art to biblical Hebrew narrative, the particular pacing of these stories contributes to a unique reading experience for readers. Alter wryly suggests that "the Hebrew writer may have known what he was doing but that we do not."[65] The speed by which these stories unfold, providing minimal commentary and clipped description of climactic moments, offers a distinctive reading experience that can leave readers with more questions than answers as one story moves to the next.

Function of the *Wayyiqtol*

The *wayyiqtol*, more than characterization or pacing, requires an investigation of the Hebrew text without reliance on translation to elucidate its function. Both the terminology and function of the presence of the *waw* with

---

62. Bar-Efrat, *Narrative Art*, 141.

63. Bar-Efrat, *Narrative Art*, 141.

64. Bar-Efrat, *Narrative Art*, 141. Bar-Efrat notes that the key difference between listening to music and reading a story is that music offers the opportunity to experience concurrent events (i.e., harmonies) at one time.

65. Alter, *Art of Biblical Narrative*, 136.

pataḥ followed by the *dagesh forte* form is a contested area of scholarship.⁶⁶ As the baseline for agreement, *The Brown-Driver-Briggs Hebrew and English Lexicon* (*BDB*) notes that the *waw-shewa* of the *wayyiqtol* "is used very freely and widely in Heb., but also with much delicacy, to express relations and shades of meaning which Western languages would usu. indicate by distinct participles."⁶⁷ In biblical Hebrew, participles are used more sparingly for "their frequent use was felt instinctively to be inconsistent with the lightness and grace of movement which the Hebrew ear loved; and thus in [translated versions] words like *or, then, but, notwithstanding, howbeit, so thus, therefore, that* constantly appear, where the Heb. has simply *waw-shewa*."⁶⁸ In later portions of the Hebrew Bible the construct of *waw-shewa* plus perfect verbs appears more frequently alongside the occurrence in the imperfect likely because of Aramaic influence on the Hebrew language.⁶⁹ While I am choosing to adopt the language of the *wayyiqtol*, there has not been consensus on this terminology through the history of scholarship.

Most often the *wayyiqtol* signals some action in the perfect tense, its use is not always related to sequence. The *wayyiqtol* can sometimes function exegetically, that is can serve to summarize or illuminate the clause that precedes it (e.g., 2 Sam 14:5: "Truly, I am a widow; *my husband has died*").⁷⁰ The *wayyiqtol* can also function in direct speech not as temporal action but volitionally as a request or command (e.g., "you shall . . . ").⁷¹ In addition to illumination and direct speech, the *wayyiqtol* can also present narrative information that breaks from a chronological unfolding to indicated a past event (e.g., Gen 31:33–34: "He came out from Leah's tent, and went into Rachel's tent, but *Rachel had taken* the household idols . . . ").⁷²

---

66. For a recent and succinct description of the state of scholarship around the *wayyiqtol*, see Poe Hays, *Function of Story*, 22–24. Poe Hays notes, "Throughout various theories about the exact nature of the *waw* consecutive or *wayyiqtol*, however, the narrative associations of the form remain central" (23).

67. Brown, Driver, and Briggs, *BDB*, 252a. In later portions of the Hebrew Bible the construct of *waw-shewa* plus perfect verbs appears more frequently alongside the occurrence in the imperfect likely because of Aramaic influence on the Hebrew language (*BDB*, 252a).

68. *BDB*, 252a.

69. *BDB*, 252b.

70. Arnold and Choi, *Guide to Biblical Hebrew Syntax*, 86.

71. Arnold and Choi, *Guide to Biblical Hebrew Syntax*, 88.

72. Arnold and Choi, *Guide to Biblical Hebrew Syntax*, 94.

For those unfamiliar with the function of the *wayyiqtol* in biblical Hebrew text, a simple example demonstrates how it works: AND *the woman woke up in the morning* AND *she got up* AND *she drank strong coffee*. Notice how the use of "AND" creates a connecting of clauses without subordination. All these clauses are identified together only because of the use of the "and." The *wayyiqtol* form functions like the "and" here, while also functioning as a punctuation mark in translation because English does not allow for progressive clauses without punctuation. Readers infer causal connections; for example, that she drank coffee *because* she needed the caffeine in the morning after a long night *or* she has a serious caffeine habit that she must break at some point but not this morning. It is up to readers to infer meaning from the gaps inherent in the unadorned narrative progression.

In *Pen of Iron: American Prose and the King James Bible*, Robert Alter argues that the King James Version (KJV) of the Bible not only reflects the style of biblical Hebrew narrative, but has also influenced prose style in America through narrative style, imagery, and themes.[73] Helpfully, Alter recognizes the play of biblical narration through its style of narration, notably in its abundant employment of the *wayyiqtol*: "the artfulness of biblical parataxis is precisely in its refusal to spell out causal connections, to interpret the reported narrative data for us."[74] The use of *wayyiqtol* in the Hebrew narrative links clauses without explanatory connections.

For Alter, the use of the *wayyiqtol*, particularly in direct speech, generates narrative silence where one might expect a subordinate clause that aids in generating interpretive connections between the linked clauses.[75] Alter identifies this negative aspect of biblical Hebrew direct speech as a reflection of the freedom of the human—that is, the "stubborn individuality" that does not allow for any universal human response to universal experiences.[76] Alter repeatedly articulates human freedom as a central part of biblical Hebrew storytelling by seeing the human as full of paradoxes and so requiring a refined art like biblical narrative to represent this human dimension sufficiently. Attending to silences in the narrative is at the same time an attendance to the human-driven character of the stories told. The *wayyiqtol* provides opportunities for interpretive play, while affirming the epistemic limits of readers.

73. Alter, *Pen of Iron*.
74. Alter, *Pen of Iron*, 133.
75. Alter, *Art of Biblical Narrative*, 79.
76. Alter, *Art of Biblical Narrative*, 129.

Sternberg's "truth and whole truth" interpretive dialectic demonstrates the interpretive play available to readers through gap-filling. This play is available through a paratactic style of narration, where causal connections and moral judgments are left to the reader. Biblical Hebrew narrative skeletal narration requires readers to put meat on the bones, as it were. Spare characterization, rapid narrative pacing, and the gapping effect of the *wayyiqtol* invite readers to explore below the surface of the narrative to provide coherence and greater significance to Hebrew stories. Paratactic storytelling demands attentive and imaginative interpretive work if readers desire to plumb the depths of meaning of any given pericope.

Conclusion

This chapter began with Auerbach's distinction between the Homeric and Hebraic epics as interpretive data residing in the overt foreground or obscure background, respectively. What Auerbach began in his description of Hebrew epic as "fraught with background," the study of biblical poetics spotlights the artistry of biblical Hebrew narrative whose bare scenes draw readers into the drama of reading. Parataxis names the gapped narrative that leaves causal connections and questions of cause, motive, judgment, etc. to the inference of readers. Characterization, pacing and the function of *wayyiqtol* demonstrate the paratactic features of biblical Hebrew narrative and the opportunities for interpretive play by readers. With the contours of biblical narrative set, the next chapter illuminates the similarities in paratactic style between ancient Hebrew stories and O'Connor's fiction by way of parallel readings of Jacob's wrestling with the angel-man in Gen 32 and the climactic scene of O'Connor's *Wise Blood*. As we will see, the climactic moments of these two narratives move through the events of transformations in their respective protagonists with a rapidity and spare quality that place great interpretive demands on readers. The paratactic style of both narrations heightens the subject-matter of the text: God's wounding blessing. It is this play of style and content that offers us a stylistic asceticism.

Chapter 4

Genesis 32 and *Wise Blood*

The Wounded Victor and
the Blinded Convert

Introduction

IN 1952, THE YEAR of *Wise Blood*'s publication, Flannery O'Connor remarked in a letter to Robert Lowell: "Harcourt sent my book to [Evelyn] Waugh and his comment was: 'If this is really the unaided work of a young lady, it is a remarkable product'" (CW, 897). Aside from the condescending tone of his assessment and O'Connor's mother Regina's humorous concern that Waugh doubted O'Connor's status as a proper lady, Waugh's comment hints at the distinctive quality of O'Connor's narrative style. Ralph Wood surmises that while Waugh likely referred to the extensive use of violence in a work of fiction written by a woman, his comment "may also have been referring to the prophetic directness of its narrative technique. The wintry plainness of her prose, its dry and tart matter-of-factness, its spare straightforwardness—none of these traits allow any lazy luxuriation in narrative eloquence."[1] Wood's regard for O'Connor's plain unadorned style provides a more generous read of Waugh's assessment of this "young lady's" technique and offers an apt characterization of O'Connor's fiction.[2]

---

1. Wood, *Christ-Haunted South*, 159.

2. O'Connor's style stands in contrast to Waugh's own elaborate and at times grandiose literary technique. Reading Waugh's *Brideshead Revisited* in my early stages of pinpointing the stylistic similarities between biblical Hebrew narrative and O'Connor's aided me in naming what the shared style was not; Waugh's extravagant means of narration placed paratactic narration in stark relief.

The bare quality of O'Connor's storytellings serves as a crucial feature of her distinctive and powerful literary voice.

O'Connor's spare narrative style was intentional and at times defied both literary convention and the explicit advice of her writing mentor Caroline Gordon. O'Connor accepted Gordon's suggested revisions only in part, reservedly appropriating Gordon's ongoing appeals to add more scenic and narrative descriptions to aid readers. Yet O'Connor maintained her spare style. I argue throughout this work that O'Connor's skeletal narrative style possesses a certain resonance with biblical Hebrew narrative. The direct quality of both biblical Hebrew and O'Connor's narratives possesses what I term a *stylistic asceticism*. That is, the spare quality of these narratives pushes readers deeper into the reading event and places demands on them in the act of interpretation analogous to the spiritual practice of asceticism. Both stylistically and thematically, O'Connor's fiction and biblical Hebrew narrative force readers to navigate how to make theologically astute interpretations from bare-bones narration.

Using the archetypal story of Jacob's wrestling on the banks of the Jabbok in Gen 32 and the climacteric of *Wise Blood*'s Hazel Motes's conversion, I show in this chapter how the syntactically paratactic style of storytelling obliquely and fittingly discloses God's grace. I establish how reading biblical Hebrew narrative alongside O'Connor's fiction illuminates the style and force of O'Connor's storytelling by transposing the biblical Hebrew narrative's *wayyiqtol* form onto *Wise Blood*'s climax. I do not argue that O'Connor's depiction of Haze's conversion necessarily implies Gen 32 in its background, nor that Gen 32 plays an essential role in understanding the events of *Wise Blood*. Instead, I draw out the similarities in style through the presence and transposition of the *wayyiqtol* to signal an underlying theological conviction concerning a fitting narration of divine self-disclosure in human activity.

Wrestling, Wounding, Naming: Jacob's 'Crippling Victory'

This case study illuminates O'Connor's literary style through a side-by-side reading with biblical Hebrew narrative. In order to accomplish such a reading, the biblical story must well represent the qualities of Hebrew narrative more generally, as discussed in the previous chapter. The narrative of Jacob's nighttime wrestling in Gen 32 provides an archetypal example.

In this well-known pericope, the patriarch Jacob finds himself wrestling through the night with an unknown figure—later disclosed as a messenger of God. At the end of the fight as dawn breaks, Jacob receives both a new limp and a new name. Though *Wise Blood* and the story of Jacob's wrestling match are set in different times, cultures, and languages, they share a spare narration of the elusive character of human encounter with the divine. In both, the authors depict this encounter as a disfiguring kind of blessing. As an entry-point into the Gen 32 story of Jacob's wrestling with the angel-man, I begin with a survey of some of the most important scholarship concerning this pericope. This brief overview demonstrates the centrality and interpretive opportunities of this story within the biblical tradition and broader literary study.

Overview: A Crippled Victor

Throughout the history of scholarship, biblical scholars have proposed ways of understanding the Jacob figure within the larger Torah tradition. Importantly, Gerhard von Rad adopts an earlier proposal—that the figure of Jacob links older and newer redacted material—and reflects on the theological impetus for the inclusion of the older Jacob tradition into the broader narration of the early history of Israel.[3] Using the example of Gen 32:22–32, Rad highlights the reappropriation of the "remote and strange" narrative of Jacob's wrestling to "the hand and words of its God, and claimed as his—Jahweh's—very own."[4] Rad's emphasis on theological

---

3. This earlier proposal was made by scholar Martin Noth. In his seminal work *A History of Pentateuchal Traditions* (*Überlieferungsgeschichte des Pentateuch*, 1948), Martin Noth identifies the patriarch Jacob as the linking figure between older Pentateuchal themes and the addition of the theme "promise to the patriarchs" (Noth, *Pentateuchal Traditions*, 56). Noth bases this linking argument on the mention of Jacob in the small credo of Deut 26:5–9, "where only Jacob is presupposed in the cultic confession" (56). The importance of Noth's claim resides in the centrality of the Jacob tradition in the formation of the Pentateuch; this tradition served as groundwork upon which the more robust patriarchal theme could build. Noth attributes the inclusion of Gen 32:23–33 to the Yahwist (J) who took the older legend of Jacob's wrestling and redacted it into the broader corpus of Yahwist material (29, 56–7). Noth's overarching argument in this work is the proposal that a P-narrative serves as the framing element of the Pentateuch; this P-narrative is the *"literary basis of the Pentateuchal narrative"* (11, italics his). Into this P-narrative framework, the JE narrative is inserted, which is made up of older sources with the E-material being inserted into the earlier J-material (see Noth, *Pentateuchal Traditions*, esp. ch.4: "J as Literary Basis of the Combined JE Narrative").

4. Rad, *Old Testament Theology*, 167. More specifically, Rad here is identifying the

reappropriation demonstrates the benefit of redacting older stories into ancient Israel's theological narration: "The narrators often digest in but a single story of only a few verses the yield of a divine history which in fact stretches from the events spoken of down into their own time."[5] In the narrative of Jacob's wrestling, Rad identifies the exemplar case of appropriating older stories into a new context.[6] The final placement of this narrative—disrupting and forestalling Jacob's meeting with Esau—indicates to Rad that the narrative serves as an interpretive key for the whole of the Jacob stories. The re-naming of Jacob as "Israel" drastically shifts Jacob from a cheater of his brother to a bearer of his people's honor. This new name also comes with an injury that will afflict him and serve as a reminder to him in each step he takes for the rest of his life.[7] Rad emphasizes that Jacob did not earn the blessing he receives through this new naming; in fact, the story itself emphasizes "God's activity, his destructive attack and his justification."[8] This emphasis on God's activity of blessing despite the questionable character of the one he blesses undergirds the broader history into which this story is received by an all-too-human nation whom God nevertheless sets apart as God's own.

In a more recent work, John E. Anderson takes up Rad's emphasis on this text as a productive interruption in the larger Jacob narrative by asking, "what if God is here acting not *against* Jacob but rather *on his behalf*?"[9] Anderson employs Roland Barthes's contention in "The Struggle with the Angel: Textual Analysis of Genesis 32" where Barthes recognizes the inconclusive and jarring effect of the passage as central to engaging its meaning.[10] Here Anderson via Barthes identifies the man-angel as fighting on behalf

---

place of the Jacob stories in the larger Yahwist (J) tradition.

Please note, the verse numeration of this narrative does not match between Hebrew and English versions. I will be using the English translation verse numeration for ease of use. This pericope is found in the Hebrew Bible as Gen 32:23–33.

5. Rad, *Old Testament Theology*, 167.

6. Rad, *Genesis*, 314.

7. Rad, *Genesis*, 316–17.

8. Rad, *Genesis*, 320.

9. Anderson, *Jacob and the Divine Trickster*, 148, italics his.

10. Barthes, *Image-Music-Text*, 125–141. Barthes notes: "what interests me most in this famous passage is not the 'folk-loristic' model but the abrasive frictions, the breaks, the discontinuities of readability, the juxtaposition of narrative entities which to some extent run free from an explicit logical articulation. One is dealing here (this at least is for me the savour of reading) with a sort of *metonymic montage*: the themes (Crossing, Struggle, Naming, Alimentary Rite) are *combined*, not 'developed.'" (140, italics his).

of Esau, so when Jacob defeats the divine figure he is also defeating his brother. Barthes recognizes in this exchange an inversion that plays out in the broader narrative. There is an inverted nature to the victory because the defeated makes the decisive blow and not the victor: "the weakest defeats the strongest, *in exchange for which* he is marked."[11] This inversion follows the whole of Jacob's life with the younger repeatedly supplanting the elder. Anderson does not find a full interpretive resolution in Barthes's argument but asserts, instead, that the narrative presents a play of deception by God on the trickster Jacob.[12] Jacob, the deceiver, is himself deceived in the wrestling match when the man strikes a blow to his hip.

Walter Brueggemann's reading of Gen 32:22–32 takes up the observations of Rad, Barthes, and Anderson by offering an interpretation that draws nearer to O'Connor's depiction of Hazel Motes in *Wise Blood*. Brueggemann summarizes this narrated event as "The Crippling Victory," where Jacob's limp thereafter "shows others (and himself) that there are no untroubled victories with the holy One."[13] Through narrative presentation, the event possesses an "ominous" quality, which Brueggemann quintessentially identifies in the "opaque portrayal of the figure" with whom Jacob wrestles.[14] A veil of mystery hangs all around Jacob's adversary, not only in his strength but also in his identity. The possibility that this adversary might be Esau, or a stand-in for him, reveals that "in the night, the divine antagonist tends to take on the feature of others with whom we struggle in the day."[15] Here, Brueggemann expands the reading of Esau in the divine wrestling match to a much broader scope than we find in the life of Jacob, the Torah, or even the world of ancient Israel: to wrestle with God entails wrestling with our own quotidian adversaries.

In the act of renaming, Brueggemann identifies a permanent change—"something happens in this transaction that is irreversible"—which might be best coined as a conversion.[16] With the appearance of the name Israel, Brueggemann argues that an important message about Israel—the person and the people—comes to the fore: "Israel is not formed by success or shrewdness or land, but by *an assault from God*. Perhaps it is grace, but not

11. Barthes, *Image-Music-Text*, 134, italics his.
12. Anderson, *Jacob and the Divine Trickster*, 156–60.
13. Brueggemann, *Genesis*, 270.
14. Brueggemann, *Genesis*, 266, 267.
15. Brueggemann, *Genesis*, 267.
16. Brueggemann, *Genesis*, 268.

the kind usually imagined."[17] O'Connor also insists that grace cannot be experienced in abstract telling but rather through showing the change—often destructive—wrought in the graced person. This insistence on showing rather than telling harmonizes with Brueggemann's reading of Jacob's experience of supernatural grace through the reception of a new name.

Importantly, Brueggemann emphasizes that Jacob's new name is inseparable from his wounding, for "the crippling is the substance of the name."[18] This crippled naming prefigures the theology undergirding the incarnation of the God-Man, where "the theology of weakness in power and power in weakness" demonstrates the inverted way of grace.[19] Jacob experiences grace in his "crippling victory." He receives a new name through weakness. Hazel Motes experiences grace in his self-blinding; he receives new sight—the mote removed from his eye—through his own crippling victory.

Transforming and Transformed Vision of Hazel Motes

The great undoing of Hazel Motes's fiercely-constructed claim, built up throughout *Wise Blood*, that "Nothing matters but that Jesus don't exist" (CW, 29), comes as Haze sets out on the road away from Taulkinham with murder in his wake. The events that follow involve a breaking down and building up of Haze that leave him radically transformed. In the following, I examine two central motifs of Haze's car and recurring mention of the sky to trace the central transformative moment and its impact on *Wise Blood*'s protagonist. This overview of the transforming and transformed vision of Haze sets the stage for this chapter's central study: a transposition of the *wayyiqtol* into the key events of Haze's conversion to demonstrate how bare narrative style functions in drawing out meaning for readers without explicit interpretive claims.

The Ruined Essex and the Depth of the Sky

The Essex. Prior to the climactic events that begin with his being pulled over and end with his intention to blind himself, Hazel Motes prepares to leave

---

17. Brueggemann, *Genesis*, 269.
18. Brueggemann, *Genesis*, 270.
19. Brueggemann, *Genesis*, 271.

Taulkinham and head to another city to preach his Church without Christ. Before the trip, he brings his car to a gas station to be serviced by a "sleeping-looking white boy" (CW, 116).[20] While Haze blasphemes Christ and praises his fine automobile, the boy works his way silently around the car before concluding that "there was a leak in the gas tank and two in the radiator and that the rear tire would probably last twenty miles if he went slow" (CW, 116). Haze replies to this dire assessment, "'Listen . . . this car is just beginning its life. A lightning bolt couldn't stop it!'" (CW, 116).

Caroline Gordon comments that Haze's "Essex is not only a means of locomotion. It is a pulpit."[21] Ralph Wood goes even further: "Motes's broken-down Essex is indeed his deity: he sleeps in it, preaches from it, and relies on it to escape from all obligations that are not of his own choosing."[22] Haze's Essex represents his self-sufficiency and self-justification, which one of Haze's most notoriously amusing lines captures: "'Nobody with a good car needs to be justified'" (CW, 64). In *A Wreck on the Road to Damascus: Innocence, Guilt and Conversion in Flannery O'Connor*, Brian Ragen expands the use of the automobile in *Wise Blood* to O'Connor's wider corpus.[23] Ragen highlights that "O'Connor often made the plots of her stories turn on what happens in—or even to—a car."[24] With the automobile comes the "myth of the American Adam" who is free to act without ties to the past or the present.[25] Included in this vision of the independent American Adam is the refusal to accept the concept of original sin, as if this autonomous creature still dwelt in innocence.[26] If the rambling man is congenitally guiltless, then he has no need of a Messiah. Ragen's description of the

---

20. Schiebe, "Car Trouble," 411.

21. Fitzgerald, "Master Class," 844.

22. Wood, *Christ-Haunted South*, 15–16. Mark Schiebe places the deification of this vehicle in its 1950s context with the explosive rise of the automobile in a post-war setting: "while O'Connor was writing and Haze was driving, automobile production and car culture was at its height in America." Drawing out Wood's statement on the connection of Haze's car to his free-choosing, Schiebe identifies the car as the "quintessential symbol of American freedom." Cf. Schiebe, "Car Trouble," 406.

23. Ragen, *Wreck on the Road*, 55–106.

24. Ragen, *Wreck on the Road*, 55. He continues, "A wreck brings the Misfit and his victims together; the loss of his Essex transforms Haze Motes; an old car is what interests Mr. Shiftlet at Mrs. Crater's farm; the bull impales Mrs. May against the hood of her automobile; and Tarwater accepts his calling after he has been molested by the man in the lavender and cream-colored car."

25. Ragen, *Wreck on the Road*, 56.

26. Ragen, *Wreck on the Road*, 56.

myth of the American Adam parallels the readers' picture of Haze Motes standing on the hood of his Essex proclaiming the Church without Christ and remaining free to move on to the next city to start anew.

The Sky. The sky motif functions throughout *Wise Blood* as a helpful demarcation of Haze's gradual transformation. *Wise Blood*'s first paragraph introduces Haze sitting on a train "looking one minute at the window as if he might want to jump out it, and the next down the aisle at the other end of the car" (CW, 3). While Haze looks *at* and not *through* the window to the view that lies beyond, a woman sitting across from Haze comments "that she thought the early evening light this was the prettiest time of day" (CW, 3). Haze, seeing the window merely as a means of escape, is contrasted with the woman who sees through the window to the "magic hour" of evening when the sun's rays strike the landscape with soft but vibrant light. A couple of days later in Taulkinham, the omniscient narrator observes that no one—Haze included—paid any attention to the "black sky that was underpinned with long silver streaks that looked like scaffolding and depth on depth behind it were thousands of stars that all seemed to be moving very slowly as if they were about some vast construction work that involved the whole order of the universe and would take all the time to complete" (CW, 19).[27] Haze's inattention to the Dantesque quality of the night sky in his early days in the city sets up a contrastive foretaste of the moment of disruption to come later.

An even more pointed allusion to Haze's relation to the sky is present in one of his most heated sermons atop the Essex:

> "I preach there are all kinds of truth, your truth and somebody else's, but behind all of them, there's only one truth and that is that there's not truth," he called. "No truth behind all truths is what I and this church preach! Where you come from is gone, where you thought you were going to never was there, and where you are is no good unless you can get away from it. Where is there a place for you to be? No place.
>
> "Nothing outside you can give you any place," he said. "You needn't to *look at the sky* because it's not going to open up and show no place behind it. You needn't to search for any hole in the ground to look through into somewhere else. You can't go neither

---

27. This is exactly the kind of description that Caroline Gordon wanted O'Connor to employ constantly, whereas its rare appearance in the novel gives it a power that repeated uses would not have achieved.

> forwards nor backwards into your daddy's time nor your children's if you have them. In yourself right now is all the place you've got. If there was any Fall, look there, if there was any Redemption, look there, and if you expect any Judgment, look there, because they all three will have to be in your time and your body and where in your time and your body can they be?
>
> "Where in your time and your body has Jesus redeemed you?" he cried. "Show me where because I don't see the place. If there *was* a place where Jesus had redeemed you that would be the place for you to be, but which of you can find it?" (CW, 93, italics added)

Haze's nihilism permeates his sermon. There is no place for you, nowhere to look for belonging, no hope for change nor absolution—all you have is yourself. Haze's fierce independence is evident in his rejection not only of any kind of kinship (seen in his humorous interactions with friendship-starved Enoch) but even of any affirmation of truth that extends beyond the self-sufficient individual—in the sky or on the earth. A train window is no more than an escape-hatch, just as a starry night is no occasion for wonder. All Haze has is his car and his determination to escape from all that does not accord with his own time and space.

Transforming Vision and a Bucket of Quicklime

Just as Jacob prepares to meet Esau, so Haze prepares his car to travel to a new city. The narrator tells us that Haze, ignoring the warning of the gas station attendant, "drove very fast out onto the highway," but also that he "had not gone five miles on the highway before he heard a siren behind him" (CW, 117). The presence of the police car disrupts Haze's plan just as Jacob's unexpected nighttime visitor at Jabbok radically disrupted the trajectory of Jacob's life.

Narrating by means of direct dialogue, O'Connor shows the exchange between the officer and Haze as quickly becoming hostile:

> "I wasn't speeding," Haze said.
>
> "No," the patrolman agreed, "you wasn't."
>
> "I was on the right side of the road."
>
> "Yes you was, that's right," the cop said.
>
> "What you want with me?"

"I just don't like your face," the patrolman said.
"Where's your license?"

"I don't like your face either," Haze said,
"and I don't have a license." (CW, 117)

Unlike Haze's previously narrated dialogue—where he and the station attendant speak past rather than to one another—this exchange registers as a confrontation and anticipates the destructive event that soon follows.

As we reach the climactic moment of Haze's conversion, the narrative itself picks up speed and intensity. With readers' attention focused in on the engagement between the officer and Haze, the essential actions constituting this climactic event come hastily one after another: the patrolman tells Haze to pull his car up to the overlook; Haze follows his instructions, getting out of the car and then looking out over the scene while the police officer pushes Haze's treasured Essex over the edge; Haze's eyes follow the car down the embankment and he stares at his idolized Essex lying in shambles resting on its hood with a tire and the motor missing while the officer proudly asserts, "Them that don't have a car, don't need a license" (CW, 118). The officer, unaware of the change occurring in Haze, repeatedly asks where Haze is heading. Upon realizing that Haze has no plan to go anywhere at all, the officer leaves Haze staring into the immensity surrounding him. The police officer's act has inadvertently, or possibly providentially, slowed down Haze long enough to look out and see what had always been before him: the infinity of the space, and thus, perhaps, the Cosmic Christ who is its Alpha and Omega.[28] Yet the narrator offers no assistance toward any such conclusion; readers are left to render their own interpretive judgment as they consider the significance of the scene.

Central to the climactic moment of Haze's transformation are his Essex and his attention to the sky. Haze's self-sufficiency, symbolized in his car, lies in ruins below his feet. This object that Haze staked so much on—his vocation as a preacher of the Church without Christ, a place to sleep when there was nowhere else to lay his head, a vehicle turned weapon that he used to commit murder, and his means of escape from one city to another—is

---

28. Ragen's discussion of the myth of the American Adam helps readers to understand precisely how this grace is experienced as Haze watches the actual vehicle of his freedom lie in ruins below his feet: "the offer of grace comes when the hero is stopped in his tracks and can run no longer. For Haze Motes that offer comes when he loses his car and with it the ability to assert his innocence and freedom by always moving on" (Ragen, *Wreck on the Road*, 105).

wrecked. Haze himself is wrecked, and in this broken state he does what he failed to do earlier in the novel—to look out and up at the "depth after depth" of the sky (CW, 118). This moment of transformed vision involves a shift of the eyes away from the Essex, symbol of his autonomy and self-worship, to the sky, which he had earlier proclaimed as nowhere to find any kind of meaning: "You needn't to look at the sky because it's not going to open up and show no place behind it" (CW, 93).

Haze sits and looks out for "a while" and then begins to walk back toward Taulkinham. The storyline here indicates a radical shift. Haze, who was adamant on getting out of town and heading somewhere new, now reverses his tracks as he begins his walk back to Taulkinham. O'Connor paints a menacing picture of what occurs once Haze returns home. He walks without comment for three hours, purchases quicklime and a bucket, carries the two items home, fills the bucket half with the caustic powder and half with water from an outside tap, and walks up the stairs and into the home with the declaration that he intends to blind himself. Whereas Asa Hawks, the false preacher, lacked the nerve to allow the quicklime to touch his eyes when he intended to blind himself, Hazel Motes, without the theatrics of Hawks, composedly follows through on his intention.

Richard Giannone, in *Flannery O'Connor and the Mystery of Love*, highlights that O'Connor sets Asa Hawks failed blinding attempt on October 4, the Feast of St. Francis of Assisi, and notes that this mention is the "only precise date given for any event in all her fiction."[29] This connection to St. Francis heightens the parallelism between Asa Hawks's failure and Hazel Motes's success and points to how readers might understand an event as grotesque as self-blinding as redemptive. Giannone terms the sight Haze receives through his physical loss of it as "Franciscan sight," where the movement towards Christ is a movement towards his death and resurrection.[30] The ascetic embraces suffering as the means of redemption.

Transformed Vision and The Pinpoint of Light

This shifting of the eyes from the car to the sky is also a shifting of the heart—of the self which for so long had been turned in on itself and now turns towards the mysterious depths that lie outside it. When we return to Hazel Motes after his blinding, he has taken on a different pattern of

29. Giannone, *Mystery of Love*, 7.
30. Giannone, *Mystery of Love*, 39.

life. Previously, he was on the road and shouting his nihilistic vision from a car hood. Now, we are told that he places glass and rocks in his shoes—as he did when he was a boy. Back then to prove that he did not need to rely on Jesus's suffering since he could provide his own, and now inversely in recognition of his reliance on Christ's cruciform love. Haze also wraps barbed wire around his chest, radically intensifying the ascetic practices of medieval mystics. No longer atop a vehicle and seeking an audience, Haze takes solitary walks around the neighborhood without drawing attention to himself and likely appearing adrift to onlookers. Whereas he earlier desired to set out to a new city, he now takes daily strolls that lead him no further than a few blocks' radius around his boardinghouse.

The landlady curiously describes the blinded Haze as having "the look of seeing something . . . of straining toward something" (CW, 120–21). After becoming attentive to the depths of space that he once ignored and subsequently blinding himself, Haze takes on a new and strange kind of sight that allows him to see differently than with his once-functioning eyes. The landlady struggles to understand the change in Haze, both in the oddness of a blind man seemingly seeing things and in his adoption of bizarre new practices:

> She could not make up her mind what would be inside his head and what out. She thought of her own head as a switchbox she controlled from; but with him, she could only imagine the outside in, the whole black world in his head and his head is bigger than the world, his head big enough to include the sky and planets and whatever was or had been or would be. How would he know if time was going backwards or forwards or if he was going with it? She imagined it was like you were walking in a tunnel and all you could see was a pin point of light. She had to imagine the pin point of light; she couldn't think of it at all without that. She saw it as some kind of a star, like the star on Christmas cards. She saw him going backwards to Bethlehem and she had to laugh. (CW, 123)

Something curious is happening in this passage. Straightforwardly, O'Connor offers readers a further description of the quizzical kind of seeing Haze has taken on after his blinding. This kind of sight is the sight of a mystic: seeing not out into the world but somehow viewing the world in himself.[31] The irony here of Haze being described as possessing mystical vi-

---

31. In thirteenth-century theologian and mystic Hildegard of Bingen's *Scivias*, she describes this kind of inward sight: "the visions I saw I did not perceive in dreams or sleep, or delirium, or by the eyes of the body, or by the ears of the outer self, or in hidden

sion should not be lost. Unlike his zealous sermon atop the Essex preaching that the world is without truth—no truth in the world, in the sky, in the past, or in the future—Haze now possesses a sight that seemingly collapses time and space. He has undergone a profound shift not only in how he conceives the world but also in how others perceive him: Mrs. Flood, his landlady, sees Haze as a pinpoint of light, recalling the Star of Bethlehem. Perhaps too threatened by this potentially transforming link, she laughs it off. While on the surface Haze's paradoxical self-blinding sight moves him *away* from the world, since he has the looking of seeing into the depths of space, the deeper truth is that he has he has discerned the metaphysical reality that roots and places him in this world no less than the other.[32]

Wise Blood closes with Mrs. Flood the landlady hovering over the corpse of Hazel Motes. The police had found Haze almost dead in a ditch after he literally fled from the landlady's advances. The narrator tells us that "[Haze] died in the squad car but [the policemen] didn't seem to notice and took him on to the landlady's" (CW, 131). Upon arrival at the boardinghouse, they place Haze on the landlady's bed and a darkly comedic one-sided conversation ensues. In rejoicing that Haze had been found, Mrs. Flood leans over the bed observing his face and trying to understand why he had rejected her offer to marry and care for him:

> She shut her eyes and saw the pin point of light but so far away that she could not hold it steady in her mind. She felt as if she were blocked at the entrance of something. She sat staring with her eyes shut, into his eyes, and felt as if she had finally got to the beginning of something she couldn't begin, and she saw him moving farther

places; but I received them while awake and seeing with a pure mind and the eyes and the ears of the inner self" (Hildegard of Bingen, *Scivias*, 60).

32. Frederick Asals identifies Haze's conversion as a radical shift from this-worldly to other-worldly orientation: "when he finally stares directly at the nothing that he has so long evaded not only does repentance set in, but Hazel Motes becomes a wholly otherworldly figure. There can be little doubt of Haze's otherworldliness in the final chapter of *Wise Blood*." Cf. Asals, *Imagination of Extremity*, 54–55. The problem with this kind of interpretation of Haze's conversion is the failure to attend to the holistic transformation that has occurred for Haze, as well as the rich Christian tradition that speaks of transformed sight (as an exemplary example consider Saul-Paul's Damascus Road conversion). Haze is described as acting strangely, yes: performing ascetic acts that have the appearance of rejecting the physical body and seeing without physical sight. But neither ascetic acts nor spiritual sight necessitate an otherworldly disposition. Notice that in the landlady's description of Haze, she speaks not of his possessing a mind emptied of this world, but filled with and encompassing it.

and farther away, farther and farther into the darkness until he was the pin point of light. (CW, 131)

Sally Fitzgerald describes this closing scene as Haze's "vision of the infinite," a "vision clarified in his blindness."[33] This final description of Haze, one conveyed to us through Mrs. Flood's own closed-eyed stare, is an image of redemption. O'Connor leaves readers with a description of Haze Motes as a pinpoint of light, not a corpse. This is one of the most established tropes in Christian imagery: from death springs new, indeed eternal, life.

The ascetic life Haze takes on after his blinding and the mystical vision he appears to attain, which Mrs. Flood crassly describes, indicates the kind of transformation Haze experienced in his looking out "depth after depth" and the shift from outward to inward vision through his radical act of self-blinding via quicklime. The denouement of the story at face-value appears to be the physical collapse of Haze that ends in his death, but on a deeper level the narrative suggests a parallel between the final months of Haze's life to the life of the great mystics—recall the life of St. Francis of Assisi, for instance—where bodily ascesis drives the whole person towards spiritual perfection. Is it possible that Haze's great bodily deformation is also a testimony of a graced life on its way to fulfilment?

The Ascetic Narrative of the Wounded Victor and the Blinded Convert

The imagery of Jacob's wrestling in Gen 32 serves as the quintessential image of a wounding blessing. The relationship between wounding and blessing is both paradoxical and a fitting description of what it means to become whole in God, which sometimes involves the humiliating act of breaking down in order to build up. The transformed vision of Hazel Motes in *Wise Blood* parallels Jacob's wounding blessing. In grotesque fashion, Haze is transformed through the disfiguration of his body, chiefly his eyes. Jacob's limp through the rest of his life serves as a reminder of God's favor; Haze blindly moves through his remaining days while acquiring a new kind of vision—a vision of the infinite.

In what follows, I explicitly draw together the narrative transformations of trickster patriarch Jacob and spitfire preacher Haze Motes in two parts. First, I explore the ways these stories about divine encounter and

---

33. Fitzgerald, "Rooms with a View," 13–14.

conversion share common themes. Second, I illustrate how these two stories share in a particular narrative quality through the transposition of the *wayyiqtol* onto *Wise Blood*'s climactic scene and an explication of the interpretive and theological return for attending to their shared style.

On Two Stories of Transformation

The stories of Jacob's nighttime wrestling and Haze's self-blinding share a number of common themes that heighten their connection as stories of wounding blessings. For instance, in both scenes Jacob and Haze are "on the move." The pericope of Jacob's wrestling begins in Gen 32:22 with Jacob sending his family and all his possessions across the Jabbok River in preparation for encountering his estranged brother, Esau. Jacob's relationship with his brother had been characterized since birth by strife and exhibited in Jacob deceiving his brother out of both birthright and blessing. Gen 32 tells us that Jacob was afraid because after years of separation from his brother he was to encounter him the next day, and he had received news that his brother brought along four hundred warriors for their visit (Gen 32:6). The movement that begins the pericope of wrestling describes Jacob's final preparations for meeting his brother. Just as Jacob completes his preparations—"and Jacob remained by himself" (Gen 32:24)—the narrative tells readers that "a man wrestled with him until daybreak." The preparations Jacob made for one type of encounter are interrupted by a different sort. Haze is also on the move. The climactic moment occurs after Haze has fled Taulkinham, suffered the destruction of his car, then left to stare at the gray sky before he begins walking back towards the town to blind himself.

Additionally, in these moments of transformation Jacob and Haze act essentially on their own. While a man (*'ysh*) wrestles with Jacob and gives him his new name, the pericope itself tells us nothing about this man. In fact, the skeletal narration of the event, with its confusion of the two "hes" (masculine pronouns) adds to the mysterious quality of the man. Jacob's proclamation offers additional information about him: "The name of this place is 'Peniel' for I saw God face to face" (Gen 32:30). Jacob evidences the elusive quality of the mysterious figure by indicating that this wrestling match was with God, not a human being. Jacob found himself alone with God. While the patrolman and the landlady make appearances in Haze's dual conversion—first in seeing depth after depth, then in blinding himself—the spare dialogue makes clear that Haze has undergone an utterly personal encounter with God. Both the patrolman's response to Haze and the landlady's innocent question about Haze's plan with the caustic bucket require the reader to discern the radical transformation that has and will occur in Haze, since neither the patrolman nor the landlady are aware of the true nature of the change underway.

In addition to the shared plot features of movement and isolation, Jacob's and Haze's divine encounters and transformation share similar characteristics. In both narratives, the conversions possess a dual quality: for Jacob and Haze their conversions involve physical and visible deformations, as well as spiritual and invisible transformations. Because of the spare style of narration, the twofold conversion moments do not draw excessive attention, nor do they overtly explain the connection between the characters' wounding and blessing. In the case of Jacob's conversion moment, the mysterious man both dislocates Jacob's hip and gives Jacob a new name. For the rest of Jacob's life, the physical reminder of this moment will follow him with a limp. This tangible element of the transformative scene is accompanied by a less-tangible yet very real gift of the new name "Israel." Similarly, Haze first receives the invisible blessing of new spiritual sight. A blessing that too hasty of a reader of *Wise Blood* might fail to recognize as a decisive moment because it is followed with the non-narrated moment just after Haze states his aim to blind himself to his landlady. A physical conversion, much like Jacob's, parallels Haze's interior moment of conversion. These dual conversion moments—visible and invisible, physical and spiritual—are two-sides of the same coin. Jacob's limp and name cannot be treated narratively apart from one another. Haze's new spiritual and physical sight go together. While the narrators do not overtly spell out the pivotal connection between the invisible and visible transformations, their paratactic style invites readers to infer such connections and perceive the significance of both the outward and inward transformations.

Jacob and Haze experience grotesque transformations. The description of Asa Hawks's scar-streaked eyes earlier in *Wise Blood* signals the damage wrought by quicklime to the face. Quicklime possesses a brutal history of violence: it has served as a weapon against enemy combatants since antiquity because of its ability to burn skin on contact once mixed with water. During the Holocaust, quicklime was used both to burn the feet of Jews as they were pack onto trains destined for work camps, as well as to cover up the smell of their decomposing bodies in mass graves. To speak of Haze's self-blinding as transformative does not erase the horror of the act. Despite the redemptive function of his blinding, the image of quicklime mixed with water conjures the violence of war-craft. O'Connor's choice to blind Haze off-stage, as it were, leaves readers with only the lean narration of Haze's gathering of supplies and acts of preparation. The artistic result does not diminish but rather heightens the horror of his mutilating act. The narration forces readers to render for themselves images of an act that if narrated could easily become either a sentimentalizing or glorification of violence.

Similarly, Jacob's wrestling—though exceedingly brief in its narration—involves a grotesque wounding. While images such as Rembrandt's painting "Jacob's Wresting with the Angel" (ca. 1659) render the wrestling match as a majestic event, with a stoic angel embracing as much as wrestling Jacob, the Hebrew narrative provides clues that suggest a much more violent scene. The verb (*ngʿ*) used in Gen 32:25 translates as "to touch or strike." While translations of the angel as "striking" Jacob's hip (literally: "the hollow of his hip") communicates a level of damage exacted on Jacob— a level described later by the narrator's comments that the injury left Jacob with a lifelong limp—the English translation does not entirely capture the force of the angel-man's act. The verb "to strike" here in its current construct and with the addition of the preposition "with" suggests a violent striking force. The same verb construct appears throughout the Hebrew Bible, for instance in the warning of God's punishment if the Ark of the Covenant is mishandled in 1 Sam 6:9 and the gale-force winds that collapse Job's house in Job 1:19. Within the Jewish tradition, Jacob's injury has been identified with the sciatic nerve, which connects the spinal cord with the muscles in the legs and feet.[34] Sciatic nerve injuries can make walking painful, and sometimes unbearable. Jacob received a serious injury in this wrestling match. Curiously, O'Connor describes Haze as developing a limp in the months following his conversion (CW, 122). Later, Haze's ascetic practice of placing rocks in his shoes explains the cause of the limp. We have no information that would suggest O'Connor had the parallel to Jacob in mind with the mention of the limp, but the shared limp nonetheless extends the similarities between the two transformed figures.

The disfigurements of Jacob and Haze are shrouded in darkness. Jacob wrestles all night and receives the match-ending blow just as dawn breaks. Haze's disfigurement results in darkness of physical sight. This thematic sharing of darkness is heightened by the elusively narrated quality of the

34. Sarna, *JPS Genesis*, 228.

events. Paralleling the physical darkness—in nighttime wrestling for Jacob and blinding for Haze—is the suggestion of an abstruse sort of divine visitation more defined by what it cannot be than what it is. One cannot see God face-to-face and live (Exod 33:20), and yet Jacob describes having seen God face-to-face and does not die. Haze looks out past the rubble of his Essex to what lies beyond "to the blank gray sky that went depth after depth into space." What does Haze see? Not simply the sky, nor nothing at all. Haze looks out with the sky as his starting to see something beyond it.

Jacob and Haze receive something revolutionarily new at the close of their divine encounters. I have already spoken of the disfigurement that accompanied the transformative moments of both protagonists. Along with Jacob's limp, he receives a new name—no small thing. The name "Israel" marks the ancient people that descend from Jacob's line as particular and set apart. The name signals both victory and blessing. Etymologically, "Israel" speaks to Jacob's seeing God face-to-face and living. Jacob wrestled with God and prevailed. Narratively, the name Israel accompanies blessing. Walter Moberly notes the choice of Jacob as the receiver of this new name that will follow the nation from hereafter: "One might have expected that someone of the character of Abraham would have this honour of being the eponymous ancestor of a nation called to be holy. Yet the fact that it is self-seeking Jacob and not faithful Abraham who gives his name to Israel speaks volumes for Israel's understanding of the nature of human life under God."[35] Not only the gift of a name for a nation but the character of the principal receiver of the name "Israel" casts forward to a fraught relationship between a faithful God and a wayward people.

The radical shift in Haze before and after his self-blinding indicates that his life has been terribly disrupted and reversed. Haze moves from a violent and antagonistic street-corner preacher to an ascetic who quietly moves through life as a monk; from sharing a bed with Sabbath Lily Hawks, a woman in whom he has no real interest, to resisting the companionship of his landlady; from trying to escape Taulkinham in his idolized Essex to pondering on the front porch the meaning of what he has discovered and taking daily walks with his shoes stuffed with stones and shards of glass. Accompanying these shifts in Haze's behavior is his ironic description of his new sight as greater than his old sight because his eyes now have no bottom.

---

35. Moberly, *Genesis 12–50*, 28.

Finally, in addition to the shared features of the two men's wounding and blessing, the most profound narrative sharing is found in the two men remaining "on the way" towards redemption after their drastic turns. Neither Jacob nor Haze is so radically transformed by his blessing that he becomes unrecognizably virtuous and without fault. Neither the biblical narrator nor O'Connor resolve their hero's encounter with divine grace through such an astonishing transformation that the figures themselves are no longer recognizable. That is, these two narratives of transformation remain credible as narratives of human encounters with the divine, not charmed fixes to the human condition.

On Two Ascetically Narrated Stories of Transformation

The similarities between the narrated conversions of Jacob and Haze extended to their narrative style. In both stories, we find divine encounter and blessed wounding events told in a spare style. In Gen 32 and *Wise Blood*'s climactic scenes, the stories unfold in rapid succession without frequent clues to *why* the events occur as they do or *what* in fact occurred in wrestling, naming, looking out, or blinding. These two stories take on an ascetic quality as they deny readers narrative details in order to draw them into a deeper sense of the text, which fittingly renders the content of the transformations: the impact of encountering divine grace.

In the last chapter, I described biblical Hebrew narrative as a paratactic style of narration in which the stories "show" more than they "tell." Parataxis, where clauses most often link together without subordination or modification, offers ample room for interpretive play on the part of readers. The function of the *wayyiqtol* in biblical Hebrew narrative evidences its paratactic narration. The Gen 32 story of Jacob's wrestling with the man serves as an emblematic example of the paratactic nature of biblical narrative through the successive use of the *wayyiqtol*. Often, translations of the biblical Hebrew text miss the force of the *wayyiqtol*'s contribution to narrative pacing and, for that reason, I here visually map the linked clauses to illustrate the *wayyiqtol*'s function more clearly for those less familiar with Hebrew:

> [2] and he arose that same night
>   and he took his two wives and his two handmaids and his eleven children
>   and he crossed over the ford of Jabbok.

GENESIS 32 AND *WISE BLOOD*

²³ and he took them
and brought them across the brook
and he brought across all that was his.
²⁴ And Jacob remained by himself
and a man wrestled[36] with him until daybreak.
²⁵ And he saw that he was not able prevail over him
and he struck[37] his hip socket
and he dislocated Jacob's hip socket while wrestling him.
²⁶ And he said: "Please, let me go for the dawn ascends."
And he said: "I will not let you go unless you bless me."
²⁷ And he said to him: "What is your name?"
And he said: "Jacob."
²⁸ And he said: "Jacob is no longer your name, but rather 'Israel' for you contended with God and with men
and you prevailed."
²⁹ And Jacob questioned
and said: "Please, tell me your name."
And he said "Why is it that you ask for my name?"
And he blessed him there.
³⁰ And Jacob declared: "The name of this place is 'Peniel' for I saw God face to face,
And yet my life is spared."
³¹ And the sun arose before him just as he left Penuel,
And he was limping because of his hip.
³² Because of this, the Israelites do not eat sinew of the hip, which is on the socket of the leg until this day for he struck the hip socket of Jacob in the sinew of the thigh.

---

36. Interestingly, the verb to wrestle (*'bq*) is a *hapax legomenon*, which only appears in this pericope, in v. 24 and the subsequent verse. This *might* give credence to Noth and Rad's proposal that this story comes from an ancient source that is later taken up by the Yahwist.

37. Translations of *ngʿ* vary widely. Nahum M. Sarna translated the verb as "wrenched"—"he wrenched Jacob's hip at its socket"—to convey the violence of the act. Cf. Sarna, *JPS Genesis*, 227. Robert Alter emphasizes that the translation "barely touch" would be more suitable than the forceful glosses often used in its place. Cf. Alter, *Five Books of Moses*, 179n26). The rationale for my translation—more straightforwardly rendered from Hebrew syntax—was argued earlier in this chapter.

Notice the way that the *wayyiqtol* paces the narrative. One of the most climactic moments in the entirety of the Jacob cycle involves wrestling with what appears to be a divine messenger in the space of a verse and a half (vv. 24b–25). The direct speech that follows the description of the wrestling match provides readers with what they need in order to understand the thrust of the discourse, but the pace moves so quickly, without any sort of modifier, that even distinguishing speakers in the dialogue is quite dizzying.

J. P. Fokkelman reflects on the diminutive length of select stories in the Hebrew Bible by noting: "Some of the profoundest and most exciting stories are remarkably short but are found close to a long text which moves at a very relaxed pace."[38] These short narratives move quickly through reports, abundantly employing the *wayyiqtol* without including many subordinating clauses. In the narrative material preceding and following the account of Gen 32:22–32, we find what Fokkelman observes regarding the pacing of narration. Before the story of his wrestling match, Jacob makes detailed preparations for meeting his estranged brother. These preparations include precise instructions to his servants, through whom Jacob hopes the giving of gifts and assuring words will soften the exchange when Esau finally encounters Jacob (Gen 32:3–5, 13–21). In addition to these preparations, the narrative also includes Jacob's prayer to God recounting God's promises to Jacob and a plea for deliverance (Gen 32:9–12). Following the wrestling account, Esau and Jacob reunite via the initial approach of Esau (Gen 33:1-3); Esau's enthusiastic response to the meeting (Gen 33:4–7); and Jacob's insistence that Esau receive his gifts (Gen 33:8–14). The narratives preceding and following Gen 32:22–32 both contain more descriptive content in proportion to the events they are detailing, including more subordinate clauses (e.g., instructions to servants, extended prayerful monologue, situating in what order Esau meets Jacob's wives and children, etc.). In short, Fokkelman's assessment that the narratives surrounding the most exciting stories appear to move "at a very relaxed slow

---

38. Fokkelman, "Genesis," 39. To elaborate his point further, he writes: "Consider chapters 22 and 24 [of Genesis]. In the Binding of Isaac, Abraham is cruelly ordered by God to sacrifice his son, the bearer of the promise, whose coming he has awaited a lifetime. The immense anxieties and incalculable implications of this situation are succinctly evoked in approximately 70 lines. Then, after the brief intervening episode of the purchase of the gravesite, we are pleasantly entertained by the calm flow, the epic breadth, and the posed harmony of characters, report, and speech in chapter 24, in which Abraham's servant seeks a bride for Isaac in Mesopotamia. By Hebrew standards, a great amount of space is devoted to ensuring that everything falls into its proper place—approximately 230 lines, at least four times the number found in the average story."

pace" holds up when reading the surrounding narratives of the exciting but brief story of Jacob's wrestling and renaming.

An examination of the impact of the *wayyiqtol* on the pacing of biblical narrative, particularly seen in Gen 32:22–32, demonstrates how pacing plays an important role in the style of storytelling involved in the climactic moments of biblical narrative. The *wayyiqtol* also amplifies the spare narrative information provided in the text. A broader investigation into the wrestling man of Gen 32 elucidates the parataxis the *wayyiqtol* offers. The elusive quality of the figure who wrestles with Jacob—referred to only as "a man" and with the pronoun "he"—takes on a more defined character when considered in light of the earlier events at the start of the chapter in Gen 32:1–2:

> ¹ and   Jacob went on his way
>   and   messengers of God met him
> ² and   when Jacob saw them, he said: "This is God's camp"
>   And   for that reason he called that place "Mahanaim
>   [literally: double camp]."

While the later identification of "the man" wrestling as a likely angel (i.e., messenger of God), is helpful, the skeletally narrated event of God's camp offers readers minimal information about who the messengers are, what their intentions might be, and the significance of Jacob encountering them. Brueggemann notes: "The affair is communicated in extreme brevity, four words in the Hebrew text [in English: 'the messengers of God met him']. The narrator gives the reader not the slightest notion of the apparently completely silent appearance, to say nothing of the fact that he wastes no words about the significance of the event for Jacob."[39] In quintessential biblical Hebrew parataxis, the textual information available in the broader chapter augments the picture of the wrestling man with an extremely bare and elusive mention of divine messengers and a double camp representing the earth and the heavens. The language of a double camp in the naming of the place as Mahanaim connects with the wrestling pericope through the man's proclamation in verse 28 that Jacob has contended with God and man. To say that the man *is* God leaves the latter duality of Jacob's struggling with a mere human out of the equation. Yet the former duality of a divine struggle signals to readers that some liminal space between human

---

39. Brueggemann, *Genesis*, 313.

and divine has been revealed in Jacob's strife.[40] Parataxis functions in both elusive pericopes of Gen 32 to leave readers with ample room for inference in light of the minimal information the narrator provides.

To summarize: where one might expect the most detail to assure that readers do not miss any important clue—as in Caroline Gordon's repeated advice to Flannery O'Connor—the story of Jacob's wrestling, wounding, and renaming leaves readers trying to catch their breath and attend to what the narrative leaves unsaid. The story requires sizable interpretive work to bear interpretive and existential fruit.

The biblical narrator's stylistic choice here should not be attributed simply to an archaic form of storytelling, though it is of course that; rather, this curt form of narration suits these particular kinds of stories concerning divine-human encounters. In the following, I analyze the spare narration of Haze Motes's conversion in *Wise Blood*'s climactic scenes. My analysis will demonstrate the similarities in paratactic style between Haze and patriarch Jacob's transformations when confronted with the divine.

O'Connor narrates the interior moment of Haze's conversion as he looks out over the embankment in a description akin to the paratactic style of the *wayyiqtol* in the Gen 32 passage recounting Jacob's wrestling event. In order to evidence the way narrative absence in O'Connor's writing parallels the *wayiqqtol* in biblical Hebrew narrative, I break down the central moment of *Wise Blood* by highlighting the presence of successive clauses without modification. Because the English language uses punctuation similarly to biblical Hebrew's use of the *wayiqqtol*, I insert a bracketed "and" to draw out the paratactic style of O'Connor's narration when the conjunction is not provided in-text.

[and]	Haze got out
and	glanced at the view. The embankment dropped down for about thirty feet,
	sheer washed-out red clay, into a partly burnt pasture where there was one scrub cow lying near a puddle. Over in the middle distance there was a one-room shack with a buzzard standing hunch-shouldered on the roof.
[and]	the patrolman got behind the Essex
and	pushed it over the embankment

---

40. The grey area between divine and human can be rendered as a "divine being," seen in the JPS Torah Commentary translation of Jacob's proclamation in v. 31 and signaling the reticence to directly name the figure God (*Elohim*); see: Sarna, *JPS Genesis*, 228.

and	the cow stumbled up
and	galloped across the field
and	into the woods;
[and]	the buzzard flapped off to a tree at the edge of the clearing.
[and]	the car landed on its top, with the three wheels that stayed on, spinning.
[and]	the motor bounced out
and	rolled down some distance away
and	various odd pieces scattered this way and that.
[and]	"Them that don't have a car don't need a license," the patrolman said, dusting his hands on his pants.
[and]	Haze stood for a few minutes, looking out over the scene.
[and]	His face seemed to reflect the entire distance across the clearing and on beyond, the entire distance that extended from his eyes to the blank gray sky that went on, depth after depth into space.
[and]	His knees bent under him
and	he sat down on the edge of the embankment with his feet hanging over. (CW, 118)

By breaking down the narrative into consecutive independent clauses, one can imagine each clause linked by the *wayyiqtol* if written in biblical Hebrew prose.[41] The litany of narrative descriptions produces a similar dizzying effect as was present in the crippling victory of Jacob in Gen 32.

When the officer departs after destroying Haze's car, readers are left with a view of Haze's back as he continues to stare at the sky. When the narration picks up again, Haze springs into action, but without readers receiving a "telling" account of the link between his staring at the sky and his decision to blind himself. Again, O'Connor describes his movements towards his exterior conversion this time in a narrated pace similar to the events of Jacob's wrestling episode with the use of the *wayyiqtol*. A

---

41. Of course, I am pointing to similarities in style with the transposition of the *wayyiqtol*, not sameness. In this passage, O'Connor includes descriptions of the landscape that are rarely found in biblical Hebrew narrative, e.g., the descriptions of the cows in the field and buzzards in the tree.

breakdown of the brief twelve lines that make up Haze's climactic decision evidences further similarity to the parataxis present in the Jacob story:

[and]	After a while Haze got up
and	started walking back to town.
[and]	It took him three hours to get inside the city again.
[and]	He stopped at the supply store
and	bought a tin bucket and a sack of quicklime
and	then he went on to where he lived, carrying these.
[and]	When he reached the house, he stopped outside on the sidewalk
and	opened the sack of lime
and	poured the bucket half full of it.
[and]	Then he went to a water spigot by the front steps
and	filled up the rest of the bucket with water
and	started up the steps.
[and]	His landlady was sitting on the porch, rocking a cat.
[and]	"What you going to do with that, Mr. Motes?" she asked.
[and]	"Blind myself," he said.
And	went on in the house.
[and]	The landlady sat there for a while longer . . . (CW, 119)

O'Connor's stripped-down paratactic style provides readers only the barest description necessary to narrate his movements from the side of the road into his room where he will blind himself. Notably, O'Connor does not narrate Haze's actual blinding in *Wise Blood*. In the subsequent chapter—and only through the landlady's account—do readers find out that Haze acted on his declaration. Rather than following Haze into the house and describing his self-blinding with quicklime, the narrator leaves readers at the end of the chapter with the landlady, Mrs. Flood, sitting on the porch, musing: "What possible reason could a sane person have for wanting to not enjoy himself any more?" (CW, 119). A description of Haze's act would have been an instance of grotesque gore, whereas her banal pronouncement that the purpose of life is to have fun stands in stark contrast to the moral and spiritual power of Haze's disfiguring act.

Here, the curt narration of Haze enacting the grace he first received as he looked out over the clearing onto his body through self-blinding confirms similarities to the narrative pacing of Gen 32. In both cases, we find narrations of a divine-human encounter leaving the protagonist drastically changed, yet the narrations are best characterized as spare and direct. In recognizing the shared ascetic quality of the two narratives, I want to point to three central shared narrative moments where the style plays an essential role in meaning-making: moments of recognition, moments of wounding, and moments of reckoning with the elusive Blesser.

Recognition. Gen 32:24 reads "*And* Jacob remained by himself *and* a man wrestled with him until daybreak." In this concise verse, made up of two independent clauses, readers receive the only hints of Jacob's confrontation with divine grace. Jacob himself is given no clue of the identity of the one with whom he contends. He might have at first supposed his brother Esau, but from what is known of the two brothers—Jacob being a shepherd and Esau a huntsman—it seems unlikely that Jacob would have proved a worthy opponent of his brawny brother. Later, in verse 29, Jacob clearly still seeks proof of his adversary when he asks for the man's name and a blessing. Ultimately, the narrative offers Jacob's full recognition of wrestling with God only after he receives a blessing. Similarly in *Wise Blood*, the narrative provides readers with only an indirect hint at what Haze sees as he stands and looks out over the embankment beyond his ruined Essex to the mysterious "depth after depth into space." Unlike the Genesis story, the narrative never overtly offers readers a hint of what Haze saw and recognized as he looked out that day. The moment of recognition serves as a fleeting moment sandwiched narratively between a comedic encounter with the patrolman and an ominous trek back into Taulkinham.

These stories obliquely render the protagonists' moments of recognizing their confrontation with the divine. Recall Maritain's insistence that art reveals the transcendent only through the humiliating effect of making readily apparent our own human finitude. Here, identifying Jacob and Haze's recognitions of divine grace only come through artistically-rendered effects. No neon lights, narrator interruptions, or inner-life of the protagonist assures readers of the divine revelation that unfolds. Throughout the Hebrew Bible, mysterious and indirect narrations of God's revelations occur. Recall, for example, the luminous darkness and burning-yet-unconsumed bush at Mount Sinai; the syntactically muddled naming of God as "YHWH"; and the still, small voice (literally: "thin silence") of God's revelation to Elijah on Mount Horeb. Correspondingly, O'Connor recognized that the writer with a theological imagination rightly formed possesses a freedom in writing "by guaranteeing his respect for mystery" (MM, 31). The ascetic quality of narration, through withholding of instantaneous and detailed descriptions of recognition when encountering the divine, unexpectedly renders even the smallest hint of recognition credible.

Wounding. Earlier, I addressed the distinctively grotesque nature of Jacob's and Haze's woundings. Intriguingly, these violent actions occupy minimal narrative space, if narrated at all. In the case of Jacob's wounding, the narrator indicates the striking and dislocating blow with succinct description. To illustrate the austere description of the wounding event, I offer a wooden translation of verse 25: "*and* he saw that he was unable to prevail over him *and* he struck his hip-socket *and* he dislocated Jacob's hip-socket while he wrestled with him." The subsequent verse shifts the scene from action to dialogue and offers no hint of the consequences of this wounding blow. Which of the two figures recognized that he was unable to win the fight? Was it Jacob, and thus the wounding was a sign of mercy? Or was it the divine figure who finally realized a cheap trick to win? How much pain did this dislocation cause? Was Jacob still able to wrestle after this blow? The very nature of the syntax amplifies these questions because of the rapidity by which story moves through the series of events. The wounding event serves as the key memorable action of this pericope, yet the narrator descriptively passes over the dislocation without comment.

Even more stark, Haze's blinding event occurs off-scene. Readers are left with Haze's answer, "Blind myself," to his landlady's inquiry about his intentions with the lime-filled bucket. In the turn of a page, readers move from Haze walking into the house with the landlady musing outside it to her reflection after the deforming act. Readers are left wondering about Haze's actions as the story remains with Mrs. Flood on her front porch. Markedly, the remainder of the chapter detailing Mrs. Flood's reflection on Haze's answer occupies double the narrative space of Haze's walk back into town and into the house.

In the central narrative actions of Jacob's wounding and Haze's self-blinding, readers encounter a surprising absence of information. Jacob's limp marks the gifting of the new name "Israel" and stands as the moment where—like Abram and Sarai—a new name serves as a seal of God's ongoing promise to his people. Haze's act of self-blinding functions as the quintessential action that marks the inner transformation he experienced out on the road, yet readers are completely denied access into the act itself. In both cases, the narrative that follows the wounding event does not directly connect with the disfiguring act and, further, occupies more narrative space. The narrative denies readers time to linger in the action the serve as the crux of the story. Why?

I want to propose that the rapidity and austerity of the wounding events creates a particular kind of interpretive experience for readers that does not allow the central transformative moments to be, in O'Connor's words, sentimentalized or pornographically rendered. The narrators do not soften the blow, as it were, to their protagonists by explaining away the wrenching of a hip from its socket or the corroding effect of quicklime. The action of grace on the characters in these narratives refuses justification or timidity. On the other hand, the narrative actions in these scenes also reject making the violent actions themselves the end or focus of the working of divine grace in Jacob and Haze. The narrated information lacks significant material detail and painful consequence of the actions. The narration of Jacob's and Haze's wounding are renunciatory in character because of the absence of what readers might expect from such central and grotesque scenes. The ascetic character of these central woundings places the onus on readers to attend to and reflect on a climactic moment that occupies so little narrated time.

Reckoning. Following the wounding events, neither narrative offers much in the way of details regarding how the protagonists reckon with a God who wounds in his blessing. In Gen 32:31, Jacob's final assessment of the wrestling event was that "I saw God face to face, and he saved my life." Jacob's declaration of God's saving act obfuscates the means of the blessing he received. The narrative offers no resolution as to *why* Jacob had to be wounded in order to be blessed. Recall that the narrative lacks clarity even on who was unable to prevail over whom. Already unclear on the motive for the initial wounding, the narrative ends with Jacob's assessment of the event as entirely salvific and without any indication of the pain incurred to achieve the good end.

In the remainder of *Wise Blood*, the narrative focus shifts almost entirely to Mrs. Flood's point of view. The narrative indicates repeatedly that Haze rarely answered the landlady's questions, and when he does respond his answers are curt. The transformation of the spitfire preacher to the nearly mute blind man heightens the transformation hinted at in the climactic moments of the Essex's demise and Haze's blinding. The only indication readers are offered on how Haze understands the blessed and blinding transformation he received are found in his explanations for his adoption of the ascetic self-denying practices. Haze insists that he has to pay (CW, 125) and is not clean (CW, 127). The mutating act of blinding himself, then, appears to be the beginning of his purgation as he moves towards paying his dues and becoming clean. While Haze refuses to indicate what he needs to pay for and purge from, his insistence to Mrs. Flood that "If you believed in Jesus, you wouldn't be so good" (CW, 125) leaves no doubt to whom he pays. His blessed new sight sets him on a path towards Jesus, the one who has blessed him. His final words as he dies in a ditch reiterate that he is on his way to redemption: "I want to go on where I'm going" (CW, 131).[42] Like Jacob's response at the close of Gen 32, Haze reckons with his wounding and blessed transformation with an inattention that offers nothing in the way of justifying or explaining away the violent work of redemption.

Conclusion

This chapter explored two sparely narrative stories of encounters with divine grace. By addressing not only their thematic but stylistic similarities, I demonstrated how the way these stories are told amplifies their theological significance. The ascetic quality of Jacob's and Haze's narratives of transformation—which the syntactic function of the *wayyiqtol* highlights—suits the subject matter of the stories themselves. The leanness of the narratives pushes readers beyond the obvious and easy answers deeper into the stories as they render visible the mysterious work of God's grace in the world.

---

42. Haze's declaration here parallels boy Bevel at the close of "The River" when the narrator tells us that "He intended not to fool with preachers any more but to Baptize himself and *to keep on going this time until he found the Kingdom of Christ in the river. He didn't mean to waste any more time*" (CW, 170, italics added).

Chapter 5

Reading Spare Stories

Introduction

IN AN ENTRY OF Flannery O'Connor's prayer journal, she begins: "Dear Lord please make me want you. It would be the greatest bliss. Not just to want You when I think about You but to want you all the time, to think about you all the time, to have the want driving in me, to have it like a cancer in me. It would kill me like a cancer and that would be the Fulfillment."[1] With what might appear as a masochistic sickness at first-glance, this prayer is in fact a confession of O'Connor's desire: she desires to desire. She longs to want God in the way of the saints: an all-consuming, all-encompassing desire of the lover for her Beloved. Ironically, at the close of her prayer, O'Connor states the root cause of her plea for God to awaken a cancerous desire in her: "Oh Lord please make this dead desire living, living in life, living as it will probably have to live in suffering. I feel too mediocre now to suffer. If suffering came to me I would not recognize it."[2] O'Connor asks for an illness tantamount to death in order to receive life, paradoxically awakening the dead desire in her through suffering, through death.

I begin this chapter with O'Connor's plea for desire because it stands at the center of my overarching interest in the impact of O'Connor's spare style on her readers. The preceding two chapters have focused on drawing

---

1. O'Connor, *Prayer Journal*, 36. Not all of O'Connor's admirers and critics are likely to find this prayer for dead desire to become alive like a cancer to be an appealing request. Sarah Gordon, in her review of *A Prayer Journal*, comments that while readers "schooled in the parochial ascetic tradition" may appreciate such prayers, "for other Christians and secular admirers of O'Connor's work, I suspect publication of this journal will be embarrassing, if not troubling indeed" (S. Gordon, "Reviewed Work, 'Prayer Journal,'" 756).

2. O'Connor, *Prayer Journal*, 36.

out the stylistically spare nature of Flannery O'Connor's fiction through the similarly narrated stories of the Hebrew Bible. In this chapter, I make the parataxis present in these stories a means for circling back around to the theological claim made in the earlier chapter on O'Connor's use of the grotesque as moments of excess. All the work of the preceding chapters comes together here in an exploration of the ways that O'Connor's paratactic narration of reality illumined by God draws readers into their own terrifying and potentially wounding encounters with divine grace.

To demonstrate this wounding effect on readers, I first outline Wolfgang Iser's account of the act of reading. Iser's insistence on the necessarily participatory nature of readers to infer a story's meaning articulates the vulnerability and entanglement of readers in the reading event. Notably, Iser emphasizes that different styles of narrative make different degrees and kinds of demands on readers. I then turn to an analogue of the vulnerability of reading found in the act of prayer as drawn out by Jean-Louis Chrétien. Chrétien articulates prayer as a wounding event, paralleling it to the wounding and blessed outcome of Jacob's wrestling with a divine visitor on the banks of the Jabbok. My exploration of the analogue of a wounding reading to a wounding prayer culminates in Bonaventure's account of St. Francis's reception of the stigmata—where the mystical seraphic vision pierces St. Francis's heart and flesh.

The Act of Reading

The paratactic style present in O'Connor's fiction and biblical Hebrew narrative makes tremendous demands on readers. Namely, readers must infer meaning—often surprising, even shocking—from a bare bones text that moves quickly, and sometimes violently, from one narrative action to another. To reflect on the theological significance of this kind of spare narrative event for readers, I turn to Wolfgang Iser's account of reading. Iser provides a framework for understanding what occurs in the act of reading. Significantly, Iser points to the interpretive work and risk required when readers confront gaps that need filling in a story.

Discovery stands at the center of Iser's exposition on the reading event.[3] In agreement with the well-known conception of the fusing of

---

3. In his essay sarcastically titled "There Is Nothing Inside the Text, or, Why No One's Heard of Wolfgang Iser," Michael Bérubé argues that Stanley Fish has dismantled any beneficial contribution of Iser's critical theory (cf. Bérubé, "There Is Nothing Inside the

horizons in Gadamerian hermeneutic theory, Iser argues that meaning arises from the engagement of the reader with the text, for "it is in the reader that the text comes to life."[4] The act of reading, then, is a "dynamic happening" where the text effects a response by the reader.[5] This dynamism produces a certain indeterminacy of meaning because meaning arises in the act of reading, not as an inert and static meaning that must be excavated from the text.

Iser's dynamic description of the reading event provides a helpful framework for understanding the impact of a particular reading experience on readers. For if reading is in fact an *event*, which involves and affects

---

Text." Bérubé points to Fish's critique of Iser's distinction between the determinacy and indeterminacy of a text's meaning (cf. Fish, "Why No One's Afraid"). In the review, Fish notes that the reason Iser lacks any notability in literary theory is that he fails to fall into one of the two reputable camps: the subversionists (to which Derrida and Fish himself belong) and those who "fight the good fight against the forces of deconstructive nihilism" (to which Hirsch and Booth belong) (Fish, "No One's Afraid," 2). Fish faults Iser for not making clear the determinate/indeterminate distinction, i.e., what qualifies as a given of the text, what is a gap to be filled, and how one arbitrates and authorizes one from the other ((Fish, "No One's Afraid," 12). Bérubé finds Fish victorious over Iser in this disagreement because Fish identifies the closest thing to a fixed fact as the social and communal interpretive influence, not something found within the fabric of the text itself (Bérubé, "Nothing Inside Text," 17). This back-and-forth between Iser and Fish echoes an earlier encounter between Iser's professor, Hans-Georg Gadamer, and Jacques Derrida. The event known as "The Gadamer-Derrida Encounter: Paris 1981" is documented in Michelfelder and Palmer, *Dialogue and Deconstruction: The Gadamer-Derrida Encounter*. Derrida's central critique of Gadamer's hermeneutics centers on the possibility for misunderstanding which, ironically, one scholar of the "encounter" deems to be the precise place of disagreement between the two great men: "a classic instance of non-communication . . . neither really making substantial contact" (Bernstein, "Conversation That Never Happened," 577). Bérubé, similarly, sees in Iser's response to Fish, an extreme misconstrual of Fish's position (Bérubé, "Nothing Inside Text," 16). The reason I cite these two disagreements is that both Iser and Gadamer fall somewhere in the no-man's land Fish identifies as lying between the deconstructionists and traditionalist. Iser recognizes the need to fit into one of Fish's two categories as problematic (Iser, "Talk Like Whales," 82–83). While some like Bérubé seek to explain why no one has heard of Iser, the solid fact remains that Iser's influence, like Gadamer's, continues to exert important sway on the understanding of texts and readers—albeit more quietly than the likes of Fish or Derrida. Eulogizing Iser in 2007, Shlomith Rimmon-Kenan celebrates Iser's "groundbreaking intellectual trajectory," noting how Iser turned the limits of human interpretation into opportunities for "plurality and productivity in reading" (Rimmon-Kenan, "Wolfgang Iser—In Memoriam," 141–44). Iser's contribution to understanding the dynamism in reading is on display here in my appropriation of his theory.

4. Iser, *Act of Reading*, 19.
5. Iser, *Act of Reading*, 22.

readers, stories offer a transformative opportunity for their audiences, potentially akin to the transformative experience of a story's protagonist. Iser identifies the implied or fictional reader as the location where readers and characters meet, the implied reader resides in the text and "prestructures the role" to be assumed by real readers.[6] The real-life readers are anticipated in the text by the fictional reader similarly to the way a work of art is created with the anticipation of being seen or a piece of music being heard. The work of art anticipates, in fact needs someone to engage it to be and become what it truly is. The work prefigures a participant. Importantly, meaning does not reside in the mind of the fictional reader; instead, the fictional reader provides a vantage point from which real readers can discover something fresh, even unexpected, within a story.

Not all readers of Iser are convinced by his proposal of the implied reader as a structural element of fiction. In the same publication year of *Act of Reading*, Wayne Booth, author of *The Rhetoric of Fiction*, poses questions related to the implied reader as construed by Iser.[7] A brief summary of this back and further helps further elucidate Iser's implied reader.

Booth argues that Iser fails to personify both implied author and reader, so that the text is left void of "matters like laughter, tears, fear, horror, disgust, joy, and celebration."[8] These responses allow for the implied reader to doubt as often as they believe the events of the narrative. Booth asks Iser: might it be possible that the implied reader—the "reader-in-the-text"—functions in the dual roles of pretender and skeptic?[9] Booth poses this question because if the implied reader is in fact a "reader" then it makes sense that she would experience the text like the real reader—who simultaneously imagines the narrative is real, while recognizing she is reading fiction.[10] Iser responds to Booth's critical question concerning the double effect of implied readers by noting that personification should and does occur in the text, but this bringing of the personal to the text arises from real readers, not anything inherent in the text. Thus, the relationship between the implied author (and implied reader) and the real reader is "all the more powerful [in contrast to an encounter with a person] as we have not encountered him in person but in a text-guided, though self-produced, image; the subsequent

6. Iser, *Act of Reading*, 34.
7. Booth, "Interview."
8. Booth, "Interview," 67.
9. Booth, "Interview," 67–68.
10. Booth, "Interview," 68.

affective reaction something which we have produced ourselves may then account for the laughter, tears, fear, horror, etc., which Professor Booth mentioned."[11] Iser agrees that there is a double-effect in reading—belief and doubt—but that this play exists within real readers for the implied reader is merely and only a literary device that real readers take up in the reading event.[12] Summarily, the implied reader serves as a role into which the real reader takes on in the act of reading. The implied reader functions, as it were, like a seat into which the real reader sits. The implied reader, then, should not be confused with the real reader.

In his earlier work, Iser describes the role of the implied reader within the text as the invitation for real readers to suspend belief and enter into a story's foreign world: "As the reader is maneuvered into this position, his reactions—which are, so to speak, prestructured by the written text—bring out the meaning of the novel."[13] Summarily, the implied reader resides in the text as a pre-structured, potential agent for meaning-making. This potential agency is taken up by the real reader who actualizes meaning.

Different kinds of stories invite different kinds of interpretive work for readers. Iser contrasts the sort of engagement available in a didactic work such as Bunyan's *Pilgrim's Progress* to a more paratactic work such as Fielding's *Joseph Andrews* and *Tom Jones*. In *Pilgrim's Progress*, we find a work that diverges from the epic style by creating characters that are like readers with concrete and relatable stories. This relatability allows Bunyan to aid the readers in seeing the condition of their own souls in the act of reading. Unlike Bunyan, Fielding's novels demand a level of participation by the reader that is absent in Bunyan's story. Fielding includes gaps in his work that both raise the awareness of the reader and require active participation for a complete "realization" of the text.[14] While Iser's reading of Bunyan

11. Booth, "Interview," 69.

12. Booth, "Interview," 70.

13. Iser, *Implied Reader*, 32.

14. Iser, *Implied Reader*, 35. Iser uses an example from *Joseph Andrews*, wherein the protagonist Joseph must resist the seduction of his late master's wife, Lady Booby, Iser writes: "Lady Booby leads on her footman [Joseph], whom she has got to sit on her bed, with all kinds of enticements, until the innocent Joseph finally recoils, calling loudly upon his virtue. Instead of describing the horror of his Potiphar, Fielding, at the height of the crisis, continues: 'You have heard, readers, poets talk of Surprise. . . . .You have seen the face, in the eighteen-penny gallery . . . could you receive such an idea of surprise as would have entered in at your eyes had they beheld Lady Booby when those last words issued out from the lips of Joseph. "Your virtue!" said the lady, recovering after a silence of two minutes; "I shall never survive it!"' As the narrative does not offer a description of

might be contested, his observations about the opportunities for involvement based on the style of the work prove helpful. Iser's contrast between the didactic style of Bunyan and the paratactic style of Fielding shows the impact of literary style on the act of reading.

The reading event involves a kind of vulnerability. In identifying spare narratives as requiring more active involvement by the reader, Iser's proposal sets the stage for more vulnerable and demanding reading experiences. The implied or fictional reader offers a built-in literary device for actual readers to suspend belief and enter an unknown fictional world. The degree of opportunity for inference made available by a sparely-wrought story (e.g., more gaps give the implied reader, and in turn real readers, more opportunities for engagement) leads to a distinctive reading experience. That is, different kinds of stories demand different kinds of actions on the part of readers. Spare stories demand more, but those demands also engage readers in uniquely transformative ways.

On the Vulnerability of Reading

Iser emphasizes the dynamism between text and reader. This reading event "creates the impression that we are involved in something real."[15] Unlike a subject before an object of study, the text invites exploration rather than investigation. Iser adopts the language of a traveler to describes the exploratory nature of the reading event: "it is only by leaving behind the familiar world of his own experience that the reader can truly participate in the *adventure* the literary text offers him."[16] Readers take on a "wandering viewpoint" as they travel within the text: "the reader's position in the text is at the point of intersection between retention and protension. Each individual sentence correlate prefigures a particular horizon, but this is immediately transformed into the background for the next correlate and

---

Lady Booby's reaction, the reader is left to provide the description, using the direction's offered him" (Iser, *Implied Reader*, 37–38; Iser is citing Fielding, *Joseph*, 20).

15. Iser, *Act of Reading*, 67. Using J. L. Austin's criteria for a successful speech-act—1) "common conventions" between speaker and hearer, 2) "procedures accepted" between the two parties, and 3) willingness to participate—Iser explores the conditions that make possible a believable reading event (Iser, *Act of Reading*, 69). While willingness lies wholly on the side of readers, the conventions and procedures for reading are first provided by the text and accepted by readers through their participation.

16. Iser, *Implied Reader*, 282, italics added.

must therefore necessarily be modified."[17] Readers wander through the text, with their expectations continually modified and reworked as they read the story. Through this backward and forward action of reading, readers bring the story alive through their participation in meaning-making. This dynamic event entangles readers in the story they are reading. Iser points to the fact that often readers feel the impulse to talk about what they have just read, "not in order to gain some distance from them so much as to find out just what it is that we are entangled in."[18] So, readers not only produce meaning through their participation in a text but are themselves meant to be transformed through their reading. This idea likely comes as no surprise to those of us who have been unable to shake off the haunting effect of a scene or a story we have read, such as the massacre of a family on the side of the road in "A Good Man Is Hard to Find" or the epic quest of brave hairy-footed hobbits in J.R.R. Tolkien's *Lord of the Rings*.

Readers' entanglement in and with the text produces a form of vulnerability. Iser emphasizes the unique form of vulnerability in readers of literature. This particular experience centers on the kind of imagination required for reading. Unlike a movie or a theatre production where the characters are present to the naked eye, characters in literature are mentally imaged through the descriptive data of the narrative. Different kinds of imaging produce different effects:

> Our mental images do not serve to make the character physically visible; their optical poverty is an indication of the fact that they illuminate the character, not as an object, but as a bearer of meaning. Even if we are given a detailed description of a character's appearance, we tend not to regard it as pure description, but try and conceive what is actually to be communicated through it.[19]

Readers are not simply reconstructing a character in their head as a one might create an online avatar. Instead, readers construct mental images of characters as agents of communication.

This need for mental imaging of characters is only one aspect of the complex imaginative work required in the act of reading. Iser identifies the information gaps in a story as the place where readers produce something new in their reading. He distinguishes between two kinds of

---

17. Iser, *Act of Reading*, 111.
18. Iser, *Act of Reading*, 131.
19. Iser, *Act of Reading*, 138.

gaps in a text: blanks and negations.[20] Blanks are simple gaps in the storytelling that require readers to fill-in; for example, O'Connor never tells us about Hazel Motes's height, so we must assign a height as we build a mental image of Haze as he stands atop his car preaching. Negations, on the other hand, function as points of tension in the narrative where the unfamiliarity of some aspect of the text pushes us to harmonize the world of the text with our own.[21] O'Connor's use of the grotesque serves as a quintessential example of this kind of negative tension in the text. The grotesque strains the expected and accepted ways of being in the real world. Between blanks and negations, the push-and-pull of the reading events is clear: even as readers fill-in blanks of a text, they are pulled out of their previous, often comfortable positions and forced to reckon with something unfamiliar through negation.

Iser's description of the effect of negation in reading parallels Rowan Williams's description of art as dispossession. We saw earlier how Williams describes art as having the potential for making the world strange. Art more generally, and here with Iser, literature more specifically, calls us out of everyday experiences to engage imaginatively with new knowledge and insights that returns us to the everyday transformed.

Within this schema, parataxis places extraordinary demands on readers because of the ample number of blanks and negations by which readers must navigate their way through unspoken aspects of a story. Paratactic narration moves quickly from event to event without modifying clauses, in stories filled with narrative gaps and without causal connection. Readers of spare narration are faced more frequently and more intensely with the tension of wrestling with what is left unsaid in the narrative.[22] Readers of

20. Iser, *Act of Reading*, 182.

21. Iser categorizing gaps as either blanks or negations partially maps onto Sternberg's distinction earlier between blanks and gaps. For both Iser and Sternberg, blanks provide less opportunities for creativity on the part of readers. Recall, Sternberg goes further than Iser in designating blanks as moments of narrative silence that are of little interest to the reader and do not require investigation to unveil more of the whole truth of a story. Iser's negations, on the other hand, function similarly to Sternberg's gaps where both are textual silences that draws readers deeper into the story.

22. I am not implying that gaps and blanks in a text equate to a paratactically narrated story; there are gaps and blanks in many narrative styles apart from parataxis. Instead, I am suggesting that paratactic narration *qua* spare narration necessarily features gaps that require filling. This is precisely the excessive demands Caroline Gordon accuses O'Connor of placing on her readers. O'Connor, in Gordon's view, is asking readers to fill in too much information, to do too much work, to arrive at a believable, satisfactory (and perhaps self-satisfied) reading of her stories.

spare stories frequently face moments that require the constructive work of gap-filling and the uncomfortable work of mediating the relation between the world of the story with their own world. In turn, readers are readily faced with the awareness of their own limits as they are required to infer meaning from a narrative that offers little clue as to what is occurring in the unnarrated portions of a story. At the same time, parataxis offers abundant opportunities for readerly involvement so as to make a story come alive in a distinctive way. Whereas a more didactic and hypotactic form of storytelling enables readers to stand more easily outside the text, taking in the information the narrative provides. Parataxis, by contrast, places readers squarely in the midst of the text, requiring readers to fill in the unnarrated portions of the fictional world and narrative events.

Readers of Flannery O'Connor

Iser's insistence on the participatory nature of reading—where both the text and readers are transformed through the reading event—returns us to the focus of this work: the effect on readers of O'Connor's stylistic asceticism. So far, I have explored the distinctive style of O'Connor's storytelling and paralleled it to the spare narrative style of Hebrew narrative to draw out its unique quality. Before exploring the theological impact of O'Connor's spare style, let me briefly summarize its distinctive nature.

O'Connor writes paratactically. Her stories are filled with straightforward descriptions that often lack dependent clauses to draw out characters, landscape, and actions. O'Connor's sparely narrated scenes echo the use of the *wayyiqtol* in biblical Hebrew narrative, where stories unfold with a series of clauses that create the effect in English of back-to-back sequential clauses (e.g., "and he walked ... and he went ... and he spoke"). This skeletal narration is precisely what O'Connor's writing mentor Caroline Gordon continually critiqued. Gordon attributed this stylistic choice to immaturity and laziness. Nonetheless, while O'Connor embraced many of Gordon's recommended changes, she never fully accepted Gordon's urging for her to create more dependent clauses that would better aid the reader in the work of interpretation.

In parallel readings of Gen 32 and *Wise Blood*, the effect on readers of sparely narrated moments of conversion speaks to the power of the style itself. Readers are moved through the climactic scenes of Jacob and Hazel's conversion at a rapid pace. Because O'Connor presents the essential scenes in such a spare form, readers are left to infer precisely what occurred in the climactic moments. In Iser's language, the abundant blanks and negations must be filled before the scene can be satisfactorily understood.

O'Connor's stories are not only sparely narrated, but the narration itself often carries with it a violent force. O'Connor narrates gruesome and morally unsettling events that fall squarely on readers without any adornment to allay the effect. As we have seen, Rowan Williams describes the narrative force of O'Connor stories as communicating "the terror of being aware of reality in the light of God."[23] O'Connor's spare and often unnerving stories require extensive readerly involvement. They are asked to fill in gaps most decisively in the climactic moments of her narrative, as they are made to ask: Is God here? Is this how God's grace could (or should) work?'

Wounding Prayer

O'Connor challenges her readers, as do few other writers, to confront the possibility that reality illumined by God is truly terrifying. I propose that the reading posture this spare style demands, particularly when it narrates this divinely-illumined reality, shares features with the kind of vulnerability and potential wounding found in contemplative prayer. Hans Urs von Balthasar describes prayer as a posture deeply rooted in the character of the human person: "Man is the being created as hearer of the Word, and only in responding to the Word rises to his full dignity. . . . His inmost being is readiness, attentiveness, perceptiveness, willingness to surrender to what is greater than he."[24] As in reading, so in prayer: they both require the passive stance of reception and the active stance of response.

The analogous postures of reading spare narrative and praying are aptly illumined by Jean-Louis Chrétien in his essay "The Wounded Word: The Phenomenology of Prayer."[25] There he argues that without prayer there would be no religious dimension for humanity because, "[i]f we are unable to address our speech to God or the gods, no other act could intend the divine."[26] Through prayer, or even the possibility of prayer, the human person makes herself vulnerable to a realm that is both invisible and intangible. Chrétien notes that in prayer the possibility of theophany,

---

23. Williams, *Grace and Necessity*, 121.
24. Balthasar, *Prayer*, 18–19.
25. Chrétien, "Wounded Word."
26. Chrétien, "Wounded Word," 147.

the manifestation of God in the world, must first begin with a kind of "anthropophany, a manifestation of man."[27] That is, prayer begins with a recognition of the limits of the human person. Prayer is that liminal place in which the finite and fallen realm of the human opens to the limitless and perfect realm of the divine. Prayer reveals the essential nature of the human, precisely because it attends to the transcendent.

The Vulnerability of Prayer

Chrétien stresses the vulnerability of prayer: "This act of presence puts man thoroughly at stake, in all dimensions of his being. It exposes him in every sense of the word *expose* and with nothing held back."[28] Making clear that he is not speaking figuratively, he continues: "[prayer] concerns our body, our bearing, our posture, our gestures, and can include certain mandatory preliminary bodily purifications such as ablutions, vestimentary requirements such as covering or uncovering certain parts of our body, bodily gestures and movements such as raising the hands or kneeling, and even certain physical orientations."[29] The effect of prayer—in its vulnerable exposure to the Divine Other—is rooted in the vulnerability of all communication. Elsewhere, Chrétien refers to this vulnerability in speech as "the naked voice" (*la voix nue*), which makes communication—most notably the communication of divine promise—possible.[30] Prayer, then, not only

27. Chrétien, "Wounded Word," 150.

28. Chrétien, "Wounded Word," 150, italics his.

29. Chrétien, "Wounded Word," 150. Later in the essay, Chrétien refers again to the body in prayer. He points to the fact that the voice is inherently enfleshed and that vocal prayer cannot be separated from the physical reality of the human person. This inherent connection between the body and vocalization of prayer is why the purity of the body in certain rituals is not separated from the purity of the prayer (168).

30. Chrétien, *La Voix Nue*, 7. Chrétien expounds on this idea of nakedness when he writes: "La nudité de la voix, nous exposant corps et âme à l'être, sans retour, frappe depuis toujours et pour toujours d'impossibilité la transparence, l' adéquation, la plénitude, la perfection, la parousie. Devancée, défaite, elle l'est en elle-même, et c'est là ce qui la fait, en toute parole, promettre, promettre ce qu'elle ne peut tenir." In "Wounded Word," Chrétien pushes back against a likening of prayer to a person speaking to himself. To be in self-dialogue, Chrétien insists, not only stands in distinction from prayer, but does violence to how we understand the phenomenon of prayer by conflating the speaker and the hearer. In prayer, there is always an other. In self-talk, there is only the singular "you" (Chrétien, "Wounded Word," 151). The language of nudity stresses this point: to stand before another naked—metaphorically or actually—creates an entirely different effect than staring at one's own reflection in a mirror. Whether the experience is

makes us aware of our own limits as humans but also places us in a posture of exposure, of vulnerability, of nakedness.

Chrétien identifies the wounding effect of prayer in two significant ways. First, prayer opens the self to another. The inner stability of self-communication gets jolted out of its normal state by making space for God: "in prayer is the first wound of the word: the yawning chasm of its addressee has broken its circle, has opened a fault that alters it. An other is silently introduced into my dialogue with myself, radically transforming and breaking it. My speech spills back over me."[31] Chrétien identifies this kind of speech as being singularly different than the speech we might utter aloud or hear addressed to us because it is wholly addressed to a Divine Other who is radically unlike ourselves. The word uttered in prayer is uttered *to* God but does not inform or modify God in any way; instead, we are shown to ourselves in prayer: "To ask of God, that is, to carry out in words an act of demanding, is, by speaking to him, to say something about him and at the same time something about ourselves. *We are made manifest to ourselves in manifesting ourselves to him.*"[32] Prayer possesses something of a boomerang effect in that what we send out in our utterances to God also come back at us with, in Chrétien's words, "sudden force."[33] The radical otherness we encounter in prayer creates a kind of unadulterated speech, where the rebounding effect of prayer brings our speech to God back on to ourselves:

> This act of a word wounded by the radical alterity of him to whom it speaks is pure address. It does not speak in order to teach something to someone, even if it always says something about ourselves and the world. It confides to the other what the other knows, and asks of him what he knows we need. Not even for a single moment is the word separate from the ordeal; it is undergone by and through itself, both by what it says and by what it does not succeed in saying and by him to whom it speaks. It itself learns from this

---

positive or negative, seeing oneself in a solitarily vulnerable posture is unlike the experience of standing before another person. In this distinction, Chrétien is pushing back against Kant and Feuerbach, both of whom liken prayer to talking to oneself (Chrétien, "Wounded Word," 151).

31. Chrétien, "Wounded Word," 153.
32. Chrétien, "Wounded Word," 153, italics added.
33. Chrétien, "Wounded Word," 153.

ordeal, and this is why this wound makes it stronger, all the stronger as it will not have sought to heal it.[34]

Prayer thus transforms the pattern of internal self-knowledge by introducing a conversation partner unlike any other conversation partner into our most interior spaces. This vulnerable exposure wounds us in our egoism, our self-deceptions, and our ignorance. Prayer wounds through a disruption that transforms our utterances to God into a new kind of utterance to ourselves.

The second wound, flowing from the first, centers on the dispossession required in prayer. This dispossession returns us to the idea of prayer as exposure, as naked speech. Chrétien uses the biblical imagery of Moses before God to draw out this particular wounding effect: "Moses responds to God that he does not know how to speak, and this is often the Prophets' first response to their vocation—that is to say, the very place where they hear it."[35] Moses hears the voice of God concurrently with the recognition of the feebleness of his own voice. Chrétien extends this image to St. Paul when he writes in Rom 8:26 that he does not know the right way to pray. This awareness of what we are called to alongside the awareness of our own lack produces a blessed kind of palindrome: "This is the circularity of prayer: the man praying prays in order to know how to pray, and first of all to learn that he does not know how, and he offers thanks for his prayer as a gift from God. One can be turned to God only in praying, and one can pray only by being turned toward God."[36] Prayer radically equalizes all those who pray, because not knowing how to pray is inherent to the act itself and yet at the same time we are gifted with the ability to pray. One cannot properly pray unless one dispossesses oneself of confidence that in prayer one knows what one is doing. Desire to pray, not technique, makes prayer possible.

Chrétien uses Kierkegaardian language to describe this paradox: "only a leap makes us enter into this circle [of prayer]."[37] There is an instability in prayer, but this instability is precisely what makes the act of praying so efficacious: "[t]he circle is not an absurd circle: it refers to the event of encounter."[38] The result of this encounter is a kind of "inner violence" where

---

34. Chrétien, "Wounded Word," 175.
35. Chrétien, "Wounded Word," 157.
36. Chrétien, "Wounded Word," 157.
37. Chrétien, "Wounded Word," 157.
38. Chrétien, "Wounded Word," 158.

we battle with the "dumbness in us."[39] Chrétien describes the rigorous battle of prayer within oneself: "The true prayer is a struggle with God where one is victorious in the victory of God."[40] Prayer wounds because it is a kind of defeat, dispossessing us in order to give victory to God. Our victory in prayer is, paradoxically, also our defeat.[41]

Chrétien links the dispossession in prayer to the vulnerability of a lover's speech: "In collapsing beneath him, prayer, like all lovers' speech, bears the weight of giving itself, that is to say, of losing itself. It suffers the other in coming unstuck from itself."[42] Prayer, like any utterance of love, is an action of self-giving. This language of intimacy and vulnerability echoes the long tradition of the mystics who liken the act of coming before God in the liminal space between where human and divine meet to consummation of the bridegroom and the bride.[43]

The language of bearing the weight of another to become unstuck from oneself evokes the image, once again, of Jacob's wrestling with the man on

---

39. Chrétien, "Wounded Word," 158.

40. Chrétien, "Wounded Word," 158.

41. In *God, Sexuality, and the Self: An Essay 'On the Trinity,'* Sarah Coakley argues that desire stands at the center of understanding the human person before God. Desire, rooted in the Trinitarian life, directs all human desire to its proper end, participation in the divine life (6). Echoing Augustine and Bernard of Clairvaux (among others) as insisting on love as rightly ordered to its proper *telos*, Coakley argues that all human desire, when properly ordered, is understood primarily through a desire for God. Asceticism stands at the center of a proper understanding of human desire, for asceticism makes space for the Holy Spirit to chasten any perversion of desire away from its proper end (11). Coakley writes: "the Spirit progressively 'breaks' sinful desires, *in and through* the passion of Christ" (14, italics hers). In tandem with ascetic practices, Coakley sees a "commitment to prayer . . . [as the] willingness to endure a form of naked dispossession before God" (19). Coakley's naming of prayer as naked dispossession echoes her discussion of contemplation in an earlier work, *Powers and Submissions: Spirituality, Philosophy, and Gender*, where she explores contemplation through the lens of St. John of the Cross's dark night of the soul as well as the passive ecstatic visions of medieval female mystics (ch. 2). Coakley emphasizes here that contemplation has everything to do with reordering the disordered desires within the contemplative, a set of acts involving both an activity and passivity on the part of the one who prays. The necessary passivity and vulnerability of the contemplative—exemplified in the female mystics—often gets ignored in considerations of what contemplation requires of us and transforms in us.

42. Chrétien, "Wounded Word," 161.

43. O'Connor largely avoids nuptial imagery in the blessed woundedness of her character, lest the implied and actual reader reduce the event to Freudian terms. Only in "Greenleaf" are there any such erotic hints. Even there, as in Teresa of Avila, the divine penetration occurs in the chest, not the loins.

the banks of the Jabbok river. In this scene of wrestling and wounding, Jacob becomes "Israel"—a naming that transforms Jacob from able-bodied trickster to a limping, yet great patriarch—through defeat. Jacob becomes unstuck from himself and available to something blessedly new through wounding. Chrétien compares the travail of the prayer event to "struggling like Jacob all night in the dust to wrest God's blessing from him" and the wounding of prayer to "[Jacob's] keeping the sign of a swaying and limping by which [his] speech is all the more confident as it is less assured of its own progress."[44] Jacob's defeat that night is also his victory. Like Jacob, we are meant to wrestle with God in prayer—to suffer the Other so as to make room for something divinely gifted within ourselves.

Akin to the limp Jacob receives, the wounding effect of prayer paradoxically strengthens the one who prays through weakness and defeat.[45] Chrétien's reference of unhealed wounds recalls his distinction explored earlier concerning two kinds of wounds: wounds that heal and wounds that do not and should not. Chrétien notes that many wounds heal over and that those scars serve as reminders of a wounding event, but there are also wounds that "must not heal" because they reflect a level of intimacy gifted that one would not want to lose.[46]

Shelly Rambo, in *Resurrecting Wounds,* refigures how we might understand the scene where the disciple Thomas encounters the resurrected Christ with the help of trauma theory to draw out the particularity of Christ's wounds: "the return of Jesus reveals something about *life in the midst of death*. If we take the line between death and life to be more porous, as the context of trauma suggests, then resurrecting is not so much about life overcoming death as it is about *life resurrecting amid the ongoingness of death*."[47] This reconfiguration of death in the resurrection event, Rambo continues, "marks a distinct territory for thinking about life as marked by wounds and yet recreated through them." Later, exploring the significance of St. Macrina's scar, Rambo notes that her wound served as a testimony that "God was here," which does not fade because the "mark remains on the body as a sign of healing; it is a mark produced not by an internal wound

---

44. Chrétien, "Wounded Word," 175.

45. In a further parallel, St. Paul's words to the Corinthian church in 2 Cor 12:9 illuminate the weakening and paradoxically strengthening work of grace: "but he said to me, 'My grace is sufficient for you, for power is made perfect in weakness.' So, I will boast all the more gladly of my weaknesses, so that the power of Christ may dwell in me" (NRSV).

46. Chrétien, *Hand to Hand,* 2.

47. Rambo, *Resurrecting Wounds,* 7, italics hers.

but by its exterior witness."[48] Rambo's notion of resurrecting wounds aligns with Chrétien's idea of wounds that must not heal, as both speak of God's ongoing albeit painful presence. Wounds that must not heal are the wounds that make us stronger through defeat, like Jacob—now Israel—whose limp does not lessen as he lives the rest of his life blessed by God.

St. Francis of Assisi's Blessed Wounds

This image of prayer as a wound that must not heal recalls another kind of blessed wound, notably received by St. Francis of Assisi (ca. 1181–1226), as St. Bonaventure recollects in *The Life of St. Francis* (*Legenda Maior*).[49] St. Francis's stigmata mark a turn in medieval mystical experience from the spiritual to the physical realm, where the spiritual mystical experience imprints itself physically onto the body.[50] To receive the stigmata is to receive on one's own body the marks of crucifixion that Christ received on the cross and retained with his resurrected body. In the preface to his account of St. Francis's life, Bonaventure extols Francis's receiving of the stigmata,

> irrefutable testimony of truth
> by the seal of the likeness of the living God,
> namely of Christ crucified,
> which was imprinted on his body
> not by natural forces or human skill
> but by the wondrous power
> of the spirit of the living God.[51]

---

48. Rambo, *Resurrecting Wounds*, 47.
49. Bonaventure, "Life of St. Francis."
50. Davidson, "Miracles of Bodily Transformation," 451–52.
 Of course, an opposite turn away from this medieval outlook occurred during the modern era. Vloeburg notes this shift in "Wounding Love." Vloeburg traces the development of modern medicine and the shift of pain from something purgative to something to be avoided (6). This shifts an account of the stigmata from a mystical encounter to a psychosomatic ailment or self-inflicted wound. The result of this shift was a kind of "battlefield" with the demythologization of the stigmata on the part of the scientific community and the exploitation of the stigmata on the part of the Church to align them with dogmatic claims (9).

51. Bonaventure, *Soul's Journey*, 182. Ewart Cousins, translator of *The Classics of Western Spirituality* collection of Bonaventure's writings, notes in his foreword that he has broken up the more poetic lines of Bonaventure's writing in "sense lines where this seemed appropriate," which takes on—as in this passage—the appearance of poetic verse (xx).

In the stigmata, Bonaventure recognizes the mark of deification where the human becomes perfected by participating in the divine life. Jesus Christ, as archetype and first fruit of perfected humanity, evidences his perfection in the cruciform image. In Bonaventure's *The Soul's Journey into God* (*Itinerarium Mentis in Deum*), he describes the mystical ascent from the world of the senses into the divine life as necessarily passing through Christ, for "Christ is the way and the door / Christ is the ladder and the vehicle."[52] The Christ Bonaventure images here is the crucified Christ, as Bonaventure summons his readers to see "him hanging upon the cross."[53]

Two years before his death, Francis received the stigmata. His stigmata aptly illustrate the relationship between wounding and blessing, vulnerability and prayer. Bonaventure depicts Francis's transformation through the crucified Christ's superabundant love. Bonaventure describes Francis praying on a mountainside at the start of a day when suddenly a Seraph—fitting the description of Isa 6:2, but with wings aflame—appears in front of him. Enclosed in the Seraph's wings was "the figure of a man crucified, with his hands and feet extended in the form of a cross and fastened to a cross."[54] Bonaventure details Francis's response to this vision: "When Francis saw this, he was overwhelmed and his heart was flooded with a mixture of joy and sorrow. He rejoiced because of the gracious way Christ looked upon him under the appearance of the Seraph, but the fact that he was fastened to a cross pierced his soul with a sword of compassionate sorrow (Luke 2:35)."[55] Overcome by emotion at this Seraphic vision, Francis understood that to be Christ's beloved is "to be totally transformed into the likeness of Christ crucified, not by the martyrdom of his flesh, but by the fire of his love consuming his soul."[56] Bonaventure goes on to describe the effect of this event on St. Francis:

> As the vision disappeared, it left in his heart a marvelous ardor and imprinted on his body markings that were no less marvelous. Immediately the marks of nails began to appear in his hands and feet just as he had seen a little before in the figure of the man crucified. His hands and feet seemed to be pierced through the center by nails, with the heads of the nails appearing on the inner side of the

---

52. Bonaventure, "Life of St. Francis," VII.1.
53. Bonaventure, "Life of St. Francis," VII.2.
54. Bonaventure, "Life of St. Francis," XIII.3.
55. Bonaventure, "Life of St. Francis," XIII.3.
56. Bonaventure, "Life of St. Francis," XIII.3.

hands and the upper side of the feet and the points on their opposite sides. The heads of the nails in his hands and feet were round and black; their points were oblong and bent as if driven back with a hammer, and they emerged from the flesh and stuck out beyond it. Also, his right side, as if pierced with a lance, was marked with a red wound from which his sacred blood often flowed, moistening his tunic and underwear.[57]

Bonaventure captures this scene with vivid imagery that draws out both the love-inducing vision of the Seraph with the cross-fixed Christ and the visceral description of the physical agony involved in receiving the stigmata.

Ilia Delio, in *Crucified Love: Bonaventure's Mysticism of the Crucified Christ*, stresses Bonaventure's emphasis on the deification of the human as involving the necessity of the whole person—the outward body and inward ensouled creature—as being in union with the crucified Christ.[58] Delio helpfully connects the image of union in *Soul's Journey* to Francis's stigmata recorded in *Life of St. Francis*: "Bonaventure views union with Christ as the power of the Spirit that both impresses and expresses. . . . In describing the Stigmata, he states that Francis was both 'inwardly inflamed and outwardly marked' indicating that Francis was both impressed by the burning love of Christ and expressed this love in his own flesh."[59] Here, Delio highlights the inherent relationship in Francis's mystical experience between the outward and inward realities of divine love. The pinnacle of Francis's mystical vision unites and integrates the invisible and intangible love of God with the visible and physical wounding of the flesh.

At the close of Bonaventure's description of Francis's stigmata, he notes that "sacred blood often flowed [from the wound on his side], moistening his tunic and underwear."[60] Bonaventure reiterates this point when discussing how Francis would try to hide his wounds and, most especially, concealing the wound on his side with clothing.[61] Bonaventure declares that this wound in particular continued to give him pain and never ceased to bleed: "Francis always wore underclothes that would reach up from his armpits to cover the wound on his side . . . the friars

---

57. Bonaventure, "Life of St. Francis," XIII.3.
58. Delio, *Crucified Love*, 80.
59. Delio, *Crucified Love*, 80.
60. Bonaventure, "Life of St. Francis," XIII.3.
61. Bonaventure, "Life of St. Francis," XIII.8.

who washed these [underclothes] or shook out his tunic from time to time . . . found these stained with blood."[62] Bonaventure describes Francis's wounds as never fully healing; in fact, it seems the wound on his side was minimally healed, if at all. These wounds are the wounds Chrétien refers to as wounds that *must* not heal, wounds that mark the dangerous gift of intimacy with God. Like Jacob, like Haze, Francis's stigmata wounds him in its blessing. The effect of the divine and human encounter marks and wounds the blessed individual.

Analogous to wounding prayer, a certain kind of reading event can make us vulnerable to wounds that bless. Namely, in reading spare narration—as we find in biblical Hebrew narrative and Flannery O'Connor's fiction—the need for inferring meaning in the ample narrative gaps puts readers at risk. Paratactic narration that discloses the possibility of God at work in the world makes readers vulnerable to their own wounding. These wounding reading events also offer a blessing to readers. Like the play of wounding and blessing in the stories of Jacob, St. Francis, and Hazel Motes, readers are invited into an act that can result not only in a deeper understanding of a story's showing of divine encounter, but also in a real encounter with divine grace.

Conclusion

This chapter began with O'Connor's plea that God bring her dead desire to life. O'Connor's prayer imagines this resurrecting of desire in her to be marked by suffering akin to the corroding and consuming effect of cancer. Her terrifying request is marked onto her stories when God's grace appears to her protagonists with violent and overwhelming force. Through an examination of Iser's description of what occurs in the event of reading and how the vulnerability of the reader more generally is intensified in the case of paratactic narration, I have shown the entanglement of readers with the stories rightly read. As with the personal entanglement inherent in good reading, I explored the spiritual and bodily entanglement inherent in prayer that wounds even as it blesses. In reading spare stories concerned with the in-breaking of the Uncreated Light into the created world, readers find an opportunity for encounter with God that shares a kinship with the vulnerability we find in prayer. An opportunity

---

62. Bonaventure, "Life of St. Francis," XIII.8.

to be met, wounded, and blessed by God. In the next chapter, I turn to O'Connor's short stories to draw out how her stylistic asceticism—spare in form and with the readerly posture of prayer—wounds in ways that humiliate, implicate, and overflow with Christ's love.

Chapter 6

Blessed Wounds of Reading

"The River," "The Enduring Chill,"
"Parker's Back"

Introduction

IN A 1970 REVIEW of *Mystery and Manners*, Miles D. Orvell writes that O'Connor's "critics and reviewers from the very first have written of her with an air of confidence and comprehension. But their own judgments and analyses have too often betrayed a groping around the peripheries of the fiction, a failure to come to grips with the mysterious reality that is at the heart of her best stories, and that seems to elude any easy specification."[1] The result is that a reader of O'Connor's fiction finds they are "like a dumb witness," Orvell surmises, where "he has had the experience—he is sure of that—but he has missed the meaning."[2] Not only does this statement succinctly summarize the confrontation of our limits when reading O'Connor's fiction, it also alludes to the experience of reading more generally. The *experience* of reading is what Orvell points to when discussing the way readers function like a "dumb witness." Building upon O'Connor's own claim that discovering a story's meaning is about experience of it rather than abstraction from it, Orvell writes: "*Experience meaning.* That is what has been missing from most discussions of O'Connor's works, as, all too often, one senses a critical faculty cut off from the resources of the whole

---

1. Orvell, "Flannery O'Connor," 184.
2. Orvell, "Flannery O'Connor," 184–85.

person."³ Deriving meaning from O'Connor's stories comes about only through readerly entanglement in her fictional world.

Reading O'Connor's skeletal and rapidly-paced narratives leave readers dizzied at a story's end. Often, this dizzying effect is not a positive one. It is not uncommon to find readers who when asked whether they have encountered any of O'Connor's stories respond with furrowed brow or pursed lips, declaring that they have read her stories and are unsure what to make of the disagreeable protagonists and considerable violence. The spare quality of these stories, lacking explanation for why the grotesque actions appear where and when they do, does not help those looking for justification for the frequent recourse to violence. Of course, this spare quality of O'Connor's fiction combined with excessive and violent scenes is also what makes her fiction both powerful and memorable. Often, the attitude towards the haunting effect of O'Connor's writing style serves as the dividing line between fans and foes of O'Connor's work.

In this chapter, I look to three stories that capture the distinctive ways O'Connor's spare style entangles readers in meaning-making and offers a kind of blessed wounding event. In a reading of "The River," I explore how the death of a young boy confounds, even humiliates, readers and makes difficult the designation of the story as either a tragedy or comedy. I turn to "The Enduring Chill" to show how O'Connor's protagonist reflects back on us as readers (and O'Connor as author) in ways that implicate us in our pride and folly. Finally, I offer a reading of "Parker's Back" that illustrates how Christ's love overflows in a stigmatic event within the story and offers an opportunity to encounter that wounding love through the act of reading. Ultimately, I show how O'Connor's spare style places us as readers in a posture akin to prayer where we may be wounded and blessed.

Wounds of Humiliation: "The River"

First, some reading wounds humiliate. When Chrétien describes the wounding effect of prayer, he emphasizes the imbalance of the encounter in a word spoken to God. To speak a word to a divine Other is to speak to a being radically different than ourselves. We, finite creatures, place ourselves before God, infinite and perfect, and await a response. That vulnerability of encounter is also found in the reading event. As seen in Iser's description of the act of reading, interpreting a text is always an adventure of inference

3. Orvell, "Flannery O'Connor," 191–92.

where the story is taken up by our imaginations. Gap-filling is part of all reading events, but paratactic narrative, with its lack of causal connections and rapid narrative pace, places greater demands on readers to fill the gaps within a text. The demanding nature of this kind of storytelling can be viewed as too challenging for modern readers, as Caroline Gordon posits regarding O'Connor's narrative style. This challenge, as I have argued, is what gives O'Connor her distinctive narrative voice and impact. To combine Chrétien's and Iser's thoughts, we might say that spare narration both places us at the limits of our understanding while simultaneously requiring abundant imaginative work to bring the narrative world to life.

Spare narration forces an awareness of our limits and places great demands on us at those limits to infer and produce meaning. This paradoxical demand reveals our inadequacy and pushes readers towards a posture of humility. Readers are humbled in reading the difficult stories that make up O'Connor's corpus because rarely can one "capture" the meaning of a story in all its complexity through an initial, or even repeated, read-through. Further, the demands and revelation of epistemic limits when reading paratactic narration can produce a more drastic effect than a posture of humility—it can *humiliate*. While humbled readers modestly recognize their own limits, humiliated readers stand overpowered in the face of their inability to fill the gaps of a story sufficiently and satisfactorily.

Consider young Bevel in "The River," a boy who commits to go down into the waters of baptism so fully that he finds the Kingdom of God, resulting in his death. Then there is nine-year-old Mary Fortune meeting her end at the hand of her seventy-nine-year-old grandfather strangling her and bashing her head repeatedly against a rock at the close of "A View of the Woods." These kinds of stories can push readers beyond wrestling with the paradoxical grotesque images of redemption via stolen wooden limbs and gorging bulls into antagonistic readings that never cease to confound and evade satisfactory interpretations. The humiliation of recognizing our own limits as readers invites a kind of limitless surrender before God. As in prayer, the humiliating wound of reading invites a posture of dispossession where we invite God into our defeat so that he might be victorious.

To explore the readerly wound of humiliation, I turn to a reading of "The River" that draws out the perplexing, muddled, and evocative nature of O'Connor's fiction. While O'Connor's stories are infamous for confounding readers with their freakish characters and bizarre scenes of redemption, none rival "The River" for its challenging picture of a young boy seeking the kingdom of heaven by baptizing himself in a river. O'Connor points to the grotesque as functioning to startle readers into paying attention to what often remains hidden under the routine of everyday life. Despite O'Connor's fiction brimming over with grotesque acts of violence, arguably the most unsettling of all climaxes for readers involves no weapons, violence, or blood as young boy Bevel pushes his head under water in what might be deemed by some as a suicide yet permeated with innocence. The unsettling quality of the climax of "The River" results from the story's unwillingness to be rendered easily as a story of tragedy or redemption.

"The River" begins with an introduction to the story's protagonist: Harry Ashfield, a boy of four or five years who lives in the city with his socialite parents. The story opens as the boy heads out for the day with the hired-help of Mrs. Connin while his parents recover from the last night's drunken social engagement. Mrs. Connin announces to the boy her plan for the day: heading to a river in the country to hear a message from the itinerant preacher Reverend Bevel Summers. With his interest piqued, Harry reports to Mrs. Connin that his name is also Bevel. The narrator tells us that boy Bevel did not mean to lie to Mrs. Connin, but instead had simply never considered until that moment that he might want to change his name (CW, 156).

The preacher's effect on the boy extends well beyond the boy's falsification of his name. When Mrs. Connin and boy Bevel arrive at the riverbank, the preacher is standing knee deep in the river insisting that what he preaches is not a quick-fix miracle but an invitation into "the River of Life, made out of Jesus' blood" (CW, 162). This river will carry those who dwell in it through their pain and into the Kingdom of Christ. At first, the boy is simply entertained by the preacher. Knowing nothing about religion and quite amused by the spectacle before him, the young Bevel comes to find these events less humorous when Bevel Summers prepares to baptize the boy. Like the adoption of the preacher's name, the boy adopts the preacher's solemnity as he is dunked upside down into the water. When the boy returns to an upright position, the preacher declares: "You count now, you didn't even count before" (CW, 165). The next day, boy Bevel returns alone to the same riverbank to "baptize himself and to keep on going this time until he found the Kingdom of Christ in the river" (CW, 171). After a first failed attempt, the boy successfully catches an undercurrent and is pulled underwater and ostensibly into the Kingdom of Christ—where he "counts." What kind of judgment are we to make about the ending of O'Connor's "The River?" Is a boy of four or five years seeking the Kingdom of God in the river's current a tragedy or a comedy? Is this a happy end or a sad one?

In *The Comedy of Redemption: Christian Faith and Comic Vision in Four American Novels*, Ralph C. Wood identifies O'Connor's stories as comedies of redemption.[4] The unsettling effect of her fiction resides in the traits of her stories' heroes: the prideful, narcissistic, judgmental, and often foolish protagonists stumble, even resist, grace when it is presented to them. Grace functions in her narratives as the ultimate referent to God's claim on the world and often appears to its receivers as a tyrant rather than friend. The confrontation of a story's hero with grace regularly takes on the appearance of violent and grotesque action.[5] These comedies of redemption often seem to be tragedies, but when readers dig deeper, Wood insists, they will find that though the climactic moments are scenes of disfigurement, violence, and often death, the intimation is grace: grace often found by the protagonist in a reluctant acknowledgement of God's love for and claim over the world.

While not all of O'Connor's protagonists accept the grace offered to them, Wood emphasizes that in confrontations with grace all the protagonists are faced with the inescapable affirmation or denial of the truth of the Gospel. Though O'Connor's fiction narrates the wounding of her heroes, the wounding only begins to narrate the conflict for the protagonist. The wounding serves as the catalyst for redemption. Thus, in the case of "The River," boy Bevel's action reflects an affirmation of the truth of the Gospel, even if the affirmation's form is crude and the one affirming has yet to reach the age of reason. In his later work, *Flannery O'Connor and the Christ-Haunted South*, Wood offers a succinct reading of the boy's final act:

> O'Connor does not narrate the inner reasoning that prompts the boy's final decision after he returns home, but the child's naïve logic is not difficult to fathom: if he were made to count so much for having stayed under the water so briefly, he could count totally if he stayed under the water permanently. Far from committing a despairing act of suicide, therefore, young Ashfield returns to the scene of his baptism to find the new life by plunging beneath the

---

4. Wood does not write specifically on "The River" in this work aside from a brief mention of a portion of preacher Bevel's sermon (91), but he also does not preclude this story from his overarching designation of "comedies of redemption." As we will see subsequently, in his later work *Christ-Haunted South* Wood leaves no doubt that he reads this story as a comedy.

5. Wood, *Comedy of Redemption*, 81.

river's surface, and thus to abandon the old death by leaving his unloving parents.[6]

Wood does not ask us to miss the childishness of Bevel as he plunges under the water; but, he also would not want us to miss the boy's desire for God in it that he first found in his baptism the day before.[7] A neglected and overlooked boy here finds Christ's love and delves into the river to become fully alive in the kingdom of God. Wood concludes of this story: "The child Ashfield enters into the community of perpetual praise by way of a *supremely happy ending* to a *supremely happy story*.[8]

In what follows, I employ Rowan Williams's work on the tragic imagination to complicate, without necessarily undercutting, Wood's argument and reading of "The River" as a comedy of redemption.[9] By complicating Wood's proposal, I do not want to do away with the ultimate claim made in these kinds of comedies: the life, death, and resurrection of Jesus Christ. This claim grounds the narrative worlds of Flannery O'Connor's stories. Instead, I want to recognize that while the comic element of a story like "The River" has merit, as a stand-alone it fails to reckon with the hardest part of this story: are we meant to celebrate this act of a neglected and attention-starved young boy? Here, we are not dealing with a hardened and disillusioned adult, but a boy at the age where he might learn to count to ten and ride a tricycle. Is deeming the story a "supremely happy" one sufficient?

Rowan Williams introduces *The Tragic Imagination* with the assertion that tragedy is "honest about what is utterly unresolved in human experience, what cannot be made sense of (if making sense means showing why it's really a good thing)."[10] Williams identifies tragedy as an opportunity to respond actively to often senseless or unanswered suffering. This tragic response does not explain away suffering but instead provides a means of imaginatively speaking about the sort of suffering that runs the risk of rendering us mute. Unspeakable injustices happen to us, yet we are still able to speak about them in some way through tragic representation.[11] Tragedy's ability to refuse reso-

---

6. Wood, *Christ-Haunted South*, 172.

7. Wood hints at this lack of idealizing when he writes that the boy seeks "in a watery and literal-minded way" death and new life in Christ through the waters of baptism (*Christ-Haunted South*, 173).

8. Wood, *Christ-Haunted South*, 172, italics added for emphasis.

9. Williams, *Tragic Imagination*.

10. Williams, *Tragic Imagination*, 1.

11. Williams writes that "the business of tragedy" involves "how *some* pain can be

lution enables its audience to approach the unresolved areas of suffering in daily life with new questions and insights. Tragic representation acknowledges the elusive elements in human experience.

Both suffering and revelation can be narratively presented in a way that opens up rather than shuts down how to speak about the seemingly unspeakably heartbreaking or elusive. As we dramatically render the tragic, we recognize that we may never truly or fully understand the stories we find so familiar and overwhelming—stories of death, heartbreak, and ruin. In narrating tragedy, Williams notes, we come "to recognize what we don't know and can't say."[12]

O'Connor's narratives, in a similar way, expose the reader's false confidence regarding how God works in the world. This moment of disillusion is also a revelation: "[i]t is a reminder of why a dramatic representation that shows us what disaster does not silence or exhaust might be called a showing of the sacred, that excess of unearned, unexpected life that sustains us in going on speaking and thinking."[13] Tragic representation centers not on explanation or absolute despair but on how we can continue to speak about some of the most difficult aspects of human existence while honestly grappling with the dimensions of suffering that elude our descriptions.

Differing from Wood in emphasis, Williams identifies a tragic dimension to the Christian faith. For example, Williams sees the Gospel of John as a tragedy in that it boldly narrates the human capacity for misrecognition when the savior is crucified by those he came to set free. Williams writes, "the Gospel of John dramatizes the connection between ignorance and refusal of the truth, loss of identity and capacity to speak, awareness of unmanageable contingency and the emergent possibility of new speech."[14] The tragic element of the Christian narrative refuses a resolution to the misrecognition of Christ as criminal and worthy of crucifixion. Christ's suffering and humanity's failure to recognize God even when he dwells among us is not "cancelled or even compensated by the hope of ultimate reconciliation."[15] But, tragedy also does not preclude hope. Instead, tragic representation reveals what suffering and injustice cannot annihilate: the

---

spoken of and understood, 'humanized', and some cannot, because the words are not yet there and, so far as we can know, may never be" (Williams, *Tragic Imagination*, 41).

12. Williams, *Tragic Imagination*, 42.
13. Williams, *Tragic Imagination*, 27.
14. Williams, *Tragic Imagination*, 121.
15. Williams, *Tragic Imagination*, 124.

human ability to represent suffering imaginatively without mitigating the pain or shutting down in the face of despair.

Returning to "The River," in its final scene boy Bevel is not alone as he tries to baptize himself once and for all. Mr. Paradise, who had appeared the day before as a mocking onlooker when the elder Bevel preached, secretly followed the boy on his return visit to the river. As the boy makes his first attempt at remaining underwater, Mr. Paradise watches him furtively from a distance. After the boy's first failed attempt, the man bounds into the water with all the grace of a giant swine shouting at the boy and waving his hands with the offer of a peppermint stick. The boy sees the man running towards him, rushes back under the river's surface, and "this time, the waiting current caught him like a long gentle hand and pulled him swiftly forward and down. For an instant he was overcome with surprise; then since he knew that he was getting somewhere, all his fury and fear left him" (CW, 171). Undoubtedly, Mr. Paradise's intentions with Bevel when he grabbed a foot-long, two-inch thick peppermint stick and followed the boy to the river are suspect. Not only are readers provided with the phallic imagery of the candy, but Mr. Paradise's aim to lure the boy with sweets suggests these are the actions of a man of ill-intention.

Does Bevel's second and successful attempt after seeing Mr. Paradise solidify the boy's death as a happy ending? Not only does he avoid returning to his neglectful home life, but he escapes the imminent danger of the man with a peppermint stick. Moreover, Bevel's permanent act of going under the waters of baptism speaks to his proper eschatological end. The Kingdom of Christ, not his absent parents or Mr. Paradise, becomes Bevel's final concern—the ultimate things triumph over the penultimate. In this way, is "The River" truly about the comedy of redemption? Maybe it is, but I do not find this answer entirely satisfying.[16]

---

16. I recall teaching this story with Ralph Wood to an honor's section of undergraduates at Baylor University. To call this reading unsatisfying undersells the reaction we received from students. Their capacity for empathy with the boy who just wanted to count and anger towards his neglectful parents was quite overwhelming. For some of the students, I could sense that their investment in the story and inability to resolve it well (especially as a good end) left a bad taste in their mouth for O'Connor. While this may seem like the kind of response an educator would not desire in the classroom, I am not sure that is the case in this instance. O'Connor's stories push readers into the uncomfortable space of reckoning with concepts that challenge, befuddle, and overwhelm readers. O'Connor's stories resist easy and pat explanations for the ways God works in the human heart and the ways we actively (or accidentally) confuse and/or resist that grace. Their response that day in class was entirely fitting for a story as difficult and evocative as "The River."

Making the definitive claim that "The River" is a comedy rather than tragedy undercuts, if not risks ignoring entirely, the sorrow that accompanies the reading of this story—even if the sorrow is mingled with joy. A young boy misunderstands the message of the Gospel, believing that baptizing himself in this way is the best means to assure that he "counts." The fact that he is an especially insightful boy, able to comprehend, in a fashion, the transformation that occurs in baptism in a way that many of the onlookers do not adds to the grief aroused at his misunderstanding. I believe that we can hold together the truth and power of what the boy finds in the preacher's words *and* affirm that the boy's final act was the result of a misunderstanding both of what baptism accomplishes and what it means "to count" in the Kingdom of God.

Boy Bevel does not only misunderstand the preacher's message, but he is a neglected child living in a home where leftover anchovy paste and room temperature ginger ale from the previous night's party serve as his last meal before he heads to the river. To add to Bevel's unfortunate situation, Bevel is unlucky enough to have the only potential savior figure outside of finding Christ in the river turn out to be a bitter man with a questionable agenda. In this story, we confront injustice committed against one of the least of these; a life of neglect and potential abuse rendered credibly because this world is full of wrongs against the innocent.

Can we hold together the affirmation of a comedic end to the story in Bevel's belief that "he was getting somewhere" (CW, 171) as the current swept him away, while also affirming the tragic and fatal end of a young boy who is caught between absent parents and a pedophile, and who holds the naïve belief that going down into the waters of baptism and staying there is the best way to assure he counts? "The River" serves as an exemplary case of the ways O'Connor's stories can humble, even humiliate readers. It remains for me a story that fails to resolve succinctly as a comedy or a tragedy, with an uncomplicated good or bad end. It continues to elude any clear and final interpretation. What I can say is this: I find the boy's desire to meet Christ in the river a good one in that he understands the truth of the Gospel in a way many of us, like the story's onlookers, miss. I want to believe that Jesus does in fact meet him on the other end of the river's current. But, I do not think that this assessment disallows sadness. In fact, I think that elements of the story invite us to hold together the joy of the boy's desire for God and the sadness of a boy of only four or five pushing himself below the water's surface at the story's close. In a similar way, I feel sadness when faced with the events at Golgotha and the wounds that Christ bears in his resurrected body, even as these things are also means and signs of a greater hope than that grief. Good Friday is in fact good, but it is also a day clothed in the color of mourning.

Wounds of Implication: "The Enduring Chill"

Flannery O'Connor's stories offer readers a fresh, sometimes disturbing, reflection of themselves. "The Enduring Chill" exemplifies how O'Connor's stories extend an opportunity to all involved—fictional and real alike—to see themselves as they truly are. Notably, in "The Enduring Chill" we find an example not only how we as readers may be implicated in O'Connor's stories, but also of how she may have seen herself in the central protagonist, Asbury Fox.

On closer examination, the kinship between O'Connor and Asbury is hard to miss. The short story begins with a train pulling into a small town, which a disembarking sickly artist begrudgingly calls home. The artist, leaving behind the culture and thrill of the big city, is greeted by a worried, overbearing mother and underwhelming skyline. O'Connor herself made the unexpected journey home half a decade before writing "The Enduring Chill." Just beginning to find a foothold in the writing world and at the start of writing her first novel, *Wise Blood*, O'Connor fell ill and made the long train ride from the Northeast to the Deep South, growing increasingly ill on her journey. Returning to Milledgeville, she initially thought her stay back in Georgia would be short-lived. In her letters it is clear that this illness took her by surprise, and she expected it to be an anomaly, writing in one letter that "This was none of my plan" and in another that she "don't expect to be ill again any time soon after such a radical cure" (CW, 886–87). While possessing a sometimes prophetic second-sight, O'Connor here did not comprehend that this health "anomaly" would become a defining feature of the remainder of her life.

Unlike his creator, Asbury's journey home was expected to be his final one. In a mawkish delight in his own death, at the start of the story he must come to terms with dying not as a starving artist in New York, but here in Timberboro, a backwater town, his home: "He had become entirely accustomed to death, but he had not become accustomed to the thought of death *here*" (CW, 548). We are offered an onslaught of reminders of what "*here*" is to Asbury in the early pages of the story, most notably and irritatingly for

Asbury by his mother, Mrs. Fox, as they pull up to his childhood home and she declares, "Home again, home again jiggity jig!" (CW, 553).

John D. Sykes Jr. notes an additional shared feature between O'Connor and Asbury that deepens the unique quality of this particular story's autobiographical nature. While a likeness to O'Connor sometimes appears in some form in her stories, it is most often in an intellectual and not, as in this story, through a self-reference as direct as a writer, with Asbury as a failed playwright.[17] In "The Enduring Chill," we find a protagonist much closer to home to O'Connor herself. In Asbury, we can imagine that O'Connor parodies not only the caricature of the inflated-ego artist, but of her own temptations for self-inflation after returning home from the big city. While I acknowledge the risk of psychologizing O'Connor, she gives us enough of herself in Asbury to recognize how close to home this story comes. An additional hint on the unique quality of Asbury is found in her consideration of using him again in a future story (HB, 261, 330). Later, in working on her final and incomplete writing project *Why Do the Heathens Rage?*, O'Connor considered using "The Enduring Chill" as its first chapter, which would place conversion at the start rather than end of her stories—a stark contrast to her usual story progression.[18] This return to Asbury in her later novel evidences that he remained with her in a unique way—she wasn't done with him yet.

Brad Gooch, in his biography of O'Connor, connects her personal and fictional life with what he calls "a coded spiritual autobiography."[19] At the close of "The Enduring Chill," protagonist Asbury lies in bed after the revelation that he is not a tortured artist on his deathbed but a fool who brought undulant fever on himself by drinking unpasteurized milk. For O'Connor to depict this scene of the prideful intellectual being wracked by fever and chills because of his own stupidity hints at the possibility that O'Connor—an intelligent woman who herself prays for a desire for God so as to wrack her with suffering—subjectively identifies with Asbury.[20] The destabilization

17. Sykes, "Portraits of the Artist," 24.
18. Wray, "Flannery O'Connor's *Why Do the Heathen Rage?*," 2.
19. Gooch, *Life of Flannery O'Connor*, 373.
20. In a later letter, written April 6, 1960 to professor of English Dr. T. R. Spivey, O'Connor clarifies her view of the gift of the Holy Spirit (specifically, as available in the Eucharist) in contrast to Spivey's: "I don't think you are unfair to me in what you say about my stage of development etc. though I have a much less romantic view of how the Holy Spirit operates than you do. The sins of pride & selfishness and reluctance to wrestle with the Spirit are certainly mine but I have been working at them a long time and will

of Asbury's confidence in his own intelligence and superiority over those around him prepares him for a mysterious encounter that at once terrifies and transforms his vision for the rest of his life.

Earlier in the story, Father Finn, the rough-hewn, unsophisticated, plain country priest, had catechized Asbury—much to his disgust—by asking him such questions as these: "How do you expect to get what you don't ask for? God does not send the Holy Ghost to those who don't ask for Him.... How can the Holy Ghost fill your soul when it's full of trash? The Holy Ghost will not come until you see yourself as you are—a lazy ignorant conceited youth!" (CW, 567). O'Connor offers us here a minimal, verging on inadequate, but ultimately effective preparation for the grace that soon comes down from his water-stained ceiling. That Asbury has made a more than nominal act of repentance is proved in his retrieving of the key to the drawer containing his blistering critique of his mother for allegedly crushing his creative powers. Now that he has been consigned to a painful sentence of lifelong illness rather than a convenient, much-desired escape via death, Asbury does not want his mother to read his awful screed of accusation against her. No sooner has he put the key back into his pocket than Asbury gazes into a bedside mirror to behold a vision of his evacuated face and eyes, now emptied of all their "trash": "They looked shocked clean as if they had been prepared for some awful vision about to come down on him" (CW, 572). Asbury's sickness, originally seen as his romanticized escape hatch from the world, now becomes a place of a healing and blessing in it: "The old life in him was exhausted. He awaited the coming of the new" (CW, 572). A new kind of suffering descends on Asbury, not of undulant fever, but of divine rapture and cleansing:

> It was then that he felt the beginning of a chill, a chill so peculiar, so light that it was like a warm ripple across a deeper sea of cold. His breathe came short. The fierce bird which through the years of his childhood and the days of his illness had been poised over his head, waiting mysteriously, appeared all at once to be in motion. Asbury blanched and the last film of illusion was torn as if by a whirlwind from his eyes. He saw that for the rest of his days, *frail, wracked, but enduring, he would live in the face of purifying terror.* A feeble cry, a last impossible protest escaped him. But the Holy

---

be still doing it when I am on my deathbed. I believe that God's love for us is so great that He does not wait until we are purified to such a great extent before He allows us to receive him" (HB, 386).

Ghost, emblazed in ice instead of fire, continued, implacable, to descend. (CW, 572, italics added)

O'Connor's prayer for her "dead desire" to be made alive is enacted in Asbury. The fever, which would wrack Asbury's body for the rest of his life, becomes like a cancer—terrorizing him with what theologian Rowan Williams terms "reality in the light of God." Again and again, O'Connor blessedly afflicts her protagonists with this terrifying blessing. Her prayer that God stir desire in her hints that this terrorizing of her protagonist is rooted in her own desire for an assault—a wounding—from God.[21]

O'Connor and Asbury share a kinship in their parallel returns home. In a way, this opportunity to return home is extended to readers. As we read stories, we both identify with and distinguish ourselves from the characters. Reading stories is unlike other narrative worlds we build—by watching cinema, beholding a piece of fine art, or taking in a play or musical. This kind of narrative encounter is distinctive because with limited information, we image a narrative world. Recall how Iser describes this need to image the world in order to occupy it as a kind of "optical poverty" that requires readers to "illuminate the character, not as an object, but as a bearer of meaning."[22] Watching movies or theatre performances does not produce this kind of poverty because the image at least in part is given to us; the character as an object stands virtually or actually before us.

---

21. Another clear example of O'Connor's protagonists' dead desire in need of awakening is found in "Greenleaf" when Mrs. May is shocked and embarrassed by Mrs. Greenleaf's ecstatic prayer: "'Oh Jesus, stab me in the heart!'" (CW, 507). While Mrs. May might insist that Mrs. Greenleaf be ashamed of herself for not acting as a good Christian, Mrs. May is the one who should truly be praying this prayer of blessed wounding. Richard Giannone, in *Flannery O'Connor, Hermit Novelist*, likens Mrs. Greenleaf's behavior to the Desert Mothers in her plea (Giannone, *Hermit Novelist*, 196). In Mrs. May, unlike Mrs. Greenleaf, Giannone argues there is also something of the asceticism of the desert dweller. But, whereas Mrs. Greenleaf enacts the life of an ancient desert mother, Mrs. May experiences the desert—at least until her final whispered confession as the bull gores her to death—without the life-giving work of the Spirit: "She [Mrs. May] is a desert person because she leads the desert life. . . . As a would-be desert-dweller, she endures its physical and psychological hardships without deriving its inward grace" (Giannone, *Hermit Novelist*, 198).

The call for a stabbed heart also echoes Julian of Norwich, who in her tenth vision, as she contemplates the wounded side of Christ, comments that his blessed heart is split in two (*Revelations of Divine Love*, Vision 10, Chapter 24). This contemplation leads Julian to rejoice that Christ's wounds have turned sorrow into joy, where Christ's split side and pierced heart are expressions of his love.

22. Iser, *Act of Reading*, 138.

Literature does not give us this image, so we must image the characters in such a way that requires our involvement in not only imagining an action but also the subject who acts.

The result of this kind of imaging produces a distinctive indwelling within the narrative, Iser notes, "because it has no existence of its own and because we are imagining and producing it, *we are actually in its presence and it is in ours.*"[23] We must occupy the narrative world in a way more immediate and intimate than some other kinds of artistic encounters because we provide some of the material goods for the narrative world and its characters in order for it to exist at all. While all literature requires this kind of imaging, the sparely-wrought narration we find in O'Connor's fiction demands greater personal investment in both imagining and indwelling a fictional world. When a character morally fails or intellectually stumbles, spare narration does not give us much in the way of a character's motive or perception of the event, nor of the narrator's judgment of the action. Readers of spare narrative are left to infer meaning for a character's actions that we were intimately involved with imaging in the first place.

This investment produces a double-edged reading effect: confrontation with a character's failings and the possibility of our own. We play a part in imaging characters who do wrong or foolish things, and we as readers are left to infer why these characters would do such an action or speak such a word. Rather than simply seeing ourselves reflected in characters, we are much more intimately involved—we are present, in some way, in them, which makes us more vulnerable to being *implicated* by their actions.

So, when we find Asbury on his death-turned-sick bed coming to terms both with his own folly that got him to this point and "the last film of illusion" being violently torn from his eyes, we might find ourselves not only imagining Asbury's terror with this new sight but asking what illusory screens stand between our eyes and seeing the world as it is. In a letter to Betty Hester, O'Connor describes Asbury's enduring chill at the story's close not so much as a conversion but as a revelation that doesn't preclude the possibility of a later conversion: "he undeniably realizes that he's going to live with the new knowledge that he knows nothing. That really is what he is frozen in—humility. Faith can come later" (HB, 261).

Maybe we find the self-absorbed and self-important Asbury a little too close to home, mirroring our own skewed vision and folly. In Asbury, we see that we also know nothing and must be frozen in humility. Maybe

---

23. Iser, *Act of Reading*, 139, italics added.

we, like O'Connor, find ourselves praying for that dead desire to be made alive in us even if it hurts, even kills us. The fact that O'Connor's fiction leaves out so much in the way of narrative details, interior motivations, and detailed dénouement following her dramatic climactic moments demands that we must earnestly entangle ourselves in these stories. Readers must provide the raw materials to imagine and interpret these gapped spaces. We must interpret the stories by not standing outside the fictional world with "suspended disbelief," but quite the opposite: by reading ourselves, our raw material, in these terrifying stories of graced encounters.[24]

Wounds That Overflow: "Parker's Back"

The undeniable quality of O'Connor's fiction is that her stories stick with readers, for good or ill. Particular images and scenes continue to challenge readers, like boy Bevel's final act, or offer the opportunity for self-reflection, like Asbury's diagnosis with undulant fever. This haunting effect can also be seen narratively within the stories, maybe most notably in "Parker's Back." Just after O.E. Parker receives Christ's face tattooed on his back, we are told: "The artist took him [Parker] roughly by the arm and propelled him between the two mirrors. 'Now *look*,' he said, angry at having his work ignored. Parker looked, turned white, and moved away. The eyes in the reflected face continued to look at him—still, straight, all-demanding, enclosed in silence" (CW, 670). The story is working its way towards its climax when Parker beholds the Christ's exacting gaze. The narrative force arrives in its fullness later, when Christ's face and Parker's back grow purple with the abuses hurled at them.

In what would be the final month of her life, O'Connor worked away on "Parker's Back." This story reflects the maturing of her skills as a writer

---

24. I use scare quotes around the language of suspending disbelief, because I do not wish to suggest that reading fiction is a suspension of our capacity for reason (in fact, I want to argue the opposite). In his exceptional essay "On Fairy-Stories," J. R. R. Tolkien rejects the notion of the "'willing suspension of disbelief'" as describing the act of reading (Tolkien, *Tolkien Reader*, 60). Tolkien argues that the moment readers feel they must suspend disbelief, the enchantment of indwelling a story is removed and readers are left "looking at the little abortive Secondary World from the outside" (60). A good storyteller creates a fictional world that enchants readers, making the fictional world true and not make-believe (60–61). Tolkien's insistence on the enchanted fictional world resonates with Iser's language of the participation required for readers of literature. Readers occupy a posture of entanglement, not laboratory observation, to produce sufficient meaning from a story.

(as well as the difficult task of distinguishing how this work might had turned out differently had O'Connor not been so ill as she completed this story). While the story offers a less spare form of storytelling with more narrative comment than we find particularly in her earlier stories, the climax of this story remains skeletal in style.

Caroline Gordon provides expansive notes on edits for "Parker's Back," which unsurprisingly include the desire for a more fleshed-out final scene with more narrative action to offer suitable weightiness to the story's close. This weightiness, Gordon argues, is needed both at the story's open and close to create a well composed narrative structure, like "that of a 'cathedral' or Roman arch."[25] Gordon describes the proclivity to "substitute comment for action" as O'Connor's "chief fault as a fiction writer."[26] That is, where O'Connor writes brief description, Gordon desires to see more expansive narrative action. Gordon identifies numerous places in the story where O'Connor should slow down "in order to give the reader time to take in what is happening."[27] This need to provide the reader more time to take in the scene is particularly important in a story like "Parker's Back," Gordon emphasizes, with meaning residing both on the literal and allegorical levels of the story.[28] As the story stands, Gordon accuses O'Connor of moving too hastily through vital scenes wherein trying to "get over the ground fast you blur the effect."[29]

We do not have to guess in this instance what O'Connor made of these comments. She writes to her friend Betty Hester: "Caroline gave me a lot of advice about the story but most if it I'm ignoring. She thinks every story must be built according to the pattern of the Roman arch and she would enlarge the beginning and the end, but I'm letting it lay. I did well to write it at all" (CW, 1218). O'Connor's melancholic response might come as a surprise to the chorus of readers who cherish "Parker's Back." I believe, however, that this story comes to us not only by way of a suffering and exhausted artist, but also from a writer whose craft had been honed for over a decade of analysis, critique, and a disciplined practice of writing. In this story, we find some of the best of O'Connor's artistry as she weaves together the cosmic

---

25. Flanagan, *Letters*, 218.
26. Flanagan, *Letters*, 219.
27. Flanagan, *Letters*, 220.
28. Flanagan, *Letters*, 220. Gordon describes the second level as "the level that says something other, something more than what has been said on the literal level" (219).
29. Flanagan, *Letters*, 219.

story of redemption with a refusal to render that redemption as cheap or implausible. O'Connor's stylistic asceticism works in this story to render reality credibly in the light of God—for Parker and for us.

In the story's early pages, we are told why Parker desires to cover his body in tattoos. As a nondescript fourteen year-old, Parker saw a man in a fair sideshow tent who was on display as a freak of nature with his nearly naked body covered in tattoos: "[t]he man, who was small and sturdy, moved about on the platform, flexing his muscles so that the arabesque of men and beasts and flowers on his skin appeared to have a subtle motion of its own" (CW, 657). While the tattooed man flexed his muscles and slowly turned to display his tattoos, young Parker stood on a bench peering over the heads of the spectators, caught up in emotion and awe: "Parker had never before felt the least motion of wonder in himself. Until he saw the man at the fair, it did not enter his head that there was anything out of the ordinary about the fact that he existed. Even then it did not enter his head, but *a peculiar unease* settled in him. It was as if a blind boy had been turned so gently in a different direction that he did not know his destination had been changed" (658, italics added). This "peculiar unease" would drive Parker to cover his body in tattoos, seeking to satisfy this growing dissatisfaction in himself.[30] While each new tattoo would make him feel sated for a brief time, he would quickly long for another. Unlike the freak at the sideshow whose tattoos appeared as "one intricate arabesque of colors," Parker's body took on the look of something "haphazard and botched" (CW, 659).

As we reach the central scenes of the story, the front of Parker's body is nearly covered with tattoos and his displeasure with life and existential dread peaked. He aims to finally get a tattoo that his wife, Sarah Ruth, "would not be able to resist" (664). He heads straight to the tattoo parlor in the city after a tractor crash that leaves him shoeless and scrambling from a raging fire. He storms into the parlor voracious for a tattoo that would satisfy Sarah Ruth and still his disquiet spirit. When he beholds the image of the Byzantine Christ, his heart races, stops, then starts again as if in rebirth. The tattoo artist asks if this is what he wants, Parker replies "'Just like it is . . . just like it is or nothing'" (667). After years of haphazard tattoos of eagles, lions, monarchs, and anchors, Parker's desire was specific, weighty, and resolute.

---

30. Andrew J. Garavel offers a helpful reading of Parker's dissatisfaction through an Augustinian lens, drawing out his compulsion for tattoos that reaches its apex in the one on his back (Bosco and Little, *Revelation and Convergence*, 146–65).

The events that follow this scene play out a transformation in Parker, which unravel and remake him as "a stranger to himself" (CW, 627). Amid this upheaval, he desires to assert some level of control over his situation and heads home to Sarah Ruth. He bangs on the door, tries the doorknob, yelling that she let him in. Despite his attempts to assert his authority over his wife, himself, and this situation, Sarah Ruth's response collapses any pretenses. She refuses to open the door until he uses his proper name, upon opening the door despises his new tattoo, and in turn beats it and him with a broom.

Here, Gordon advises that the story needs more narrative action—more detail to fill in the events that unfold. Instead, O'Connor offers her readers the barest descriptions of one of the most dramatic conversion moments in all her short stories. With Parker's back bruised and Christ's face covered in welts, we are left watching Parker through Sarah Ruth's eyes as he is "leaning against the tree, crying like a baby" (675). How are we to read this story's close? Why does Parker cry like a baby? Are these tears of despair, disappointment, relief, wonder?

The final pages of "Parker's Back" match the distinctive spare style of O'Connor's fiction. We are not offered a clear delineation of the literal versus allegorical levels of the story. We are not told outright the quality of Parker's tears. The elements lacking in this story's close, however, place into stark relief the narrative information we are offered. When Parker arrives home and demands Sarah Ruth let him in, she asks him once again who is there in an attempt to get him to go by his full name Obadiah Elihue, rather than his preferred initials O. E. As she demands incessantly, "'Who's there?:'"

> Parker turned his head as if he expected someone behind him to give him the answer. The sky had lightened slightly and there were two or three streaks of yellow floating above the horizon. Then as he stood there, a tree of light burst over the skyline.
> Parker fell back against the door as if he had been pinned there by a lance . . .
> Parker bent down and put his mouth near the stuffed keyhole. 'Obadiah,' he whispered and all at once he felt the light pouring through him, turning his spiderweb soul into a perfect arabesque of colors, a garden of trees and birds and beasts.

In this climactic moment, Gordon warns O'Connor against the "natural inclination" to move too hastily through a central moment and instead to "stand still or move very slowly."³¹ Yet, this closing scene—with its rapid movement from the turn of Parker's head to the burst of light to the piercing, naming, and illumination—results in quite the demanding read.

The quick succession of events at the climax of the story is not a result of O'Connor's fatigue but of her distinctive style, particularly when narrating divine action in the created order. Here, we do not find the allegorical and literal levels of storytelling so much as the reality of a world created and upheld by God. For O'Connor to slow down and spell out what happens to Parker in this moment would deny readers the opportunity to discern God's mysterious work in the world.

In this moment, Parker is transfigured into the tattooed freak at the fair. He becomes the cause for wonder he first felt as a teenage boy. Not only in O'Connor's fiction, but throughout the Christian tradition, light plays a central role in communicating the presence of the transcendent. Here, with Parker on his front stoop, we find a cryptic, yet suggestive image of being pierced with light echoing rather directly the wound in Christ's side with the piercing of a lance.³² Parker, pierced like Christ, whispers his proper name, Obadiah, and "all at once he felt the light pouring through him" (CW, 673). He whispers his true name again, this time in full, "Obadiah Elihue!," as if to confirm both who he truly is and the light that fills him.

This story receives a lot of attention for its magnificent rendering of Parker receiving the tattoo of Christ on his back, Christ's eye's demanding Parker's attention. But, the climax of "Parker's Back" is not in the reception of the tattoo, but in this moment at the close of the story when Parker submits to his true name, Obadiah, servant of God. Richard Giannone richly describes the impact of this moment of naming: "After he murmurs his first name, light pours through his body as a promise of joy.... Having become a paradise of wonder, Obadiah freely gives his second name, Elihue, which affirms the God he serves. *Elihue* means 'my God is he.' With the initials O.E. acquiring substance, Parker's flesh is now made word. He feels himself to be the visible dwelling of glory."³³ Here, in this sparely wrought scene at

---

31. Flanagan, *Letters*, 220.

32. The Lance of Longinus or Holy Lance has a legendary tradition as a relic, first recorded in 570 CE by a pilgrim to Jerusalem (Nickell, *Relics of Christ*, 108). Longinus is the name assigned to the soldier who pierced Jesus's side in John 19. The legendary name is most likely derived not from a soldier's name, but instead from the Greek that suggests the one who lances (Nickell, *Relics of Christ*, 107).

33. Giannone, *Mystery of Love*, 229, italics his.

his front door, Parker experiences the culmination of the work of conversion that began in earnest in the upper room tattoo parlor.

Parker finds himself in the morning twilight "overwhelmed and his heart flooded with a mixture of joy and sorrow," in the words of St. Bonaventure recounting St. Francis's seraphic vision.[34] The wonder he first experienced as a young man beholding the sideshow freak with his beautifully tattooed skin now illuminates Parker's soul. Parker's striving to make himself wondrous through slapdash tattoos across his arms, legs, and chest failed to produce the effect, but this moment of divine illumination pierces, wounds, and imprints him with a gift all his striving could never achieve. Now, pierced with love, Parker shares in his suffering as Sarah Ruth beholds Christ's face imprinted on Parker's back and begins to thrash him with a broom.

This description of Parker's pierced body matches the intensity of many of O'Connor's final scenes. Sykes highlights that, for O'Connor, the effect of her storytelling carries with it a force that impacts readers in a particularly violent fashion: "O'Connor intends readerly violence to all her readers, believers and unbelievers alike, not excluding herself. For, ultimately, she hopes to precipitate an act of reading that is itself a kind of *imitatio Christi*, or more accurately, an *imitatio crucis*."[35] Sykes goes on to clarify why violence—for both characters and readers—plays such a central role. Violence ties in to three central theological principles Sykes identifies in O'Connor's work: the centrality of the body in human salvation, the importance of suffering as seen in the tradition of monastic asceticism, and the conception of evil as *privatio boni*.[36] Sykes uses the image of Hazel Motes at the close of *Wise Blood* to evidence the theological underpinnings of violence, for Haze's asceticism reflects the role of the body in his salvation and the centrality of physical suffering to confront and expunge the evil within him. Haze's ascetical practices are understood as imitating Christ to become like him in suffering and death. We can see this same idea at work in "Parker's Back" with the clear role of his body in his salvation, his shared suffering with Christ at the story's close, and the vacuous nature of Parker's soul as one rattled with holes like a "spider web" to one transformed and filled with color and life (CW, 673).

---

34. Bonaventure, "Life of St. Francis," XIII.3.
35. Sykes, *Aesthetic of Revelation*, 44.
36. Sykes, *Aesthetic of Revelation*, 45.

The result of a narrative style that aims to produce an *imitatio crucis* reading experience leads to a wound that overflows with Christ's love. To speak of a reading experience as imitating not only the life but the crucifixion of Christ returns us to St. Francis's stigmata. The vision of Christ crucified remains with and transforms St. Francis for the remaining years of his life. His stigmata are an exemplary case of *imitatio Christi, imitatio crucis*. O'Connor's stylistic asceticism invites its own wounding and blessing event akin, in some way, to the reception of the stigmata. Readers can receive their own wounds of love in reading, as they fill in the gaps and infer their painfully redemptive implications. This occurs when, like St. Francis, the vision of Christ crucified wounds with an overflow of love that "imprints" the beholder with the vision beheld. This wound of overflow, of excessive love, recalls Chrétien's language of prayer being like a lover's speech, where the language of love for another dispossesses the speaker of his or her own power. It is the speech of self-giving, like the cruciform image of self-giving. The laborious work of interpreting spare stories leaves readers vulnerable to their own seraphic vision, where they encounter not only their own limits or character flaws but the radical demonstration of love in Christ crucified.

Parker's luminous stigma invites us to share in this transformation, this wounding that transfigures his soul. The story's close offers us just enough to know that something has profoundly transformed Parker. Not only has he taken on his true name, he also responds radically differently to things not going the way he had planned. Throughout the story, we see Parker flitting like a hummingbird from one source to another to satisfy his wants and to be an object of desire. But, here, after his plan to impress Sarah Ruth goes radically awry, Parker does not take off to the city for another tattoo and instead accepts his wife's fury, makes his way out of the house, then settles down and sobs under the pecan tree in the front yard. By spending time in these final pages, we are invited into the discreet, but thorough alteration of Parker's desires through this stigmatic event. We encounter Christ's love indirectly yet profoundly through this sparely narrated moment of blessed wounding.

Conclusion

Here, in these three short stories, we see how O'Connor's style draws out substance through a stylistic asceticism. In them, we are invited into readings that humiliate, implicate, and overflow with Christ's love in ways that wound us even as they bless. As we read O'Connor's fiction we not only encounter stories of wounding invitations of grace, but are offered through them an invitation of our own.

Conclusion

Stylistic Asceticism

O'Connor knew well the difficulty many readers have with her style of storytelling and the subject matter she undertakes. She initially proposed *Wise Blood* to Rinehart & Co. before publishing with Harcourt, Brace & Co. The Rinehart editor, John Selby, did not see in O'Connor the same artistry and potential that many would find in her work. O'Connor comments to her literary agent, Elizabeth McKee, that Rinehart's "criticism is vague and really tells me nothing except that they don't like it. I feel like the objections they raise are connected with its virtues, and the thought of working with them specifically to correct these lacks they mention is repulsive to me" (CW, 880). O'Connor responds to Selby in-kind, noting that she is not setting out to write "a conventional novel" and that the kind she is writing "will derive precisely from the peculiarity or aloneness, if you will, of the experience I write from." She closes the letter noting that the final book "will be just as odd if not odder than the nine chapters you have now" (CW, 881). Similarly, the reception of *Wise Blood* received mix reviews, which she speaks to in the author's note to the work's second edition:

> *Wise Blood* was written by an author congenitally innocent of theory, but one with certain preoccupations. That belief in Christ is to some a matter of life and death has been a stumbling block for readers who would prefer to think it a matter of no great consequence. For them Hazel Motes' integrity lies in his trying with such vigor to get rid of the ragged figure who moves from tree to tree in the back of his mind. For the author Hazel's integrity lies in his not being able to. Does one's integrity ever lie in what he is not able to do? I think that it usually does, for free will does not mean one will, but many wills conflicting in one man. Freedom cannot

be conceived simply. It is a mystery and one which a novel, even a comic novel, can only be asked to deepen.[1]

Precisely where reader's recognize Haze's virtue, O'Connor sees vice. For O'Connor, Haze's submission to a will other than his own drive for self-autonomy, exemplified in his Church without Christ, is his true act of freedom. Here, we find a submission that many a modern reader would find old-fashioned, stifling, and even offensive rather than liberating.

Because of O'Connor's brilliance as a fiction writer, her unyielding theological convictions add dimension to her stories rather than collapsing them into soppy or didactic Christian tropes. As we have seen, a key aspect of her success as a Catholic novelist is her spare style, particularly in climactic moments, which allows for the possibility of God's work in the world without neon signs or other grand narrative gestures. Rather delightfully, one of O'Connor's most frequently quoted lines, "to the hard of hearing you shout, and to the almost blind you draw large and startling figures" (CW, 806), can be nearly turned on its head in terms of the work of divine grace in her stories. By employing grotesque action, O'Connor communicates to a secularized readership the presence of distorted wills and misdirected desires. These are the moments of excess which signal but do not equal the working of grace within a story.

Grace at work in her stories comes by way of the lean, discreet, and spare in contrast to the forceful, grotesque, and sometimes violent narrative action by which O'Connor fiction is often recognized. The crux of my contention in this book lies in the value of those lean and discreet moments alongside the "large and startling." The style of O'Connor's fiction, most importantly and notably in the climactic moments of competing wills and the possibility of redemption, invites readers more deeply into the mystery of conversion. The stylistic austerity stands out all the more with the freakish and grotesque character of O'Connor's stories. And, as I have shown, this working of grace sparely-wrought in the stories also opens up prayerful opportunities in the act of reading.

In his ascetical homilies, St. Isaac the Syrian writes that "Perception of God is an abyss of humility."[2] This humility is found "[w]hen a man goes far away from men and concentrates himself, then immediately the thoughts of repentance will be imprinted in his understanding."[3] In the

---

1. See "Author's Note to the Second Edition (1962)," in O'Connor, *Wise Blood*.
2. See "Homily 64" in Isaac the Syrian, *Ascetical Homilies*, 448.
3. See "Homily 64" in Isaac the Syrian, *Ascetical Homilies*, 447.

practices of isolation and stillness, the ascetic is ushered into a posture of humility through contrition. This ancient idea is an evergreen one that modern people appreciate, often seen in our *avoidance* of isolation and stillness. When we are left without the clutter, the distraction, and the noise, we can more easily see ourselves as we truly are. The absence of distraction pushes us towards doing the work of self-reflection and it is here, in this uncluttered space that we perceive God in our humility because it is God at work in us. In the words of St. Isaac, "Do not think that without divine grace contrition can descend on the mind."[4] Frequently, these revelations through divine grace are accompanied by a wounding of the self, be it in humility, judgment, or a blessed stigmatic event.

There is a kinship between the effect of ascetical practices, like those of which St. Isaac speaks, and the spare narrations of the reality of the world and ourselves in the light of God. The spare narrations of divine grace in O'Connor's fiction share a kinship with ancient biblical narratives in their proclivity to give the readers a minimum amount of narrative detail at the most pivotal moments of the story. The difficulty of reading spare narration puts clear demands on readers that require a more substantial investment than some other kinds of storytelling. The term "stylistic asceticism" is an attempt to capture this spare narrative style that is grounded in and pointed towards the conviction that in blessing there can also be a kind of wounding, that by taking on the spare form we invite ourselves into that uncluttered space where divine grace leads to contrition and transformation.

In closing, I want to return us to the exemplar case of blessed wounding in Jacob's wrestling with the angel-man. In the chapel of the Parisian church of Saint-Sulpice stands a painting by nineteenth-century painter Eugène Delacroix. It features Jacob wrestling with an angel. The painting foregrounds the wrestlers, with a deserted landscape looming behind, and with weapons and Jacob's outer clothing piled in the foreground. The very edge of the Jabbok river shimmers in blue from one side of the painting, while the other side captures the scene of the gifts being sent to Esau ahead of his estranged brother Jacob's visit; the herders and servants take no notice of the remarkable wrangling scene occurring on the riverbank. The production of this painting became an antagonistic experience for Delacroix, as the work unexpectedly occupied twelve of the last fourteen years of his life. Like Jacob, Delacroix did not anticipate the solitary struggle that would result in both exhaustion and grandeur. Jean-Louis

---

4. See "Homily 64" in Isaac the Syrian, *Ascetical Homilies*, 447.

Chrétien, reflecting on the transferred impact of the subject matter of the painting onto its creator, comments, "in the very year in which the work was finished, Delacroix imagines himself dying at his task, in front of an unfinished, unfinishable work . . . but in the end he too became Jacob, and his wounds a blessing."[5] The events of Gen 32's wrangling and blessing capture in literal terms the entanglement of wounding and blessing, which resonates well beyond the event itself: often a great gift—of a blessed new name or work of art—comes at great cost.

My exploration in this work of the crippled victor Jacob and blinded convert Hazel displays two protagonists who know well the effect of blessed wounds. This blessed wounding extends out from the narrative art itself and puts readers at risk of their own wrangling and transformation. Analogous to the artist laboring over his work in the image of Delacroix wearily working away on his painting for twelve years, readers engage these sparely narrated stories as an event—a participation of readers with the text that requires their creativity and vulnerability to produce a credible interpretation of the story. To narrate grace effectively and believably is difficult. An examination of the spare style of these narratives of grace reveals the role style plays in meaning. Grace hypotactically rendered runs the risk of saying too much about an event veiled in mystery. Paratactic narration, as in the apophatic theological tradition, recognizes how speaking in negation and leaving room for silence can open up meaning rather than shutting it down.

In a theological reflection on Shūsaku Endō's *Silence*, Makoto Fujimura observes how the authorial choice to withhold narrative information often leads to frustration on the part of readers: "The author's [Endō's] attempt to communicate nuanced truth about a God who is greater than propositions . . . is often met with a demand to clarify."[6] Like Endō, the biblical writers' and O'Connor's employment of parataxis, notably in narrating transformative grace, resists demands to render grace clearly and explicitly. Instead, readers are offered an experience that invites the prayerful posture of vulnerability, openness, and contrition. "Art is not anything that goes on 'among' people, not the art of the novel anyway," O'Connor notes. "It is something that one experiences alone and for the purpose of realizing in a fresh way, through the senses, the mystery of existence" (CW, 988). O'Connor's spare style invites us as readers to delve

---

5. Chrétien, *Hand to Hand*, 7–8.
6. Fujimura, *Silence and Beauty*, 49.

into the mysterious action of divine grace in the fictional world and our own. The presence of grace, of God's work in the world and Christ's invitation to us, comes to us not in the "large and startling" but in the lean and discreet moments of transformed vision.

Bibliography

Alter, Robert. *The Art of Biblical Narrative*. 2nd ed. New York: Basic Books, 2011.
———. *The Five Books of Moses: A Translation with Commentary*. New York: Norton, 2008.
———. *Pen of Iron: American Prose and the King James Bible*. Princeton, NJ: Princeton University Press, 2010.
Anderson, John E. *Jacob and the Divine Trickster: A Theology of Deception and Yhwh's Fidelity to the Ancestral Promise in the Jacob Cycle*. Winona Lake, IN: Eisenbrauns, 2011.
Aquinas, Thomas. *The Summa Theologica of St. Thomas Aquinas*. Translated by Fathers of the Dominican Province. New York: Christian Classics, 1981.
Arnold, Bill T., and John H. Choi. *A Guide to Biblical Hebrew Syntax*. New York: Cambridge University Press, 2003.
Asals, Frederick. *Flannery O'Connor: The Imagination of Extremity*. Athens, GA: University of Georgia Press, 1986.
Auerbach, Erich. *Mimesis: The Representation of Reality in Western Literature*. Princeton, NJ: Princeton University Press, 2013.
Balthasar, Hans Urs von. *Prayer*. New York: Paulist, 1967.
Bar-Efrat, Shimon. *Narrative Art in the Bible*. London: Bloomsbury T. & T. Clark, 2004.
Barthes, Roland. *Image-Music-Text*. Translated by Stephen Heath. New York: Hill and Wang, 1978.
Basselin, Timothy J. *Flannery O'Connor: Writing a Theology of Disabled Humanity*. Waco, TX: Baylor University Press, 2013.
Berlin, Adele. *Poetics and Interpretation of Biblical Narrative*. Winona Lake, IN: Eisenbrauns, 1994.
Bernstein, Richard J. "The Conversation That Never Happened [Gadamer/Derrida]." *The Review of Metaphysics* 61.3 (2008) 577–603.
Bérubé, Michael. "There Is Nothing Inside the Text, Or, Why No One's Heard of Wolfgang Iser." In *Postmodern Sophistry: Stanley Fish and the Critical Enterprise*, edited by Gary A. Olson and Lynn Worsham, 11–26. Albany, NY: SUNY Press, 2004.
Bettenhausen, Elizabeth. "Foreword." In *Christianity, Patriarchy and Abuse: A Feminist Critique*, edited by Joanne Carlson Brown and Carole R. Bohn, xi–xii. New York: Pilgrim, 1989.

BIBLIOGRAPHY

Bonaventure. "The Life of St. Francis." In *Bonaventure: The Soul's Journey into God, the Tree of Life, the Life of St. Francis*, translated by Ewert Cousins, 177–327. New York: Paulist, 1978.

———. "The Soul's Journey into God." In *Bonaventure: The Soul's Journey into God, the Tree of Life, the Life of St. Francis*, translated by Ewert Cousins, 51–116. New York: Paulist, 1978.

Bong, Sharon A. "The Suffering Christ and the Asian Body." In *Feminism and Theology*, edited by Janet Martin Soskice and Diana Lipton, 356–64. New York: Oxford University Press, 2003.

Booth, Wayne C. "Interview: Wolfgang Iser." *Diacritics* 10.2 (1980) 57–74.

———. *The Rhetoric of Fiction*. 2nd ed. Chicago: University of Chicago Press, 1983.

Bosco, Mark, and Brent Little, eds. *Revelation and Convergence: Flannery O'Connor and the Catholic Intellectual Tradition*. Washington, DC: Catholic University of America Press, 2017.

Boyarin, Daniel. *Intertextuality and the Reading of Midrash*. Bloomington, IN: Indiana University Press, 1994.

Brinkmeyer, Robert H., Jr. *The Art and Vision of Flannery O'Connor*. Baton Rouge, LA: Louisiana State University Press, 1989.

Brooks, Cleanth, Jr., and Robert Penn Warren. *Understanding Fiction*. 2nd ed. New York: Appleton–Century–Crofts, 1959.

Brown, Francis, et al. *The Brown-Driver-Briggs Hebrew and English Lexicon*. 1906. Reprint. Peabody, MA: Hendrickson, 1994.

Brown, Joanne Carlson, and Rebecca Parker. "For God So Loved the World." In *Christianity, Patriarchy and Abuse: A Feminist Critique*, edited by Joanne Carlson Brown and Carole R. Bohn, 1–30. New York: Pilgrim, 1989.

Brueggemann, Walter. *Genesis*. Interpretation: A Bible Commentary for Teaching and Preaching. Atlanta, GA: John Knox Press, 1986.

Bruner, Michael Mears. *A Subversive Gospel: Flannery O'Connor and the Reimagining of Beauty, Goodness, and Truth*. Downers Grove, IL: Intervarsity Press Academic, 2017.

Cain, William E. *Literary Criticism*. Vol. 5. The Cambridge History of American Literature, edited by Sacvan Bercovitch and Cyrus R. K. Patell. Cambridge: Cambridge University Press, 1994.

Carnes, Natalie. *Beauty: A Theological Engagement with Gregory of Nyssa*. Eugene, OR: Cascade, 2014.

Chrétien, Jean-Louis. *Hand to Hand: Listening to the Work of Art*. Translated by Stephen E. Lewis. New York: Fordham University Press, 2003.

———. *La Voix Nue: Phénoménologie de la Promesse*. Paris: Les Éditions de Minuit, 1990.

———. "The Wounded Word: The Phenomenology of Prayer." In *Phenomenology and the Theological Turn: The French Debate*, 147–75. New York: Fordham University Press, 2001.

Coakley, Sarah. *God, Sexuality, and the Self: An Essay "On the Trinity."* Cambridge: Cambridge University Press, 2013.

———. *Powers and Submissions: Spirituality, Philosophy and Gender*. Oxford: Wiley-Blackwell, 2002.

Cofer, Jordan. *The Gospel According to Flannery O'Connor: Examining the Role of the Bible in Flannery O'Connor's Fiction*. New York: Bloomsbury Academic, 2014.

Davidson, Arnold I. "Miracles of Bodily Transformation, or How St. Francis Received the Stigmata." Translated by Maggie Fritz-Morkin. *Critiqical Inquiry* 35.3 (2009) 451–80.

Delio, Ilia. *Crucified Love: Bonaventure's Mysticism of the Crucified Christ*. Quincy, IL: Franciscan Media, 1999.
Etsy, William. "In America, Intellectual Bomb Shelters." *Commonweal* 67.7 (1958) 586–88.
Ewell, Barbara C., et al., eds. *Southern Local Color: Stories of Region, Race, and Gender*. Athens, GA: University of Georgia Press, 2002.
Fielding, Henry. *Joseph Andrews*. Everyman's Library 467. London: Dent, 1910.
Fish, Stanley. "Why No One's Afraid of Wolfgang Iser." *Diacritics* 11.1 (1981) 2–13.
Fishbane, Michael. *Biblical Text and Texture: A Literary Reading of Selected Texts*. Oxford: Oneworld, 1998.
Fisk, Anna. *Sex, Sin, and Our Selves: Encounters in Feminist Theology and Contemporary Women's Literature*. Eugene, OR: Wipf & Stock, 2014.
Fitzgerald, Robert. "Introduction." In *Everything That Rises Must Converge*, by Flannery O'Connor, 5–30. New York: Farrar, Straus & Giroux, 1965.
Fitzgerald, Sally. "A Master Class: From the Correspondence of Caroline Gordon and Flannery O'Connor." *The Georgia Review* 33 (1979) 827–46.
———. "McMullen's Choice: A Recent Appraisal of Flannery O'Connor." *Religion and the Arts* 2.4 (1998) 519–29.
———. "Rooms with a View." *Flannery O'Connor Bulletin* 10 (1981) 5–22.
Flanagan, Christine, ed. *The Letters of Flannery O'Connor and Caroline Gordon*. Atlanta: University of Georgia Press, 2018.
Fokkelman, J. P. "Genesis." In *The Literary Guide to the Bible*, edited by Robert Alter and Frank Kermode, 36–55. Cambridge, MA: Belknap, 1990.
Friedman, Richard Elliot. *The Bible with Sources Revealed*. San Francisco: HarperOne, 2005.
Fujimura. *Silence and Beauty: Hidden Faith Born of Suffering*. Downers Grove, IL: InterVarsity, 2016.
Gadamer, Hans-Georg. *Truth and Method*. Translated by J. Weinsheimer and D. G. Marshall. 2nd rev. ed. New York: Continuum, 2004.
Gentry, Marshall Bruce. *Flannery O'Connor's Religion of the Grotesque*. Jackson, MS: University Press of Mississippi, 1986.
Giannone, Richard. *Flannery O'Connor and the Mystery of Love*. New York: Fordham University Press, 1999.
———. *Flannery O'Connor, Hermit Novelist*. Urbana, IL: University of Illinois Press, 200AD.
Gooch, Brad. *Flannery: A Life of Flannery O'Connor*. New York: Back Bay, 2010.
Gordon, Caroline. *Old Red and Other Stories*. New York: Scribner's, 1963.
Gordon, Sarah. *Flannery O'Connor: The Obedient Imagination*. Athens, GA: University of Georgia Press, 2003.
———. "'Reviewed Work: "A Prayer Journal" by Flannery O'Connor.'" *The Georgia Review* 67 (2013) 754–56.
Hardy, Donald E. *Narrating Knowledge in Flannery O'Connor's Fiction*. Columbia, SC: University of South Carolina Press, 2003.
Higton, Mike. *Wrestling with Angels: Conversations in Modern Theology*. Grand Rapids, MI: Eerdmans, 2007.
Hildegard of Bingen. *Scivias*. The Classics of Western Spirituality. New York: Paulist, 1990.
Isaac the Syrian. *Ascetical Homilies of St Isaac the Syrian*. 2nd ed. Boston: Holy Transfiguration Monastery, 2011.

BIBLIOGRAPHY

Iser, Wolfgang. *The Act of Reading: A Theory of Aesthetic Response*. Baltimore, MD: Johns Hopkins University Press, 1980.

———. *The Implied Reader: Patterns of Communication in Prose Fiction from Bunyan to Beckett*. Baltimore, MD: Johns Hopkins University Press, 1974.

———. "Talk Like Whales: A Reply to Stanley Fish." *Diacritics* 11.3 (1981) 82–87.

Kayser, Wolfgang. *The Grotesque in Art and Literature*. Translated by Ulrich Weisstein. Bloomington, IN: Indiana University Press, 1963.

Kinney, Arthur F. *Flannery O'Connor's Library: Resources of Being*. Athens, GA: University of Georgia Press, 1985.

Landess, Tom. *The Short Fiction of Caroline Gordon: A Critical Symposium*. Southern Series. Irving, TX: University of Dallas Press, 1972.

Lanham, Richard. *Analyzing Prose: Second Edition*. New York: Bloomsbury Academic, 2003.

Long, V. Philips. *The Art of Biblical History*. Grand Rapids, MI: Zondervan, 1994.

Maritain, Jacques. *Art and Scholasticism: With Other Essays*. Translated by J. F. Scanlan. New York: Scribner's, 1947.

———. *Creative Intuition in Art and Poetry: The A.W. Mellon Lectures in the Fine Arts*. New York: Meridian, 1955.

May, John R. *The Pruning Word: The Parables of Flannery O'Connor*. 1st ed. Notre Dame, IN: University of Notre Dame Press, 1976.

McMullen, Joann Halleran. *Writing Against God: Language as Message in the Literature of Flannery O'Connor*. Macon, GA: Mercer University Press, 1998.

Michaels, J. Ramsey. *Passing by the Dragon: The Biblical Tales of Flannery O'Connor*. Eugene, OR: Cascade, 2013.

Michelfelder, Diane P., and Richard E. Palmer, eds. *Dialogue and Deconstruction: The Gadamer-Derrida Encounter*. Albany, NY: SUNY Press, 1989.

Moberly, R. W. L. *Genesis 12–50*. Old Testament Guides 2. Sheffield: Bloomsbury T. & T. Clark, 1992.

Moran, Daniel. *Creating Flannery O'Connor: Her Critics, Her Publishers, Her Readers*. Athens, GA: University of Georgia Press, 2016.

Nickell, Joe. *Relics of Christ*. Lexington, KY: University Press of Kentucky, 2007.

Noth, Martin. *A History of Pentateuchal Traditions*. Translated by Bernhard W. Anderson. Englewood Cliffs, NJ: Prentice-Hall, 1972.

O'Connor, Flannery. *Collected Works: Wise Blood, A Good Man Is Hard to Find, The Violent Bear It Away, Everything That Rises Must Converge, Essays and Letters*. New York: Library of America, 1988.

———. *Everything That Rises Must Converge*. New York: Farrar, Straus & Giroux, 1965.

———. *The Habit of Being: Letters of Flannery O'Connor*. Edited by Sally Fitzgerald. 1979. Reprint. New York: Farrar, Straus & Giroux, 1988.

———. *Mystery and Manners: Occasional Prose*. Edited by Sally Fitzgerald and Robert Fitzgerald. New York: Farrar, Straus & Giroux, 1970.

———. *A Prayer Journal*. Edited by W. A. Sessions. New York: Farrar, Straus & Giroux, 2013.

———. *Wise Blood*. 2nd ed. New York: Farrar, Straus & Giroux, 1962.

Orvell, Miles D. "Review: Flannery O'Connor." *The Sewanee Review* 78.1 (1970) 184–92.

Poe Hays, Rebecca W. *The Function of Story in the Hebrew Psalter*. Lanham, MD: Lexington, 2021.

BIBLIOGRAPHY

Rad, Gerhard von. *Old Testament Theology*. Vol. 1, *The Theology of Israel's Historical Traditions*. Translated by D. M. G. Stalker. Louisville, KY: Westminster John Knox Press, 2001.

Ragen, Brian Abel. *A Wreck on the Road to Damascus: Innocence, Guilt, & Conversion in Flannery O'Connor*. Chicago: Loyola University Press, 1989.

Rambo, Shelly. *Resurrecting Wounds: Living in the Afterlife of Trauma*. Waco, TX: Baylor University Press, 2017.

Rimmon-Kenan, Shlomith. *Narrative Fiction: Contemporary Poetics*. 2nd ed. London: Routledge, 2002.

———. "Wolfgang Iser—In Memoriam." *Partial Answers: Journal of Literature and History of Ideas* 5.2 (2007) 141–44.

Ruether, Rosemary Radford. *Sexism and God-Talk: Toward a Feminist Theology*. Boston: Beacon, 1993.

Sarna, Nahum M. *The JPS Torah Commentary: Genesis*. Philadelphia: Jewish Publication Society, 2001.

Schiebe, Mark. "Car Trouble: Haze Motes and the Fifties Counterculture." In *Wise Blood: A Re-Consideration*, edited by John J. Han, 405–23. New York: Editions Rodopi, 2011.

Shloss, Carol. *Flannery O'Connor's Dark Comedies: The Limits of Inference*. Baton Rouge, LA: Louisiana State University Press, 1980.

Scott, R. Neil. *Flannery O'Connor: An Annotated Reference Guide to Criticism*. Milledgeville, GA: Timberlane, 2002.

Ska, Jean Louis. *Our Fathers Have Told Us: Introduction to the Analysis of Hebrew Narratives*. Rome: Gregorian & Biblical Press, 2000.

Sternberg, Meir. *The Poetics of Biblical Narrative: Ideological Literature and the Drama of Reading*. 2nd ed. Bloomington, IN: Indiana University Press, 1987.

Sykes, John D., Jr. *Flannery O'Connor, Walker Percy, and the Aesthetic of Revelation*. Columbia, MO: University of Missouri Press, 2007.

———. "Portraits of the Artist." *Flannery O'Connor Review* 8 (2010) 22–30.

Tolkien, J. R. R. *The Tolkien Reader*. New York: Ballantine, 1986.

Tonstad, Linn Marie. *God and Difference: The Trinity, Sexuality, and the Tranformation of Finitude*. New York: Routledge, 2016.

Vloeburg, Sander. "Wounding Love: A Mystical–Theological Exploration of Stigmatization." *International Journal of Philosophy and Theology* 77.1–2 (2016) 1–29.

Ware, Kallistos. "The Way of the Ascetics: Negative or Affirmative?" In *Asceticism*, edited by Vincent L. Wimbush and Richard Valantasis, 3–15. New York: Oxford University Press, 1998.

Wiggins, Robert A. "Caroline Gordon: 'Old Red and Other Stories' (Book Review)." *Studies in Short Fiction* 1.1 (1963) 67–69.

Williams, Rowan. *The Edge of Words: God and the Habits of Language*. London: Bloomsbury Academic, 2014.

———. *Grace and Necessity: Reflections on Art and Love*. Harrisburg, PA: Bloomsbury Academic, 2006.

———. *On Christian Theology*. Oxford: Wiley-Blackwell, 1999.

———. *The Tragic Imagination: The Literary Agenda*. New York: Oxford University Press, 2016.

———. *The Wound of Knowledge: Christian Spirituality from the New Testament to St. John of the Cross*. 2nd rev. ed. Cambridge, MA: Cowley, 2003.

BIBLIOGRAPHY

Wood, Ralph C. *The Comedy of Redemption: Christian Faith & Comic Vision in Four American Novelists.* Notre Dame: University of Notre Dame Press, 1991.

———. *Flannery O'Connor and the Christ-Haunted South.* Grand Rapids, MI: Eerdmans, 2005.

Wray, Virginia. "Flannery O'Connor's *Why Do the Heathen Rage?* and the Quotidian 'Larger Things.'" *Flannery O'Connor Review* 23 (1994–95) 1–29.

Index

Alter, Robert, 7, 71n11, 72–74, 78, 80, 82, 86, 88, 109n37
Anderson, John E., 93–94
angel-man. *See entry for* Genesis 32 (Jacob Wrestling at the Jabbock)
Aquinas, St. Thomas. *See entry for* Saints
Asa Hawks, 35, 100, 105
Asals, Frederick, 11, 102n32
Asbury Fox, 31n38, 148–53
asceticism, the spiritual practice (*for stylistic asceticism, see entry for* parataxis)
    as *askesis/ascesis*, 2–3, 103
    as fasting, 3
    as moderation, 3
    as natural asceticism, 3
    as prayer, 3, 66, 132n41, 138, 151n21, 159
    as self-denial, 3, 17
    as unnatural asceticism, 3
    the spiritual practice of, 3, 14, 91, 118, 132, 158, 163
atonement, 15–16
Auerbach, Erich, 68–69, 71n14, 76–77, 78n43, 89

Bakhtin, Mikhail, 52n36
Balthasar, Hans Urs von, 55n47, 128
baptism, 14, 18, 141, 143–44, 146–47
Bar-Efrat, Shimon, 7n17, 84–86
Barthes, Roland, 93–94
Basselin, Timothy J., 56
Berlin, Adele, 7n17, 71–74, 80

Bernstein, Richard J., 121n3
Bérubé, Michael, 120–21n3,
Bettenhausen, Elizabeth, 16
Bevel Summers, 142
Bible, 5, 7–8, 19, 69, 73n21, 75, 77n35, 82n58, 87–88, 93n4, 106, 110, 115, 120
    and the King James Version, 7, 88
biblical Hebrew narrative, ix, 2–8, 9n27, 12–13, 15, 68, 70–73, 76–77, 80, 82–83, 85–91, 108, 111–13, 120, 127, 137
blessed wounding, 2, 14, 41, 61, 108, 117–18, 120, 131, 133–34, 137, 140, 151, 159, 163–64
Bong, Sharon, 16n39
Booth, Wayne, 76–77, 78–79n46, 121n3, 122–23
Boy Bevel, 14, 118n42, 141–44, 146–47, 153
Boyarin, Daniel, 82n57–58
Brinkmeyer, Robert H. Jr., 52–52n36, 58n55
Brooks, Cleanth Jr., 4n11, 26–28
Brown, Joanne Carlson, 16n39
Brueggemann, Walter, 94–95, 111
Bunyan, John, 123–24

Cain, William E., 25n22, 25n23–27
Carnes, Natalie, ix, 43n8, 65n78
Chrétien, Jean-Louis, ix, 14, 42, 59–61, 66, 120, 128–34, 137, 140–41, 159, 164

173

INDEX

Coakley, Sarah, 18n51, 63n69, 132n41
Cofer, Jordan, 8
conversion, 13, 31, 38–39, 65, 91, 94–96, 99, 102n32, 104–6, 108, 112–13, 127, 149, 152, 156, 162
Cousins, Ewart, 134n51

Davidson, Arnold I., 134n50
Delacroix, Eugène, 163–64
Delio, Ilia, 136
Derrida, Jacques, 121n3
desire, 9, 18n51, 19, 28–29, 37, 63n69, 64–66, 89, 119, 131, 132n41, 137, 144, 147, 149–51, 153–56, 159, 162

Endō, Shūsaku, 164
Enoch Emery, 33–37, 98
Esau, brother of Jacob, 83–84, 93–94, 98, 104, 110, 115, 163
essays and other writings of Flannery O'Connor
  Mystery and Manners, 45, 139
  A Memoir of Mary Ann (FO wrote forward), 48, 63n71
eucharist, 53, 149n20

Father Finn, 150
feminism/feminist, 15–17, 19, 25n19
Feuerbach, Ludwig, 130n30
Fielding, Henry, 79n46, 123–24
Fish, Stanley, 120–21n3
Fishbane, Michael, 7n17, 69, 70n8
Fisk, Anna, 15–17, 19
Fitzgerald, Robert, 2–3, 29
Fitzgerald, Sally, x, 10, 20nn1–4, 32n43, 33n44, 33n46, 34nn47–48, 35n50, 36nn54–56, 37n57, 37n59, 38nn60–61, 39n64, 67n83, 96n21, 103
Flanagan, Christine, 21–22n5, 30–32nn36–42, 154n25–29, 157n31
Fokkelman, J. P., 110
Friedman, Richard Elliot, 73n21
Fujimura, Makoto, 164n6

Gadamer, Hans-Georg, 42n4, 121

Garavel, Andrew J., 155n30
Genesis 22 (Binding of Isaac), 68, 69n6, 110n38
Genesis 32 (Jacob Wrestling at the Jabbok), 13, 78, 81 85–86, 89, 90–118
Gentry, Marshall Bruce, 58n55
Giannone, Richard, 100, 151n21, 157
God. *See entries for* Jesus Christ, Holy Spirit
Gooch, Brad, 149
Gordon, Caroline, 12, 20–25, 28–40, 52n34, 58, 70, 91, 96, 97n27, 112, 126n22, 127, 141, 154, 156
  and mentorship of O'Connor, 10, 12, 21, 28–29, 32–34, 38–39, 91, 127
  and "Old Red", 21–23, 28–29
  and New Criticism, 12, 20–21, 24, 28
Gordon, Sarah, 10–11, 25, 28–29, 53n36, 119n1
grace, 3–5, 9n27, 12–13, 15, 19, 38–40, 42, 54, 55n47, 56–61, 63–65, 87, 91, 94–95, 99n28, 103, 108, 114–15, 117–18, 120, 128, 133n45, 137, 143, 146, 150, 151n21, 153, 160, 162–65
  as excess, 39–40, 55n47, 56–58, 120, 162
  as violence, 5, 15, 19, 54, 56, 58, 63–64, 66, 143
  as paradox, 5, 42, 54, 58, 103, 133n45

Hall, Eileen, 51, 54n40, 58
Hardy, Donald, 11
Harry Ashfield. *See entry for Boy Bevel*
Hazel/Haze Motes, 5, 13–14, 20–21, 33–40, 91, 94–108, 112–18, 126–27, 137, 158, 161–62, 164
  and his Essex, 38n60, 95–97, 99–100, 102, 107, 112, 117
  description of, 38, 102n32, 103
  on his asceticism, 13–14, 39, 100–101, 102n32, 103, 106–8, 116–18, 158
  self-blinding of, 5, 13–14, 21, 36, 39, 95, 100–105, 107, 113–14, 116–18, 164

INDEX

Hester, Betty, 29, 38, 152, 154
Holy Spirit, 31n38, 132n41, 149n20
Homer, 68–69, 71n14, 76–77, 89
Hopps, Gavin, ix, 2n5
humor, 1, 55, 56n47, 98, 142
humiliation/humility, 14, 17–18, 21n5, 50, 53, 59, 62, 103, 115, 138, 140–41, 147, 152, 159, 162–63

irony, 2, 52–54, 56, 78–79n46, 101, 107
Isaac, father of Jacob and Esau, 68, 69n6, 83–84, 110n38,
Iser, Wolfgang, 13, 120–28, 137, 140–41, 151–52, 153n24

Jacob, 5, 13–14, 19, 41, 49, 58–61, 66, 79, 81–86, 89, 91–95, 98, 103–18, 120, 127, 132–34, 137, 163–64
 and Esau, 83–84, 93–94, 98, 104, 110, 115, 163
 as the eponym of wounding, 61, 107
 the blessing of, 5, 19, 41, 49, 59, 61, 79, 82–84, 89, 92–93, 103–5, 107–8, 115, 117, 133, 137, 163–64
 the wounding of, 5, 13–14, 19, 41, 49, 58–61, 66, 79, 89, 91, 95, 103–6, 108, 112, 115–18, 120, 132–34, 137, 163–64
 see also Genesis 32 (Jacob Wrestling at the Jabbock)
Jesus/Jesus Christ, 1, 36, 62, 95, 98, 101, 118, 133, 135, 142, 144, 147, 151n21, 157n32
 and the Incarnation, 9, 18n51, 53, 62, 64–65, 95
 the crucifixion of, 17, 134–36, 145, 159
Jones, David, 42

Kant, Immanuel, 130
Kayser, Wolfgang, 55
Kierkegaard, Søren, 131
Kingdom of God, 14, 141, 143–44, 146–47
Kinney, Arthur F., 5n14, 49n26

Landess, Tom, 22n6
Lanham, Richard A., 76
Leah, wife of Jacob, 87
Long, V. Philips, 74–75
Lowell, Robert, 90
Lytle, Andrew, 19

Maritain, Jacques, 12, 41–50, 52, 57, 66, 115
 and influence on O'Connor, 41–42, 46, 49, 52
 and Thomistic aesthetics, 12, 41–42, 50
Mary Fortune, 141
McKee, Elizabeth, 161
McMullen, Joann Halleran, 2n2, 8–10
Moberly, Walter, 107
Moran, Daniel, 34n49
Mr. Paradise, 146
Mrs. Connin, 142
Mrs. Flood, 102–3, 114, 116–18
Mrs. Fox, 149

Nickell, Joe, 157n32
Noth, Martin, 92n3, 109n36

O. E. Parker (Obadiah Elihue Parker), 29–30, 40, 153–59
O'Connor, Flannery
 and her publishers (Harcourt, Brace, & Co.; Rinehart & Co.), 90, 161
 on her Catholic faith, 9–11, 24–25, 51–53, 56n47, 57–58, 162
 on her demands of the reader, 2, 9–10, 12–15, 20–21, 23, 32–33, 39, 70, 89, 91, 120, 124, 126, 128, 141, 152–53, 157, 163–64
 on her literary style. *See entries for* the grotesque *and* parataxis
 on her Thomistic view of art, 11n36, 12, 28, 41–42
 on professional writing career, 12, 21, 29, 39–40, 70
Orvell, Miles D., 139–40

INDEX

parataxis/paratactic narration or style, 4–7, 11–13, 15, 23, 40, 70–71, 76–77, 80, 82, 88–89, 90n2, 91, 105, 108, 111–12, 114, 120, 123–24, 126–27, 141, 164
    as lean narration/style, 4n12, 11–12, 21, 106, 162, 165
    as gapped narration/style, 4, 6, 12, 79, 89, 153
    as skeletal narration/style, 2–3, 4n12, 12–13, 89, 91, 104, 111, 127, 140, 154
    as stylistic asceticism, 3, 6n16, 14, 91, 127, 138, 159, 163
    versus hypotaxis/hypotactic style, 4, 11, 15, 23, 40, 76–77, 127, 164
Parker, Rebecca, 16n39
Percy, Walker, 24
Poe Hays, Rebecca, x, 87n66
point of view, 27, 29–31, 71, 72n16, 117
    and omniscient narrator, 7, 29, 31–32, 53n36, 84–85, 97
prayer, 3, 14, 66, 110, 119–20, 128–35, 137–38, 140–41, 151, 159, 162, 164
    the effects of, 120, 129–37, 140
    the vulnerability of, 14, 120, 128–32, 135, 137, 140, 159, 164
prophetic vision/voice, 8, 24, 34, 46, 148
    and the prophet, 8, 37, 131

Rachel, wife of Jacob, 83, 87
Rad, Gerhard von, 92
Ragen, Brian, 96, 99n28
Rambo, Shelly, 17n48, 133–34
Rebekah, mother of Jacob and Esau, 83–84
repentance, 102n32, 150, 162
revelation, 4, 13, 15, 50, 52, 56–57, 59, 61, 115, 141, 145, 152
Rijn, Rembrandt von, 106
Rilke, Rainer Maria, 59–60
Rimmon-Kenan, Shlomith, 7n17, 121n3
Roman Catholicism, 9–11, 24–25, 51–53, 56n47, 57–58, 162
Ruether, Rosemary Radford, 17, 18n49

Sabbath Lily Hawks, 33, 35–37, 107
saints, 62, 119
    Anselm of Canterbury, 15
    Antony, 3
    Augustine of Hippo, 11n36, 65–66, 132n41
    Bernard of Clairvaux, 132n41
    Bonaventure, 14, 65n78, 120, 134–37, 158
    Francis of Assisi, 14, 100, 103, 120, 134–37, 158–59
    Hildegard of Bingen, 101–102n31
    Isaac the Syrian, 162–63
    Julian of Norwich, 151n21
    John of the Cross, 61, 132n41
    Macrina, 133
    Paul the Apostle, 64, 102n32, 131, 133n45
    Teresa of Ávila, 61, 65n78, 132n43
    Thomas Aquinas, 11n36, 42–43, 46, 49, 56
        and Thomistic theological aesthetics, 43, 49, 56
    Thomas, disciple of Jesus, 133
Sarah Ruth Parker, 155–56, 158–59
Sarna, Nahum M., 106n34, 109n37, 112n40
Schiebe, Mark, 96n20, 96n22
Scott, R. Neil, 56n47
Selby, John, 161
sentimentality, 54.n40, 56
Shloss, Carol, 56n47
short stories, 1, 3, 14, 22, 28–29, 45, 110, 138, 148, 156, 159
    A Good Man Is Hard to Find (1955 collection), 29
    "A Good Man Is Hard to Find", 1, 4n11, 31, 56n48, 125
    "The River", 14, 118n42, 140–44, 146–47
    Everything that Rises Must Converge (1965 collection), 3, 29
    "A View of the Woods", 34n49, 141
    "Greenleaf", 132n43, 151n21
    "Parker's Back", 14, 29–30, 140, 153–58

"The Enduring Chill", 14, 31n38, 140, 148–49
Ska, Jean Louis, 72n16
spare style. *See entry for* parataxis
Spivey, T. R., 149n20
Sternberg, Meier, 5, 7, 70, 71n11, 77–83, 89, 126n21
stigmata, 14, 120, 134–37, 159
   and Christ's blood, 136–37
   and seraphic vision, 14, 120, 135–36, 159
   and the Holy Lance, 136
   and transformation, 134–35, 159
   See also entry for Francis of Assisi *under* Saints
stylistic asceticism. *See entry for* parataxis
suffering, 15–19, 56, 63n71, 64–65, 67n83, 100–101, 119, 137, 144–46, 149–50, 154, 158
Sykes, John D. Jr., 24–25, 26n25, 34n49, 149, 158
   and *imitatio Christi . . . imitatio crucis*, 158

Tate, Allen. *See entry for* Gordon, Caroline
the grotesque, 2, 4, 6, 8, 12, 40–42, 48, 50n33, 51, 53–58, 126, 140–43, 162
   and the origins of, 55
   as disfiguration, 48, 54, 103, 106, 114, 117, 143
   as disruption, 50–51, 56, 58, 66–67
   as estrangement, 55
   as excess, 12, 40, 51, 55–58, 140, 162
   as ugliness, 47–49, 66
   in the Bible, 8, 106
The Misfit, 1, 4n11, 31, 54, 56n48, 96n24
Tolkien, J. R. R., 125, 153n24
Tonstad, Linn Marie, 18n51

violence, 1–2, 5, 8n23, 12, 15–19, 50, 54, 56, 58, 63–64, 66, 90, 105–6, 109n37, 129n30, 131, 140, 142–43, 158
   as redemption, 1, 5, 8n23, 15, 18, 58, 63, 142–43
Violent Bear It Away, The, 29
vision, 8, 10–11, 14, 25, 30, 31n38, 34, 46–47, 49, 52, 53n36, 56n47, 58, 95–96, 100–101, 103, 120, 132n41, 135–36, 143, 150, 151n21, 152, 158–59, 165
   and quicklime, 98, 100, 103
   transformation of, 103, 135, 159
Vloeburg, Sander, 134n50

Ware, Kallistos, 3
Warren, Robert Penn, 4n11, 26–28
   and New Criticism, 26, 28
Waugh, Evelyn, 90
wayyiqtol, 5–6, 7n20, 12–13, 70, 82, 86–89, 91, 95, 104, 108, 110–13, 118, 127
Wesley, Charles, 41
Why Do the Heathens Rage?, 149
Wiggins, Robert A., 23n10–11
Williams, Rowan, 2, 6, 12, 18, 39, 42–43, 46–47, 49–50, 52–59, 61–66, 126, 128, 144, 145
   and tragic representation, 49–50, 55n47, 57, 144–45
   on O'Connor, 2, 42–43, 46, 52–59, 128
   the theology of, 12, 18
Wise Blood, 5, 11n35, 12–13, 20–21, 25, 28–29, 32–36, 39–40, 70, 89–92, 94–97, 102–5, 108, 112, 114–15, 117, 127, 148, 158, 161
Wood, Ralph C., *ix*, 5, 38n63, 90, 96, 143–45, 146n16
   and the comedy of redemption, 5n15, 143–44

www.ingramcontent.com/pod-product-compliance
Lightning Source LLC
Chambersburg PA
CBHW062047220426
43662CB00010B/1682